D1064590

For a thousand years, from 2100 B.C., Thebes dominated the religious and political scene of ancient Egypt. Her Eleventh Dynasty rulers became kings of the whole country and, though their successors of the Thirteenth Dynasty lost control of the north to the Hyksos, it was regained at the beginning of the Eighteenth Dynasty by another Theban family.

Amon, who had begun as a local deity of Thebes, became the chief national god. The wealth derived from conquest poured into his treasury and captives and subject peoples were put to work on his estates and on his temple, until the latter became the largest—and one of the most splendid —the world has ever seen. Other great sanctuaries were built in the vicinity, including the mortuary temples of the kings of the Eleventh, Eighteenth, Nineteenth and Twentieth Dynasties. The tombs of these rulers and of their families and the tomb chapels of the officials of the realm, of which almost five hundred have been unearthed and studied, show—as do the structures, reliefs and sculptures of the temples themselves—the high degree of skill attained by the artists, architects and sculptors of ancient Egypt.

Many of the Theban monuments were known to Greek travellers at the beginning of our era, but it was not until the middle of the nineteenth century that Luxor, the largest town in the area, became a centre of attraction for visitors who today arrive in ever-increasing numbers. Here they can contemplate the greatest number of ancient monuments—and some of the most impressive—which have survived from the ancient world. In this splendid volume the author reconstructs Egyptian history in the light of the latest discoveries in Thebes and illustrates his narrative with a profusion of photographs specially taken in the tombs for this volume.

Charles F. Nims has spent twenty-three years in archaeological work in Egypt, all but two of them with the Epigraphic Survey of the Oriental Institute of the University of Chicago at Luxor, of which he is at present the Field Director.

THEBES OF THE PHARAOHS

THEBES
OF THE PHARAOHS

Pattern for Every City

Charles F. Nims

Photographs by Wim Swaan

DISCARDED BY THE
CCAD PACKARD LIBRARY

Elek Books   London

913.32
N619t

Published in Great Britain by
ELEK BOOKS LIMITED
2 All Saints Street London N I

and simultaneously in Canada by
THE RYERSON PRESS
299 Queen Street West Toronto 2

.

© Paul Elek Productions Limited 1965

Istituto Geografico De Agostini S.p.A. - Novara 1965
Printed in Italy

THE PACKARD LIBRARY

DEC 3 0 1974

OF THE COLUMBUS GALLERY OF FINE ARTS
AND THE COLUMBUS COLLEGE OF ART AND DESIGN

Contents

* The hieroglyphic text on the title page is translated at the beginning of this Chapter.

Plates

7

MAP AND PLANS

Jacket illustrations: *front:* Bas-relief of the head of the Goddess Hathor, tomb of Haremhab

back: Wall painting of the Mayor of Thebes, Sennefer, and his wife, Meryt. Theban tomb no. 96

End papers: *front:* Hieroglyphic text from the stele of Djari

back left: Bas-relief of Senusert I embraced by the god Atum, Karnak

back right: Hieroglyphics from the shrine of Senusert I

Binding Brass: Hieroglyphic writing of " Waset " the Egyptian name of the ancient town we call " Thebes ".

Preface

" CAN YOU RECOMMEND a book about Thebes? " This is the most frequent question asked me by the many visitors to Luxor whom I meet each winter. I have had to reply, " There isn't any." Thus I was most happy when Paul Elek asked me to write a monograph on Thebes for his series on ancient cities. This book does not tell everything about Thebes; that would require a large encyclopedia. It does attempt to select the most interesting and important facts and to present them in such a way that the general reader will feel more at home in the ancient city. It is not possible to make absolute statements about every aspect of an ancient culture; some may feel that I have been positive about too few matters; my professional colleagues may think I have been positive about too many. The latter will recognize that some of my conclusions are not those generally held; for most I have supporting evidence, but some may be due to my ignorance. The translations of texts are my own; they are freer than those usually published and as a consequence are, I trust, less wooden.

To Wim Swaan I express my admiration for the large collection of fine photographs from which the selection has been made. He brought to his task the eye of the artist, which often saw things which had escaped the eye of the archaeologist. He has asked me to express his gratitude for the co-operation he received from members of the Egyptian Department of Antiquities, to Sobhy el-Bakri, the Chief Inspector of Antiquities for Upper Egypt, and his associates, the local inspectors at Thebes, to Victor Girgis, Director of the Egyptian Museum, Cairo, and the curators with him, Abd-el-Mohsen el-Khashab, Abd-el-Qadir Selim, and Gamal Salim. Without their assistance the illustrations in this book would not have been possible. I am indebted to my colleagues George R. Hughes and Edward F. Wente, the former for his willingness to take over tasks properly mine so as to give me time to write, the latter for carefully reading the first chapters, and to both for discussing with me many of the problems. The cover design, the text on the title page, the plans and map are the work of my colleague Reginald Coleman. His wife, Marie Coleman, and Emma Jean Rasmussen typed the manuscript. To all of these I express my gratitude, and above all to my wife, Myrtle, who has borne with me in a year when each of us has assumed new responsibility, and who has seen that neither household nor social obligations kept me from completing this volume.

Chicago House - Luxor
United Arab Republic - 10 April 1964

Introduction

NINETY MINUTES or less after the aeroplane has left Cairo it begins its descent to Luxor, dipping down over the 1300 foot peak west of the river, crossing the patchwork bands of cultivation which border the ribbon of the Nile river, and sometimes giving the passengers a fleeting glimpse of one of the temples of Thebes. It touches down at the international airport in the desert east of the cultivation, and within a few minutes the bus starts the short trip to the town, to deposit the traveller at his hotel.

If he comes by train, the visitor has a ten to twelve hour journey in an air-conditioned sleeper or coach. Thus the train is comfortable in the warmer weather, from the end of March to the beginning of November. Since the Nile valley south of Cairo gets no rain to mention, the train moves in a cloud of dust which is sucked in at every crack, but in the air-conditioned cars this nuisance is eliminated. Many hotel rooms, too, are air-conditioned.

Travellers of the nineteenth century had no such comforts. They came up river by boat, taking two to four weeks from Cairo. There were no hotels until the later part of this period. Many had house boats on which they lived for some months. In the first third of this century travel became more convenient, but only a little less leisurely, and Luxor was a favourite winter resort where habitués returned for several weeks each year. Today the bulk of visitors stay a day or two, and are whisked rapidly through the ancient monuments, hardly digesting what they are ill-prepared to view.

Some of the information they receive is not very helpful. Even the ancient name of the place " Thebes " is variously applied. Many of the guides have fallen into the habit of using it to describe the necropolis area to the west of the river and some modern map-makers have fallen into the same error. The chief ancient town was about the temple of Amon at Karnak; the Greeks gave it the name of Thebes and thought of it as encompassing all of the monuments in the district. It is usually this wider designation which is used in this volume. Within this area are a greater number of ancient monuments, temples, tombs, and tomb chapels, than in any other comparable area in the world.

On the east side of the river two temples gave their Arabic names to the towns which grew up round them, Luxor and Karnak. Luxor means " the castles " from the great columns which remain standing, and Karnak is an old word for " fortress ". The area of the largest enclosure at Karnak, which contains the great temple of Amon, the temple of Khonsu, and other smaller temples, chapels and shrines, is

60 acres; the whole area is more than twice as great. There are large sections which have still not been explored properly, and the task of a thorough investigation is greater than can be supported by the resources likely to be available to archaeologists in the foreseeable future.

On the west side of the river some of the place-names such as the Valley of the Tombs of the Kings are self-explanatory. Deir el-Bahri and Deir el-Medineh mean the " Northern Monastery " and the " Monastery of the City ", the city being Medinet Habu; there is no satisfactory explanation of the second word in this name. The Ramesseum takes its name from its builder, Ramesses II. The " Tombs of the Nobles ", more properly the " Tomb Chapels of the Theban Officials ", stretch out along the edge of the mountain, the various sections having different names. Between the road to the Valley of the Tombs of the Kings and that to Deir el Bahri is Dra Abu-el-Naga, " the Arm of Abu-el-Naga ", a local saint. The valley before Deir el-Bahri is the Asasif, an obscure word which perhaps means " labyrinth ". The next hill is called Khokha, " nectarine ". South of this lies the hill of Sheikh Abd-el-Gurna, named after a local and entirely mythical Moslem saint who, like many Christian saints, is a survival from pagan days, and goes back to the worship of the peak, the Gurn. The district of Sheikh Abd-el-Gurna includes the Lower Enclosure, an ancient quarry to the north-east of the hill, the Upper Enclosure, which surrounds the tomb chapels on the east side of the hill, and the tomb chapels in the plain which stretches toward the Ramesseum. The last hill with tomb chapels is Gurnet Murai, named after another local saint.

The visitor is faced by unfamiliar ideas. The " picture writing " carved or painted on a wall is hard to associate with methods of inscribing our own languages, yet hieroglyphic inscriptions are not greatly different from the printing in a newspaper of today. Egyptian hieroglyphs are similar to a rebus in which the picture of an object is used to represent its sound, even when the object has no relation to the word in which its sound occurs. James Henry Breasted illustrated this by a picture of a *bee* and a *leaf* which together made the English word *belief*, an inexact parallel since hieroglyphic writing showed neither vowels nor syllables. The Egyptian took a picture of a house, the name of which sounded something like *per*, and wrote with the same picture the word *peri*, meaning " to go out ". The picture of a game board for draughts, which was called *men*, was used for the second and third consonants of the name of the god Amon. The Egyptians did not write vowels, but only the 24 consonants of their language. There were one or more signs for each of these, and many other signs, like those just mentioned, which stood for two, or even three, consonants.

Such pictures were taken over by Semite miners employed by the Egyptians in Sinai about the time of Hatshepsut, and given Semitic names. From this crude writing developed the alphabet used by the Canaanites and the Phoenicians. The Greeks took over the signs of the latter and even some of the names for them, and many of these letters passed into the alphabets of Europe. A few of the original pictures can be recognized today; A is the head and horns of an ox turned upside down; M is ripples or waves of water; O is the pupil of the eye.

The kings of the period of Theban greatness had five names; the last two the prenomen, or throne name, and the nomen, or personal name, were enclosed in a *cartouche*, an elongated loop with a line at the base. This should not be confused with a similar oval surmounted by the bust of a foreigner which enclosed the name of a captured or subject city or community in lists of places conquered.

Egyptian historians divided the long list of their rulers into thirty families or dynasties; the division is still followed though it is now known that it is not always quite accurate. There is no standard spelling of Egyptian proper names; the practice adopted in this volume is to follow the consonantal structure of the Egyptian language, and most of the spellings have been used by others before me. Some scholars prefer to use Greek versions where these exist, but it seems inconsistent to write Montuhotep, for which there is no Greek witness, but to reject Amenhotep in favour of the Greek form, Amenophis. However, consistency has not always been maintained; Nitocris, for instance, might have been written Neitiker.

Egyptian architecture is not like Greek architecture, but it has had to borrow the terminology of the latter. The terms used therefore do not always represent the same things as in classical architecture. An architrave in an Egyptian building is the stone beam which rests on the abaci above the capitals of columns and supports the roof. Any hall whose roof is supported by columns is a hypostyle hall; when that built at Karnak by Seti I and Ramesses II is meant, it is capitalized as the Hypostyle Hall. One term has become almost the exclusive property of Egyptian architecture, the pylon. This consists of two towers on either side of a doorway, each rectangular in ground plan and with the rising surfaces sloping inwards, and joined by a porch over the doorway. In most of the larger pylons a stairway leads from one end to the porch and thence to the top of one or both of the towers.

Two sorts of relief were used, one raised, where the background is cut away, here designated *bas-relief* which means " low relief ", and the other where the figures or hieroglyphs are cut into the surface, designated " incised relief ". Within a figure in incised relief the details are always in bas-relief. Except for occasional remarks, no attempt has been made to discuss the concepts which guided the ancient artist; such discussions belong to more specialized publications. There is no difference in the artistic principles on which rested the wall paintings and the reliefs, and most reliefs were also painted. While in tomb chapels many paintings are on plaster surfaces, they are not frescoes, and this technique was not used in ancient Egypt.

The beginning of the Egyptian year was tied to the heliacal rising of Sirius, the Dog Star, about 19 July which coincided with the time that the river should begin to rise. In the prehistoric and protodynastic period New Year's day was determined by observation, but within one or two years of 2780, in the Third Dynasty, it was set by calculation as 365 days after the previous New Year, one-quarter of a day short of the actual length of the year. By the time it became evident that New Year's day no longer corresponded to the astronomical phenomenon, the conservatism of the Egyptians kept them from changing an established custom. Indeed, it may be that they had no accurate count of the years elapsed since the calendar was correct. In 1,460 years (four times 365), the " Sothic Cycle ", it was accurate again; this was in 1320-1317, approximately the date of the accession of Seti I. The lunar calendar, which determined many of the feasts, was adjusted regularly so that the principal festivity of each lunar month would fall in the proper month of the civil calendar. These peculiarities have aided greatly in working out ancient chronology, as in a few instances there are records of the day in the civil calendar on which the heliacal rising of the Dog Star was observed.

The river at Luxor flows approximately north-east, but the Egyptian thought of it as flowing north, and, except for the compass designations on the plans, all directions are given in terms of river north. The ancient people always spoke as if south was at the top of the map; for those of us who have become used to the opposite viewpoint it is difficult to think of " up south " and " down north ".

It may seem to those who see the ancient monuments of Thebes for the first time that the inhabitants were equally obscure about many things. As one comes to have some understanding of them, of why they erected temples to their gods and their chapels and tombs for their dead, they will appear as a people of great achievement, of great hope, and as the creators of one of the great civilizations which underlie our own.

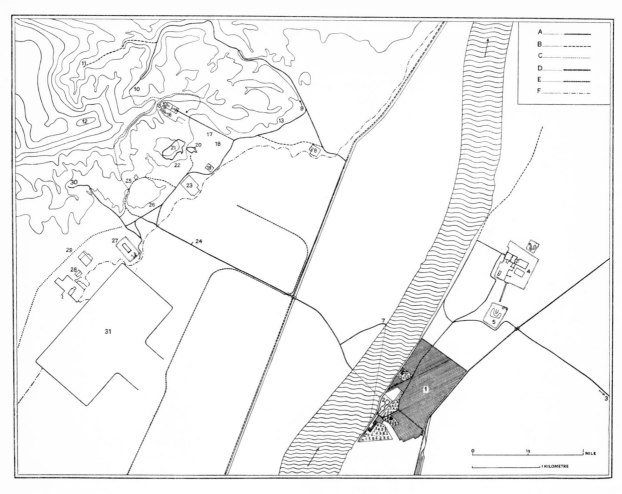

MAP OF THEBES

A Black-top road	9 Road to the Valley of the Tombs of the Kings	20 Sheikh Abd-el-Gurna, Lower Enclosure
B Dust Road		21 Sheikh Abd-el-Gurna, Upper Enclosure
C Foot Path	10 Valley of the Tombs of the Kings	22 Sheikh Abd-el-Gurna, plain
D Main railroad	11 West valley	
E Local railroad	12 The peak, el-Gurn, " The Horn "	23 The Ramesseum
F Edge of cultivation	13 Dra Abu-el-Naga	24 The Colossi of Memnon
	14 Deir el-Bahri, mortuary temple of Hatshepsut	25 Deir el Medineh
1 Luxor		26 Gurnet Murai
2 Luxor Temple	15 Deir el-Bahri, temple of Thutmosis III	27 Medinet Habu
3 Road to airport	16 Deir el-Bahri, mortuary temple of Mentuhotep II	28 Palace of Amenhotep III
4 Temenos of Amon		29 Ancient graded road
5 Temenos of Mut	17 Asasif	30 Valley of the Tombs of the Queens
6 Temenos of Montu	18 Khokha	
7 Landing on west bank of river	19 Mortuary temple of Thutmosis III, in ruins	31 Lake or harbur of Amenhotep III
8 Mortuary temple of Seti I		

14

Historical sketch

When Homer sang of Hundred-gated Thebes, her magnificence was fading. Through most of the second millenium before our era Amon, her god, had dominated the religious scene of Egypt and her leaders held sway over the land and built its empire. Much booty from their conquests had been dedicated to the Theban gods, whose temples had grown in size and wealth almost beyond imagination. In the western cliffs and valleys her royalty and officials were buried in splendour. The objects interred with them, the decorations of their tombs and tomb chapels and the endowments for their services sought to assure that the life they had lived along the Nile would continue in the world of the dead.

Toward the end of this period the centre of political power moved elsewhere; economic decay set in; most of her burials were violated. Yet for another thousand years the state sanctuaries continued to function, to be refurbished and at times enlarged. Even in their decadence the great sandstone temples of Thebes were famed throughout the world. The Egyptian name of the temple of Amon at Karnak sounded to Greek ears like that of their Boeotian city, so they bestowed on the Egyptian centre the name " Thebes ", which has been used ever since for the great area of temples and tombs near the modern town of Luxor.

The Assyrian invaders and the contemporary Hebrew prophets knew Thebes by the designation which became familiar when the city attained prominence in the Eighteenth Dynasty. Jeremiah (XLVI, 25) promised that punishment would be brought upon Amon of No, and Nahum (III, 8) pointed to the destruction of No-Amon as a lesson to Nineveh. This was their vocalization of the words we translate as " The City " and " The City of Amon ". The Greeks translated the latter as Diospolis. Its own countrymen also spoke of it as the " Southern City ". Since Amon was identified with the sun god Re, by comparison with the ancient seat of this god, On (Heliopolis of the Greeks), Thebes also was known as " Southern On ".

Her actual name was yet another, Waset; this was first the name of the nome, or province, in which Thebes was situated. Early in the Old Kingdom Upper Egypt, the Nile Valley between Memphis and the island of Elephantine, was already divided into twenty-two nomes, of which Thebes was the fourth from the south. Among the several statue groups from the valley temple of the pyramid of king Menkaure (Mycerinus) is one showing the monarch with the Theban nome personified as a god standing by his side (Pl. 5). The symbol of the nome was a peculiar sceptre, or staff, decorated with an ostrich feather and tied with a ribbon. Originally this was a branching limb trimmed to this design. In temple reliefs this unadorned staff is

15

often carried by the gods. As a hieroglyph it means " dominion " and while there is no connection between this meaning and the symbol which designates the nome and the city, it may be seen as an accidental foreshadowing of the time of Thebes' pre-eminence in the Middle and New Kingdoms, when it was known as the " Mistress of Every City ".

The prehistoric river Nile cut its way down through the North African plateau by stages, leaving terraces as evidence of each deepening cut. The lower four show increasing evidence of stone age artifacts as man, driven from the drying plateau, sought food along the water's edge. The river, having reached its historic level, built up a flood plain by the deposit of silt in its annual inundations. Small elevations which were slightly above the highest waters gave refuge to man and suggested to him that on such a mound, first uncovered from the primeval waters which enveloped the world, the creator god had made his home and mankind had come into being.

The Nile, coming from the south, turns north-east at El-Rizeikat and continues in that general direction for twenty-five miles before turning northward again. Just above this town the desert comes down to the river on either bank; this was the southern boundary of the Theban nome. To the north on the eastern bank the desert touches the river at Khizam, where the stream turns north; here was the northern boundary of the nome on that side. On the western bank the desert comes to the river near the Eleventh Dynasty cemetery opposite Karnak. Here once stood the town of Heri-her-Amon, " My face is upon Amon ", which was the northern boundary of the nome there. The distance from El-Rizeikat to Heri-her-Amon corresponds closely to the length of the Theban nome given on the shrine of Senusert I, three *schoeni*, just short of twenty miles.

In the Theban nome the arable land was divided into three segments, the meandering river forming the arcs and the desert edge the chords. Each had its cult centre, the ancient names preserved in the designations of the modern towns. On the western bank the segment goes from border to border, with Armant the chief town. On the eastern bank a small southern segment had its centre at Tod; the northern segment, roughly equal in area to that on the western bank, had Meda-mud as the cult centre. In each town the chief god was Montu, a human figure with a hawk head, but also described as a bull. Montu was the god of the Theban nome throughout the pre-Christian history of Egypt.

During the first five dynasties of Egypt the Theban nome seems to have been of little importance. The administrative centre was at Memphis and while there was continuous traffic on the river, granite for the pyramids coming down from Assuan and expeditions going to and coming from Nubia, there are only traces of activity in the Theban towns. However, it may be that there were more extensive building operations in these places than indicated, the evidence having been removed in subsequent reconstruction. Throughout the period the mastaba tomb chapels of the chief officials were near the pyramids of the kings they served, but at the begin-ning of the Sixth Dynasty a gradual decentralization of administration set in and the nome officials often were interred in their home communities. In the Theban nome at least four nomarchs (rulers of a nome) cut their tombs into the hill now known as Khokha, opposite the settlement on the east bank which, when it first appeared in the inscriptions, was known as Waset and is now known as the city of Thebes.

In 2182 the Old Kingdom ended in chaos. For a short period there were nume-rous claimants to the throne, a situation reflected in the later tradition of seventy kings in seventy days for the Seventh Dynasty. For about two decades the Eighth Dynasty ruled from Memphis; the combined length of reign for four of its kings was twelve years, so that the succession of the other eleven was rapid. In Upper Egypt they had a centre at Koptos, twenty-five miles north of Thebes. One of the rulers appointed Idy, a son of Shamay, the Vizier of Upper Egypt, to be in charge of the seven southernmost nomes. This was the district known as the " Head of the South ", first mentioned in the Sixth Dynasty, which later included the eighth and ninth nomes. The succeeding Ninth Dynasty, which ruled for thirty years, made its administrative centre at Heracleopolis, about sixty miles south of Memphis.

During this half-century the hold of the northern rulers on the Head of the South was precarious. The inscriptions of the nomarchs of this district and of Middle Egypt tell of local fighting and famine, with an allegation of cannibalism. Almost coincidentally with the assumption of power by the Ninth Dynasty a leader named Intef became, according to his descendants, " Hereditary Prince and Count, Nomarch of the Theban Nome, Keeper of the Door of the South ", the last title a claim to the control of Elephantine. Those who followed in power looked upon him as the founder of the line which produced the Eleventh and Twelfth Dynasties. He was succeeded by two or three nomarchs of the same name who were in continual warfare with the chieftains of nearby nomes.

Though these Intefs gave nominal allegiance to the kings at Heracleopolis, they consolidated their hold on the Head of the South. In 2133 Montuhotep I, son of the last nomarch Intef, broke with the northern ruler and proclaimed himself king. Within three years the Ninth Dynasty was followed by the Tenth. Montuhotep was soon succeeded by his son Intef I who died in 2118; his young son Intef II succeeded him. He boasts that at Thebes he " filled the temple (of a god whose name the Amarna zealots erased) with sacred libation vases ", and for other gods " built their temples, their steps being clay-whitened, their door frames made steady, and their offering endowments established ". In his reign Thebes was able to enjoy some peace and prosperity. For fifty years he dominated the Head of the South and was succeeded by his son Intef III who, already advanced in age, died after a rule of eight years.

Like his town Waset, Amon, whose name means " hidden ", was at first of little importance. His origin is obscure. In the Pyramid Texts, extensive religious and mortuary compilations found on the walls of the tomb chambers of the last king of the Fifth Dynasty and of the kings of the Sixth, this god and his female counterpart Amonet appear as the primordial deities of southern Upper Egypt, in association with similar deities from Hermopolis of Middle Egypt and Heliopolis of the Delta. Twice more he appears in these texts, once in a reference to the " Throne of Amon " and once where a parallel text mentions Min, the ithyphallic god of Koptos and Akhmim with whom Amon became identified.[1]

The first documentary localization of Amon at Thebes is in an inscription of the nomarch Rehuy who lived after the end of the Sixth Dynasty; he " delivered provisions to the temple of Amon during the years of famine ". An official who served under an unnamed king, perhaps Intef I, tells that his master performed services for Amon and other gods.

The Head of the South was comparatively quiet when Montuhotep II ascended the throne in 2060. His court was made up mainly of officials of Theban birth, and his wives and concubines were clothed in splendour, if the remains of jewelry found on their bodies are an indication.

The peace did not continue. About 2040 the eighth nome revolted and the suppression of the insurrection was continued by a military campaign northward, resulting in the fall of the Heracleopolitan kingdom. Now Thebes was truly the Mistress of Every City in Egypt. Whatever buildings befitting her new position may have been erected, subsequent building and alteration in Karnak has removed all evidence, though in the other towns of the Theban nome traces of temples of this time survive. On the west bank the monarch erected his mortuary temple, the lower parts of which are still to be seen.

After a reign of half a century Montuhotep II was followed by his aging son Montuhotep III in 2009. In the eighth year of his reign, a landholder named Hekanakht, away from home on business, wrote back letters with detailed instructions concerning the care of his home and his household. These indicated that there was a shortage of food throughout the country.

It is significant that famine was still a threat at the end of the Eleventh Dynasty, when the country had become stable. It may be that the chaotic conditions following the end of the Sixth Dynasty were due to an extended period of low inundations and scarcity of water rather than that the shortage of food was due to the fragmentation of the country. The " prophecy " of Neferty, a political tract written a few years later, speaks of low Niles in the preceding years, but the tendentious nature of the work suggests that it should not be relied on as historical evidence. The principal motive of the Theban nomarchs in securing control of the Head of the South may well have been the need to assure adequate provisions for their people.

In 1997 the fourth and last of the Montuhoteps began his reign. His vizier Amenemhat (Greek, Ammenemes) took over full control of the kingdom in 1991, beginning the Twelfth Dynasty. He represented himself, while vizier, as loyal to his royal lord and commemorated Montuhotep IV in his monuments. His successors claimed to be the rightful successors of the kings of the previous dynasty and there is no reason to suppose that Amenemhat's assumption of the kingship was an usurpation.

The name borne by the new king was known as early as the reign of Intef III and the sheets in which were wrapped the bodies of sixty soldiers who had fallen in the siege of some fortress in a campaign of Montuhotep II have in ten instances names compounded with Amon. One already shows Amon's claims to power, Sankh-Amensekhemtawy, meaning, " Amon, the (most) powerful (god) of the Two Lands, sustains life ". But while names compounded with Amon were popular in court circles, none occurs in the list of more than eighty persons in the letters of Hekanakht and another contemporary archive. However, in the latter a blessing is pronounced in the name of Amon-re, the earliest evidence of Amon's identification with the ancient sun god.

The kings of the Eleventh Dynasty had ruled their country from Thebes, making frequent trips throughout the land with a show both of friendship and of force. Amenemhat found his native city too distant from the rest of the country for the exercise of adequate control, and, on the border between Upper and Lower Egypt, established a residence which he named Ity-tawy, " Seizer of the Two Lands ". For two centuries he and his descendants, the Senuserts (Greek, Sesostris) and the Amenemhats, led their country in a period of advancing culture and prosperity. They and their officials were buried in pyramids and tombs in a stretch of desert southwards from Dahshur to the mouth of the Fayyum.

Though Thebes was no longer the main arena of political activity, its prominence as a religious centre was assured. An extant altar from the temple of Amenemhat at Karnak was dedicated to Amon-re, Lord of the Thrones of the Two Lands, an epithet foreshadowed in the Pyramid Texts. Senusert I added spectacular buildings for Amon, among them a limestone chapel described on page 75. Here Amon is shown in human form wearing two plumes on his head. In more than two-thirds of the representations he appears in the ithyphallic form. In addition to the epithet already mentioned, he has those of " Foremost of Ipet-esut " and " King of the Gods ". Though the compound name Amon-re is usual, Re may be omitted; this seems to have been of little consequence. Thus at the beginning of the Twelfth Dynasty Amon already appears essentially as he was to continue thereafter.

Amenemhat I, after twenty years of reign, made his son Senusert coregent. The wisdom of this act was proven when, ten years later, the king was assassinated in

1. Painted sandstone statue of Montuhotep II in jubilee attire, found in a " tomb " at his mortuary temple, Deir el-Bahri. *Cairo Museum*

2. The mortuary temples of Montuhotep II (left) and Hatshepsut (right) at Deir el-Bahri. The ruins of the newly discovered temple of Thutmosis III are to the left of the upper terrace of Hatshepsut's temple.

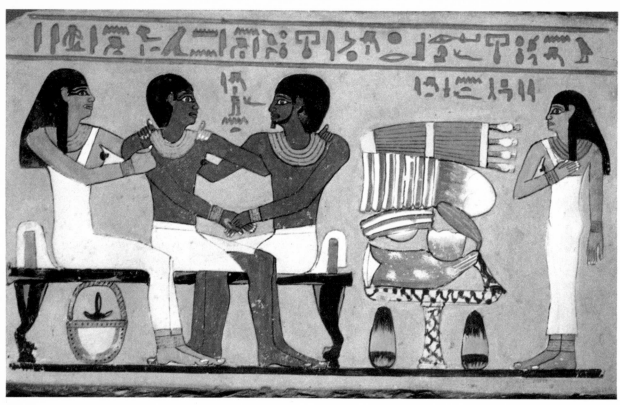

his bedchamber at night by a dissident faction. Senusert, returning from a campaign in the north-western desert when he heard the news, left immediately for the Residence and was able to prevent the expected civil war.

Throughout this dynasty the rulers associated their heirs with them on the throne. Their concern for the welfare of Egypt and the strengthening of the central power was shown by the pacification of Nubia, the eventual elimination of the nomarchs, the reclamation of the Fayyum, and administrative reforms. Under Senusert III, whose rule began in 1878, the country was divided into three departments, the southernmost of which was the Department of the Head of the South, with its administrative centre at Thebes. Reports to and from the Residence were channelled through the Reporter of the Southern City and most of the high government officials had their representatives resident in Thebes.

The Twelfth Dynasty came to an end in 1786. With the Thirteenth Dynasty there was a great shift in the centre of authority. The office of vizier became the hereditary right of a powerful family. Yet the average reign of the kings was two and a half years and, except for two brothers, there is no sign of interrelationship. Upper Egypt and Nubia continued without great change and many monuments were erected in Thebes. A papyrus from there of about 1740 records the acquisition by a private person of ninety or more household slaves, of whom half were Asiatics. This indicates that there was an increasing infiltration of these people into the north-eastern delta.

The history of the entrance of the Asiatics is not clear, but by 1720 they had established a centre in Avaris and by 1674 overwhelmed the Egyptian ruler in Lisht. At a later time they were remembered as the Hyksos, a name derived from the Egyptian words for " Rulers of Foreign Countries ". Nubia broke away from Egypt and its rulers became allied with the Hyksos. Thebes reasserted her independence and, though tributary to the Hyksos, controlled the southern fourteen nomes. There was an understanding between the foreigners in the north and the earlier rulers of the Seventeenth Dynasty in Thebes by which the Hyksos were allowed to quarry granite in Assuan and the Thebans could pasture their cattle in the delta marshes and import from the north emmer for their swine.

Many of the rulers of the Seventeenth Dynasty were buried beneath small pyramids which stood in a row along the foot of the hill of Dra Abu-el-Naga at Thebes. Several added monuments at Karnak; Sebekemsaf, about 1645-1630, was remembered in the reign of Ramesses IX because " he made ten notable works for Amon-re, King of the Gods, whose monuments still stand within " (Karnak).

Toward the end of this dynasty difficulties arose between the Hyksos and the Theban dynasts. A fragment of a papyrus recounts the visit of a messenger from the Hyksos prince Apophis to the court of Sekenenre Tao II, called " the Brave". The northern ruler complained that the bellowing of hippopotami in a pool at Thebes kept him awake at night. The Egyptians considered the hippopotamus an animal of the god Set with whom they identified the chief deity of the Hyksos. The harpooning of the hippopotamus was a sacred rite in Egypt and this would be a scandal to those who held Set in reverence. The legend related a trial of strength between Amon, whom Sekenenre served, and Set, whom Apophis worshipped. The outcome of the contest is not recorded, but it can be certain that Amon was victorious.

Sekenenre Tao II and his queen Ahhotep were the children of a like-named king and his queen Tetisheri. An exquisite statue in the British Museum shows the queen mother in her younger years. A mummy of a little, old balding lady now in the Egyptian Museum in Cairo possibly is hers. She lived into the next dynasty and future generations held her in great reverence. Her son, the hero of the legend, met a violent death, perhaps at the hands of the Hyksos. Her daughter,

3. Painted funerary stele of Amenemhat, in incised relief, found near Deir el-Bahri. Twelfth Dynasty. Cairo Museum

4. Model of fishing canoes, from the tomb of Meket-re. End of Eleventh Dynasty. Cairo Museum

Queen Ahhotep, was buried with the finest collection of jewelry, other than the Tutankhamon treasure, ever found at Thebes.

Kamose, son of Sekenenre Tao II, carried on the quarrel. At Karnak he erected two stelae telling of his campaign against the Hyksos. The beginning of one had been known for half a century from a copy a schoolboy made on his writing board; it was authenticated by fragments of a stele found later at Karnak. The second stele was discovered in A. D. 1954, re-used as a foundation of a statue of Ramesses II in front of the Second Pylon at Karnak. These records tell that Kamose, in his third year, against the advice of his courtiers, went down to attack the Hyksos outposts. He pushed northwards sixty miles beyond his boundary at Cusae and scouts on his flanks caught a messenger from Apophis bearing a letter to his ally the ruler of Nubia, pleading for a united campaign against the Theban king.

Kamose died soon after his triumphal return to Thebes and was succeeded in 1570 by his younger brother Ahmose, who married his full sister Ahmose-Nefertari. He drove the Hyksos out of Egypt, pursuing them beyond the north-eastern border. Then he quelled his foes in Nubia and put down rebels in Egypt. Just when these events took place in his reign of a quarter of a century it is not possible to determine.[2]

Though Ahmose and his son and successor Amenhotep I were direct descendants of the last rulers of the Seventeenth Dynasty, Egyptologists follow the ancient tradition in beginning the Eighteenth Dynasty with the expulsion of the Hyksos and with Ahmose as its first king. Under Amenhotep I, who began his twenty year reign in 1546, a new building phase began at Karnak. In later generations this ruler, with his mother Ahmose-Nefertari, became the patrons of the Theban necropolis. With Amenhotep I the practice began of separating the place of royal burial from the chapel, resulting in the use of the Valley of the Tombs of the Kings for interment while the mortuary temples were built along the edge of the western desert.

Amenhotep I continued to expand into Nubia and to consolidate Theban power in Egypt. He married two of his sisters, Ahhotep II and Ahmose Merit-Amon. By the first he had a son who died in infancy and at his death there was no prince of his line to succeed him. He had designated as his heir the husband of his younger sister, also called Ahmose. This man, Thutmosis I, was a soldier, born of a non-royal mother; he may have been related to the royal family.

It has been asserted that the legitimacy of an Egyptian monarch was based on his marriage to the daughter of the chief queen. This hypothesis has been used to explain the brother-sister marriages of the Eighteenth Dynasty. Whatever the truth of such a view may be, the real strength of the ruler lay in his own ability and the loyalty of the chief civil servants who administered his realm. Often these continued their positions from one reign to another, supervising the military forces, the temples and their priesthoods, and economic affairs. In the Eighteenth Dynasty many were buried in the Theban necropolis. Their accounts of their services and rewards and the pictures on the walls of their tomb chapels are primary sources of our knowledge of the history and culture of their times.

Thutmosis I followed the example of his predecessors by campaigning in Nubia and also took his army northward to the Euphrates. He was hardly more fortunate in his heirs than Amenhotep I; his two eldest sons predeceased him and he was followed in about 1512 by a third son by a younger princess, who took the same throne name as his father. The young Thutmosis II was married to his half-sister Hatshepsut, daughter of Ahmose II. Again there was no male heir in the direct line and when the king died in 1504 the throne fell to the son of Isis, one of the women of the king's harem.

This boy, named like his father and grandfather, became known to history as

5. King Menkaure with personified nome of Thebes, from the valley temple of this king at Giza. Fourth Dynasty. *Cairo Museum*

6
7

Thutmosis III. At his father's death he was between six and ten years old. In his later years he tells both that he had been made coregent by his father and that Amon had designated him when he was serving the god at Karnak. He certainly was the chosen successor, but as he was a minor, his father's chief queen, Hatshepsut, acted as regent. She and Thutmosis III are two of the most remarkable persons in Egyptian history.

Hatshepsut was undoubtedly able and ambitious. It has been customary in judging her to follow the understandable animosity shown towards her by Thutmosis III after her death. The gravest charge that has to be brought against her is that, in the second year of her regency, she decided to take the office as well as the responsibility of rule. During one of the feasts of the god she went up river in a towed barge, the king and the bark of Amon with her, and in the Luxor Temple was crowned king. The festivities featured music and acrobatic dancers. That these were part of the god's festivities and not special for the occasion is indicated by similar performances shown in a depiction of the Feast of Opet during the reign of Tutankhamon. Following the ceremonies Hatshepsut, the newly crowned king, and her now coregent Thutmosis III returned to the palace attached to the temple of Amon at Karnak. Thereafter representations show her dressed in male garb and she is often referred to by masculine pronouns. She claimed that she had been crowned first by her father Thutmosis I and devoted a wall of her mortuary temple to the legend that she was the child of Amon himself. It may well be that this claim was made by every monarch.

Helped by able administrators, Hatshepsut embarked on a vast building programme throughout Egypt. In Karnak she erected a central sanctuary for Amon and set up two pairs of obelisks. The most spectacular of her works was her mortuary temple at Deir el-Bahri, the architect of which was Senmut, her chief adviser and closest confidant. She sponsored a Red Sea expedition to Punt and once led troops into Nubia. Most of her inscriptions were only in her name and Thutmosis III was generally ignored. Yet on her sanctuary for the bark of Amon he frequently appears, especially in the scenes of the major feasts, and his own mortuary temple, and the canal before it, are named.

As Thutmosis III grew older he gradually increased his power. Senmut died about the seventeenth year of the joint reign; in his tomb sometimes his name was erased, but not that of Hatshepsut. The last dated monument giving her name jointly with that of Thutmosis III is in the twentieth year. Between then and the twenty-second year she died, and sometime thereafter Thutmosis removed from office most of the senior officials who had served her, but his eventual erasure of her name and figure on the monuments was later than generally assumed. He lost no time in embarking on a campaign into Syria, subsequently followed by others and accounts of these military exploits are written on walls in Karnak. The great temple of Amon was further enlarged, but it was only in the latter years of his reign that he replaced Hatshepsut's sanctuary. He was the greatest conqueror his country ever had and under him the Egyptian empire reached its fullest extent.

On his death in the fifty-fourth year of his reign, 1450, Thutmosis III was succeeded by his son Amenhotep II. The mummy of the deceased king shows him to have been a short man, about five feet two inches in height; his son was taller by almost two and a half inches. Both boasted of their prowess with a bow; a description of the latter's ability is given on a granite stele in Karnak. Amenhotep II's military leadership was similar to that of his father. In 1425 he was succeeded by his son Thutmosis IV who, after a reign of eight years, was followed by his son Amenhotep III.

For a century and a half before Amenhotep III came to the throne in 1417, the

6. Painted bas-relief of the vulture goddess Nekhbet, Anubis shrine, mortuary temple of Hatshepsut, Deir el-Bahri.

7. Painted bas-relief of Hatshepsut's offerings to Amon, Anubis shrine, mortuary temple of Hatshepsut Deir el-Bahri.

rulers of Egypt found much of their time taken by the enlarging and defence of their empire in Nubia and Asia. It is true that their officials supervised the erection and repair of temples throughout the land and that Thebes benefitted as much as, if not more than, any locality. When other tasks permitted, the kings were present to participate in the great feasts at Thebes, but there is no certainty that they stayed there long or that they made it their chief residence. Indeed, there is some indication that Amenhotep III's immediate three forefathers spent much of their time between military campaigns in Memphis.

Now the empire appeared secure, and it was only in the early years of his reign that Amenhotep III made any pretence of military activity. He constructed a large palace compound in the desert to the south of his mortuary temple and in front of it excavated a large lake or basin. By the time he came to the throne he was married to a commoner named Tiy. She was the king's " great wife ", the chief queen, and almost as remarkable a woman as was Hatshepsut. Amenhotep III remained close to her all his life. Often she is shown with him in statues and on reliefs; a colossal representation of the pair is the largest piece of sculpture in the Cairo Museum. Tiy had much influence in the affairs of the empire. After the death of her royal husband, King Tushratta of Mitanni wrote her two letters asking that the good relations between the two countries be maintained through the reign of her son.

Amenhotep III was fond of issuing large commemorative scarabs. Five such are known; the earliest fixes the title of Tiy as the ranking queen. In the second year of the reign another recounts the capture of a hundred wild bulls in a two-day royal hunt, and in the tenth year yet another recalls that since his accession Amenhotep had killed 102 lions in his hunting preserves. In the same year a scarab was issued to announce the reception of the daughter of the king of Mitanni and her 317 attendants into the royal harem, and the last, in the eleventh year, gives an account of the building of a pleasure lake for Tiy near Akhmim, similar to the one before his Theban palace. It is recorded that it was 6400 feet long by 1200 feet wide, and was dug in fifteen days.

In the Theban region Amenhotep III replaced the temple at Luxor and the one in the southern region of Karnak dedicated to Mut, the goddess of the Theban triad. The Third Pylon at Karnak is his; in this, fortunately for posterity, he used blocks from earlier structures for the foundations and the core. He planned, if he did not actually begin, the Tenth Pylon. His mortuary temple on the edge of the western desert was the largest ever constructed, but today the colossi which stood before it are the only remains immediately noticeable.

Like his predecessors he was served by able officials, and to his favourites he granted tomb chapels more magnificent than had been given to private persons hitherto. One of the most outstanding of these was the Royal Scribe Amenhotep, son of Hapu, who may have been in charge of the building activities of his ruler and who brought from Gebel Ahmar, near Cairo, a block of red sandstone for the great colossus which once stood before the Tenth Pylon at Karnak. He was given his own funerary temple to the south of that of his lord and a number of statues of him were placed about Karnak. He was past eighty when he died; later he became a god of healing and was so regarded down into the Roman period.

After the first ten years of his reign Amenhotep III lost interest in physical activity. During the following twenty-eight years the internal affairs of Egypt seem to reflect peace and well-being, yet in retrospect one realizes that there was a serious malaise in which the religious establishments were involved.

From the beginning of the Twelfth Dynasty Amon had been the national god, identified from that time with Re, the sun god of Heliopolis. Whether then Amon's endowments grew out of proportion to those of other gods is not known. In the

Eighteenth Dynasty certainly more attention was given to the Theban god than to Re of Heliopolis and probably more than to Ptah of Memphis.

The sun had been personified as Re and other names were given to its various attributes. From the Middle Kingdom the word " aten " had been used as the name of the physical disc. Under Amenhotep III this word came into more common use, but just when in this reign the " aten " became considered a god is not clear. On the death of Amenhotep III in 1379, his son Amenhotep IV came to the throne. Until his fifth year he continued to use this name. Somewhere in Karnak he erected a temple to Re, where he appeared in conventional representation worshipping Re-Harakhty, " Re-Horus-of-the-horizon ", and with an epithet which included the name of " Aten ". Soon after he took the name of Akhenaten, " It is well with the Aten ", and moved his residence to the area now known as El-Amarna, where he remained until his death. To what extent political strife or jealousy of the priesthood of Amon influenced the change is a matter for speculation.

The temple which Akhenaten built for Aten at Karnak, where he erected the grotesque colossal statues of himself, was torn down at the end of his reign. The change from the conventional art to the new Amarna style appears in the tomb chapel of the Vizier Ramose, However, it is mostly the negative aspects of the Amarna revolution which concerned Thebes. When Aten was proclaimed the sole god the other temples were closed; the figures and names of the gods, and even the word " gods ", were erased. Much of this defacement was done carelessly, some by illiterate workmen who hacked out other words which had a resemblance to the name of Amon.

During the Amarna period, which lasted about a decade and a half, the king adopted a practical monotheism in religion, while the art forms became less formalized and sometimes approached caricature. The written language changed from the classical expressions of the Middle Kingdom to usages much closer to colloquial speech. It was in this period that the word " pharaoh ", meaning " the great house ", was applied regularly to the person of the ruler rather than to his palace, a usage that goes back to the reign of Thutmosis III. Following the abandonment of the Amarna experiment there was an attempt to return to classical usages in written accounts, but it was never quite successful. Letters and reports written by Thebans during the next two centuries are in a style which is designated " Late Egyptian ", the usage which came in during the Amarna period.

There is no period of Egyptian history which has intrigued recent generations so much as that of the Amarna interlude. The monotheistic faith has appealed to many as the forerunner of Judeo-Christian belief. Yet it was largely an intellectual exercise practised by an effete clique surrounding the king and had little effect on the general populace. Internal dissension and lack of general support brought the episode to an end with the death of Akhenaten in 1362. Even before his death he seems to have compromised his cult: in about 1364 he appointed his son-in-law Smenkhkare coregent and sent him to Thebes to make peace with the priests of the traditional religion of Amon.

It is doubtful that Smenkhkare outlived his father-in-law by more than a few months. He was followed, in 1361, by a youth who had lived in El-Amarna and who, with his young wife, the daughter of Akhenaten, changed his name to conform to the return to the ancient religious heritage. Had it not been for the almost miraculous preservation of the funerary equipment in his tomb, Tutankhamon and his queen Ankhesenamon would hardly have been noticed in the course of history. In the eight years of Tutankhamon's reign valiant attempts were made to restore the former order, attempts which were continued by his successor, the elderly priest Ay, whose family seems to have had some connection with that of Queen Tiy.

When this aged king died in 1348 there was no legitimate heir. The throne was taken by the general Haremhab who had been responsible for much of the administration under Tutankhamon and perhaps even under Akhenaten. While still the ruler's chief deputy he had built a tomb at Memphis. At the beginning of his reign he came to Thebes for the Feast of Opet and was crowned in the temple of Luxor, as had been Hatshepsut. At the close of the ceremony Amon returned to Thebes and Haremhab fared northward to his residence. Never thereafter did any major ruler make his headquarters in Thebes, though the pharaohs often visited it. But Amon remained the national god and his temples in the Theban district made this city the religious centre of Egypt. Haremhab's desire to placate the priesthood of Amon is shown not only by the addition to his name of " beloved of Amon ", common to many rulers, but also by his choice of the epithet, " Great of Marvels in Karnak ", as part of his five-fold titulary.

This was no idle boast for he built or completed three of the great pylons for the temple of Amon. On a stele at the rear of the pylon now designated as the tenth, he recounts a great administrative reform. Many of the chief officials of Amenhotep III had ceased functioning when the Amarna revolution began and certainly those whom Akhenaten had appointed were too closely identified with his heresy and perhaps too inefficient to continue in office after him. A large number of Haremhab's appointments to office, including the priesthood, were outstanding soldiers. In many temples he restored the scenes and inscriptions which Akhenaten's agents had mutilated. His successors did not recognize the reign of Akhenaten and those of his immediate followers and credited the reign of Haremhab with the years from the death of Amenhotep III.

As his successor Haremhab chose his deputy in the army, Paramessu. When this elderly officer became king in 1320, he took the name of Ramesses, the first of that name. With him began, according to Egyptian tradition, the Nineteenth Dynasty. Though he lived little over a year thereafter, apparently he planned, and may even have begun, the great Hypostyle Hall at Karnak. His son, Seti I, continued this work throughout a reign of approximately fifteen years, during which he was occupied by military campaigns. He did not live to see the completion of his building projects at Thebes. One of these was his mortuary temple in which there was a chapel dedicated to his father.

Seti I died in 1304. His son and successor, Ramesses II, claimed that he had been chosen by his father as a youth. Because there seems to have been an older son who predeceased Seti, some have doubted this, but it must have been essentially true. In fact, there is evidence that Ramesses II was coregent with his father; the dating of Ramesses II's reign, however, starts only with his independent rule.

In the remaining sixty-seven years of his life the great event was his campaign which took place in the fifth year of his reign against a Hittite confederation with headquarters in Kadesh on the Orontes river in Syria. In his eagerness to attack, the king, with one of his four divisions, advanced beyond the main part of his troops and found himself trapped by the enemy. With a great deal of courage he fought his way free, aided, no doubt, by the arrival of reinforcements. Afterwards he deemed it a great victory and had scenes and accounts of the battle carved on the walls of his great temples. Sixteen years later Ramesses II concluded a peace treaty with the Hittite king. The Egyptian version is at Karnak, while a Hittite version translated into Akkadian is also in existence on two clay tablets. In the thirty-fourth year of his reign the king added to his harem a daughter of the reigning Hittite ruler, an event which he commemorated in a long text, two copies of which are at Karnak.

The intention of Ramesses II to patronize Amon shows in the monarch's appearance, in the first year of his reign, at the Feast of Opet. It was then that he appointed Nebwenenef as the High Priest of Amon. Whether the previous incumbent

8. Ships taking the Mayor of Thebes, Sennefer, and his wife, Meryt, on the funerary voyage to Abydos and back. Wall painting in the burial chamber. Reign of Amenhotep II. Theban Tomb No. 96

had died about the same time as Seti I, or whether Ramesses II was determined to have his own man in this office we do not know. The priest had his tomb chapel in the Theban hills, but was also accorded a mortuary temple just south of that of Seti I. He is the only commoner besides Amenhotep, son of Hapu, known to have been so honoured.

Ramesses II in his long reign was not only a prodigious builder but, by usurping the names of his ancestors and predecessors, took credit for their monuments as well. Because of these acts and his boasts, it has become fashionable to drop the epithet, " the Great ", that scholars of the nineteenth century of our era bestowed on him, and to regard him, with some distaste, as a megalomaniac. The truth is that the length of his reign, the prosperity of the country which the Amarna interlude had little diminished, and the comparative peace of the times enabled him to build to an extent previously unequalled. Some have complained that the style of the decoration of his temples is decadent. In part this is due to the coarser sandstone which the large buildings made necessary, but one does feel that Seti I's artists did finer work on the same material. As for his usurpation, most of the kings of preceding dynasties tore down the temples of earlier rulers that they might erect grander ones. Nor was Ramesses more boastful than other monarchs, though he was certainly more wordy. The very conception of Egyptian kingship placed the sovereign in a unique position. He, a god himself, acted as the mediator between the gods and Egypt, and as he served the gods according to their traditional desires, so the material prosperity of the land increased. Certainly in Thebes Ramesses built to the glory of Amon and he clearly expected, as other rulers had, that such honouring of the god would honour him also.

It may be that the building programme was too great for the good of the country. When Ramesses II died in 1237 at about the age of ninety, he was succeeded by his fourteenth son Merenptah, the older sons having predeceased their father. The new pharaoh seems to have obtained most of the stone for his monuments by quarrying other structures. He used the back of a stele of Amenhotep III to make one of the records of the greatest crisis of his reign. Tribes from the eastern islands and the north-eastern littoral of the Mediterranean, driven from their homes at the time of the Trojan War, plied the sea looking for plunder and places to settle. Merenptah repulsed their attempt to invade the north-east delta in his fifth year. As an appendage to the account of his victory erected in his mortuary temple, he also boasts of minor conquests, including the assertion, " Israel is wasted; non-existent is its offspring ". This sole mention of these Biblical people in all Egyptian records has made this account known as the " Israel Stele ".

The beginning of Theban ascendancy was in a period of economic difficulty; the nearing close of her time of greatness was in another. The real prosperity of the land depended on the delicate balance between the amount of food available and the needs of the populace. It is estimated that the agricultural worker and his family could live on half his produce, the other half going to support the rest of the population.

The cycle of the farming year in the region of Thebes is as follows. In the last third of July the Nile begins to rise, reaching its height about the end of August, normally covering all the land to the edge of the desert. The water begins to subside about the end of September. Dykes kept the water out of some fields which could be planted as soon as the water was high enough for them to be irrigated. In various areas other dykes trapped the high water which was gradually released in the ensuing months to irrigate other fields. Planting began as soon as the water was off the fields, starting in October for the plots inundated and drained immediately. The crop was harvested in February and March, with threshing any time in the dry months ahead. Since rain was extremely rare, it played no part in the agricultural cycle.

9. Head of figure of Senusert I garbed as Osiris, from Karnak. Cairo Museum

Military campaigns into Syria were planned, whenever possible, to follow closely after the Egyptian harvest. Thus not only was the local food supply not diminished, but also the harvests to the north could be used or destroyed. We have little information about the season for building. However, advantage could be taken of the dry period to quarry stone and move it to the site by river during the inundation.

The temples had a great number of workers attached to their foundations, many of them slaves, including captives. Certain Egyptian officials had the right to impress the citizenry for government service and penalties for evasion were severe. In the Middle Kingdom the corvée was handled by the Department of Labour Procurement. If this labour was recruited at a time when it was not needed to build dykes or till fields, no serious dislocation of the economy would occur.

If, however, a heavy building programme or unseasonal military effort drew off personnel who would otherwise be engaged in food production, the economy would decline. Another cause of insufficient food was inundation levels which were either above or below normal. For a few years this situation could be met by reducing rations and drawing on stored supplies, but prolonged low Niles would bring about serious dislocation of the normal way of life and great suffering. The various accounts and traditions of famine years from lack of water indicate that this did happen.

Lack of diligence in attending to irrigation and cultivation would bring about the same result. Much has been made of the idea that efficient irrigation depended on a strong central power. This can be overstressed; in the Theban nome a strong local government could plan and execute the necessary work and almost certainly did so in the Eleventh Dynasty. However, when there was a total centralization of power in the national government, there may have been insufficient local initiative and authority to supervise such matters when the national government weakened.

Thus the reasons for a failing economy may be complex, and with little data available no clear picture of the reasons for the decline of Egypt can be outlined. However, it is as possible that long years of low inundation were responsible for the breakdown of the economy as that the weakness of the central administration caused the periods of depression.

The death of Merenptah occurred between 1225 and 1220; his immediate successor was Amenmose who was followed by Seti II. A contemporary record dates the latter's death to his sixth year. Then came to the throne the child Siptah, apparently Seti II's son by a woman in his harem, with Seti's widow Tausert acting as regent. The actual power was wielded by the Chancellor Bay. Siptah died after a few years and Tausert assumed the kingship. All these had tombs in the Valley of the Tombs of the Kings.

The Chancellor Bay may have been the " Syrian who made himself chief ", as recounted in Papyrus Harris I. The account given in this document pictures the land as being in chaos, much as the " prophet " Neferti described it before the coming of Amenemhat I or the Eighteenth Dynasty pictured it under the Hyksos.

In this case the saviour king, as described by his descendants, was Setnakht, the founder of the Twentieth Dynasty, who took over the rule in about 1200. His antecedents and the circumstances of his coming to power are unknown. It is likely that he was from the army. He died within two years and his son Ramesses III became pharaoh. This king patterned his name after that of his famous predecessor and made the latter's mortuary temple a model for his own. In the delta he faced attacks from the Libyans in his fifth and eleventh years, while in his eighth year the Sea Peoples whom Merenptah had driven off half a century earlier tried again to settle in Egypt. The king had accounts of these struggles carved on the walls of his mortuary temple at Medinet Habu in Western Thebes.

From this dynasty and the beginning of the next we have a great number of original documents. Many come from the government archives which for a time were

10. Interior of Hathor Chapel of Thutmosis III at Deir el-Bahri. *Cairo Museum*

11. Amenhotep II nursed by Hathor-cow, relief found in the Hathor chapel. *Cairo Museum*

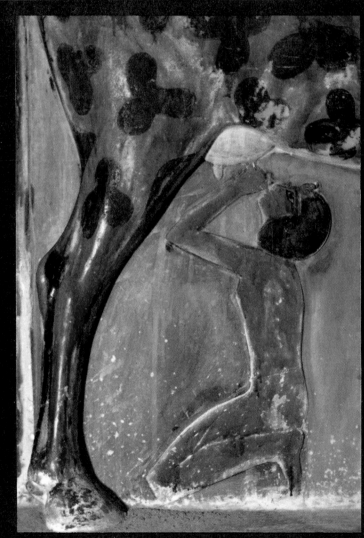

12

13

gathered at Medinet Habu or from collections belonging to officials of the necropolis which had its offices there. There are also writings on limestone flakes and potsherds, some used for accounts, letters, and personal notations, others the practice exercises of schoolboys studying to be scribes. These latter come from Deir el-Medineh, the village which housed the men working on the royal tombs and where the scribal school was situated. Not all are yet published; when they can be fully studied they will give a well rounded account of life in this small group of officials and workers.

One of these documents tells of a strike in the twenty-ninth year of Ramesses III. The workers on the royal tomb, angered by continual delays in the delivery of their monthly rations of grain, left their work and sat down by one of the mortuary temples. This action was successful in getting some satisfaction for the moment, but the delays were repeated. That there was a shortage of food is evident from the general tenor of the document; the vizier, a native of their village, sent them a message as he was passing on the river on official duties. " Even when there was nothing in the (government) granaries, I gave you what I found (elsewhere)." He was able to send them only half their usual rations. From a letter later in this century we know that one temple storehouse was bare and evidently even the gods went hungry.

It was probably soon after these strikes that Ramesses III was plotted against in the palace. Certain high officials administering the harem and some of the women therein tried to assassinate the monarch and replace him with one of the princes. The conspirators were caught, tried and punished, but the attempt on his life may have been successful. In the summary of the trial Ramesses III speaks from the realm of the glorious dead, suggesting that, whenever the plot took place, the record of it was compiled posthumously. It has been said that since the king's body showed no wounds, he was not murdered. But in the conspiracy magic writings and wax images were used. In other places this sort of witchcraft was often accompanied by the use of poison. Among the members of the household found guilty were several who, unsuspected by the king, could have administered such poison. If Ramesses III succumbed to this assassination attempt, it certainly took place in Thebes, for he died there.

Another posthumous document is Papyrus Harris I, already mentioned. It is mainly a long and detailed list of Ramesses III's benefactions to the temples of Egypt. In the concluding historical section the unsettled conditions preceding the reign of Setnakht are mentioned, followed by a brief account of Ramesses III's wars, his foreign commercial ventures, and a claim that he had secured the peace and prosperity of the Egyptian people. In this document the sovereign again speaks from the realm of the dead.

It is clear that this account was prepared by his son Ramesses IV who immediately succeeded him when he died in 1166. The new pharaoh claimed, no doubt correctly, that his father had designated him as his successor. Down to the end of the dynasty in 1085 there were a series of rulers, each named Ramesses, about whose reigns not much is known except that the internal situation continued to deteriorate. The wealth of the temples in Thebes remained great, but there was a general feeling of unrest in the land. One reads of defalcation by various persons. Bands of marauders roamed the land; it is said that they were of foreign descent. Some attacked the fortified area of Medinet Habu and breached the outer walls. The High Priest of Amon, Amenhotep, came to office under Ramesses IX and in 1130 had himself represented on a wall at Karnak as equal in importance with the pharaoh. It was probably in the early years of Ramesses XI, who came to throne in about 1112, that the High Priest came to open warfare with the bandits by whom he was temporarily bested. It seems to have been following this that the Nubian Viceroy led a rebellion, with most of the fighting further north.

12. The chief of Punt and his obese wife, painted bas-relief, mortuary temple of Hatshepsut, Deir el-Bahri. *Cairo Museum*

13. The donkey which carried the wife of the chief of Punt, and attendants, mortuary temple of Hatshepsut, Deir el-Bahri. *Cairo Museum*

It was in the sixteenth year of Ramesses IX that the systematic plundering of royal burials was first brought to official attention. A fuller account of this will be given later; it must now suffice only to mention that by the end of the dynasty all the then known tombs of the kings had been robbed and that soon after the mummies which remained were removed to places of safety.

Soon after the middle of the reign of Ramesses XI there appears a man who was active in directing the affairs of Amon and of Thebes, as did his descendants after him. Herihor first appears in the Temple of Khonsu at Karnak with the titles " High Priest of Amon, Generalissimo, Leader ", and is shown conducting services for the gods in the position traditionally occupied by the pharaoh. He also claims that it was he who erected this part of the building. Of course, the priests, and not the king, officiated in the temples most of the time and the construction and care of temples must have been in great measure due to their suggestion and enterprise, but this is the first time that the monarch was not *credited* with such acts in the temples themselves.

Soon Herihor proclaimed himself ruler, assuming the full titles and regalia of royalty in the scenes and inscriptions in the court of the temple of Khonsu. This may have coincided with the beginning of the era of " Repeating of Births ", signifying a renaissance, in the nineteenth year of Ramesses XI. Among the several dates assigned to this era only the last known, in the seventh year, mentions Ramesses XI. Among the records so assigned are documents about the looting of royal tombs and dockets concerning the reburial of former rulers. The most interesting account concerns the adventures of Wenamon whom Herihor sent to Byblos in the fifth year of the renaissance to obtain timber for a new river bark of Amon; this story will be recounted later.

Herihor died before the end of the seventh year; his son Piankh succeeded in all offices but that of ruler. A letter from Piankh, with the troops in Nubia, has a veiled allusion to the pharaoh which may refer to Ramesses XI's incapacity to rule. With the death of this last Ramesses in 1085 the dynasty came to an end; this date is usually considered to mark the end of Theban supremacy. Yet Amon remained the national god and his priests continued to conduct services in his temple for at least a millenium to come.

The kings of the Twenty-first Dynasty ruled from Tanis; they were on good terms with the High Priests of Amon at Thebes, many of whom their daughters married. The first of the line was Nesbanebdjedet (Greek, Smendes), already established as chief in Tanis when Wenamon began his voyage. After he had proclaimed himself king he sent a gang of 3000 workmen to repair the flood wall at the Luxor temple. Thebes continued to be controlled by the High Priests of Amon. They bore the title of " Generalissimo " and often those of " Vizier " and " Viceroy of Kush " (Nubia), having in their charge the control of Upper Egypt and the Nile Valley south of Assuan.

Pinodjem, son of Piankh, continued the decoration of the temple of Khonsu and refurbished the temples at Medinet Habu and minor monuments at Karnak. Toward the end of his life he assumed the title of king, but his rule, like that of his grandfather, was confined to Thebes. His grandson, Pinodjem II, in the latter years of his High Priesthood, about 1000, was confronted by a scandal in official circles.

The malefactors were identified vaguely as " the scribes, inspectors and high officials who did evil acts within No, Amon's city ". After a sixty-six day conference between Pinodjem and Amon, the god pointed out the miscreants and they were punished. Because of the investigation of this villainy the great Feast of Opet was not held this year. The actual investigation was in the hands of a minor temple functionary, Thutmose, who recounts his history in a chapel built against the outer wall of the court near the eastern end of the Tenth Pylon at Karnak. The inscription tells of further reforms and the rise of Thutmose to higher offices; his confirmation in his highest office took place in the fifth year of the reign of Siamon during the Feast of Opet.

Toward the end of that year Neskhonsu, wife of Pinodjem II, was buried in the cliff tomb south of Deir el-Bahri to which the mummies of many ancient rulers had by now been transferred. On the same day that Pinodjem II was buried there five years later, the first three kings of the Nineteenth Dynasty were re-interred in the same tomb. Except for the burial of a priest in the fifth year of Shoshenk I, the first ruler of the Twenty-second Dynasty, this tomb remained undisturbed until the latter part of the nineteenth century of our era.

Shoshenk I, the Shishak of the Old Testament, was of Libyan origin, a descendant of chiefs whose peoples had served in the Egyptian army and had settled in Egypt some centuries before. In his twenty-first year, about 925, he directed one of his officials to build a court before the Second Pylon at Karnak, and on a section of the outer wall he inscribed a list of places he had captured during a campaign into Palestine in the fifth year of Rehoboam, king of Judah.

About 850 Osorkon II, the third successor of Shoshenk I, granted practical autonomy to Thebes. The eldest son of Takelot II, the succeeding king, also named Osorkon, became the nominal High Priest of Amon, residing at El-Hibeh, considerably to the north. About 835 Osorkon went south to quell an insurrection in Thebes and in subsequent years was several times faced by such revolts, the last being in 785. Yet as early as 817 another, Harsiese, claimed the office of High Priest in Thebes, giving his allegiance to King Petubast, the founder of the rival Twenty-third Dynasty also in the north. Later Harsiese proclaimed himself pharaoh, and as such was buried in a tomb alongside of the Eighteenth Dynasty temple at Medinet Habu. His skull, found beside his plundered sarcophagus, had a hole in the forehead, an injury received some years before his death. Did he receive this wound in battle?

Thus there were rival claimants to the office of High Priest of Amon at Karnak. Perhaps the Theban High Priest withdrew at the news of the approach of Osorkon, to return again when he had departed. Apparently he used, or was used by, the rival kingdom in the north, but the obscurity of this period warns that such suggestions be put forward with caution.

All the claimants to the throne of Egypt gave allegiance to Amon. In the Sudanese kingdom centred at Napata, just south of the Fourth Cataract, there was another centre of Amon worship. This had been an outpost of the empire in the Eighteenth Dynasty, but when Egyptian control weakened a local kingdom arose, the rulers following their version of Egyptian culture and giving their allegiance to the Theban god.

Even before 730 the king in Napata, Kashata, had made his influence felt in Thebes. From the Twenty-first Dynasty the title "God's Wife of Amon" was borne by a daughter of the king. This priestess officiated in the Theban religious rites in the place traditionally occupied by the king, had her name in a cartouche, received income from the temple estates, and exercised great political power. Kashata persuaded the incumbent God's Wife of Amon, Shepenwepet I, daughter of the last king Osorkon of the Twenty-third Dynasty, to adopt his daughter Amenartis I.

Her brother Piankhi, Kashata's successor, invaded Egypt in his twenty-first year, about 730, in response to pleas from the Egyptians who claimed to be oppressed by the pharaoh Teftnakht of the Twenty-fourth Dynasty, then reigning in the delta. Sending his army ahead, he later came to command the attack in person, pausing in Thebes to celebrate the New Year's Festival and the Feast of Opet two months later. After conquering the north he returned to his far-off kingdom, and before his death commanded his sister to adopt his daughter, Shepenwepet II, that she might succeed as God's Wife of Amon.

Piankhi's successor was his brother Shabako; then came Pianki's sons Shabataka and Taharka. Their names occur frequently on Theban monuments and they built an addition before the Eighteenth Dynasty Temple at Medinet Habu. It was during the reign of Taharka, which began in 689, that the Assyrians first approached Egypt, and Taharka's intention, apparently unrealized, was to proceed into Palestine and meet Sennacherib, as reported in II Kings XIX, 9. Esarhaddon invaded the delta as far as Memphis, taking many captives, among them a son of Taharka. In 667 Ashurbanipal invaded and briefly occupied Egypt, and in his second campaign in 663 sacked Memphis. Taharka had died a few months earlier and the Assyrian was opposed by his nephew and successor, Tanuatamon.

Ashurbanipal's account of his invasion names a number of Egyptian "kings", actually local governors, appointed by his father, who had defected to Taharka. One was Montuemhat, Fourth Prophet of Amon and Prince of Thebes. In spite of his fourth position in the hierarchy of Amon he was the most powerful civil servant in Upper Egypt, and he served loyally under each succeeding native ruler. When Psametik I (Psammetichus) founded the Twenty-sixth Dynasty in Sais in the delta following the Assyrian withdrawal and extended his rule over all Egypt, Montuemhat acknowledged his sovereignty. At the time that Psametik had his daughter Nitocris adopted by Shepenwepet II to be her successor as God's Wife of Amon, Montuemhat was one of those who made large contributions to her support. He lived to an old age and was buried in the valley of Asasif, in a tomb which was grander than that of any commoner before him and probably surpassed in magnificence those of the sovereigns under whom he served.

The Twenty-sixth Dynasty continued in power until the Persian conquest in 525; the rulers added a few monuments in Karnak and made further additions to the Eighteenth Dynasty temple at Medinet Habu.

During the next century and a quarter the Persian rulers of the Twenty-seventh Dynasty gave scant, if any, attention to Thebes, though Cambyses passed through on his march to Nubia. In the Twenty-ninth Dynasty, 399-380, two rulers, Pshenmut (Psammuthis) and Hakor (Achoris), were credited with small buildings and repairs in Thebes.

With the last native dynasty, the Thirtieth, began a great campaign of building and restoration in the temples of Egypt and the state temples at Thebes received their share of attention. Nekhtnebef (Nechtanebo I) began the First Pylon and built gateways and the extensive mud brick temenos wall about the temple of Amon. Djedhor (Teos), before his capture by the Persians, and Nekhtharheb (Nechtanebo II) continued the policy of refurbishing. In view of the fact that these rulers were continually at war with the Persians, the amount of work done in the temples is remarkable. The foreigners finally triumphed, bringing an end to the dynasty in 343. In 332 Alexander the Great, fresh from his victories in Asia Minor, entered Egypt.

The Egyptians had, almost from the beginning of hieroglyphic inscriptions, a written form of the signs for use on papyrus which is now called "hieratic". In the Twenty-Sixth Dynasty a new, more cursive form of writing, now called "demotic", made its appearance. It became used throughout Egypt for legal contracts and letters and later an extensive literature was written in it. On the famous Rosetta Stone and other stelae it was used as a translation of or an addition to the hieroglyphic and Greek texts. With the coming of the Ptolemies other papyri were written in Greek and some legal archives have both demotic and Greek documents

14. Hieroglyphs on the reconstructed limestone way-station of Senusert I, Karnak.

relating to the same matters.

On the death of Alexander his general Ptolemy became first regent and then

14

ruler of Egypt. He was followed by his descendants for more than a hundred and fifty years. The assimilation of Greek culture, which had begun earlier, became more rapid, but was mainly confined to Greek settlements. The native population continued to follow their old customs. To placate the local inhabitants new temples were erected throughout Egypt and old ones repaired and extended. Much attention was given to Thebes and there is hardly a Ptolemy whose name does not appear on Theban temples. It has often been noted that the building activities of the Ptolemaic rulers was less comprehensive in Thebes than elsewhere; this was because the fabric of the Theban temples in actual use still was sound.

In spite of the honour paid to the Theban gods, the area was restive under the rule of non-Egyptians. Thebes was in revolt around 200, and again in 130, this time taking sides in a dynastic quarrel. Again in 88-85 Thebes fought for independence, and the repression of the uprising was accompanied by the destruction of the villages in the district. Under the last Cleopatra the priests of Amon erected a stele in honour of a Greek official who had helped to restore Thebes following this destruction, and they seem to have been conducting their own affairs independently of the government in Alexandria.

With the suicide of Cleopatra in 30, Ptolemaic rule came to an end and the country became the property of the Roman Caesars. On this occasion Thebes again revolted, and in the suppression of this another destruction ensued. Work on the temple of Khonsu and the adjoining temple of Ipet in Karnak, and on the outer wall of the Ptolemaic temple at Deir el-Medineh, was done under Augustus.

From the time the Greeks first took an interest in Egypt in the Twenty-Sixth Dynasty, foreign travellers began to tour the country. Whether Herodotus went to Thebes when he visited Egypt during the middle of the fifth century is uncertain; his description of it could be from hearsay. From the end of the third century B. C. and down into the second century of our era great numbers of Greek-speaking tourists came to Thebes to see the ancient wonders. Their chief interest was in the colossi which stood before the destroyed mortuary temple of Amenhotep III and in the vacant long passages of the Tombs of the Kings, which they called syrinxes, " tubes ". On these monuments they carved their names and often accounts of their impressions. The most famous of these tourists was Hadrian who visited Thebes with his entourage in A. D. 130. In his time the temple of Isis at Deir Shelwit, on the desert edge south of the lake of Amenhotep III, had much of its decoration completed. There and at Medinet Habu the last work was done under his successor Antoninus Pius. These are the last dated hieroglyphic inscriptions in the region, though some crude attempts at the ancient writing and decoration may be later.

Christianity had a firm hold in Egypt by the end of the second century of our era. In 292, under Diocletian, Thebes again was in insurrection. Then, or earlier, a Roman legion was stationed in the Luxor Temple and its environs; there is a Greek inscription of Constantine on a pedestal still in that temple. By the end of the fourth century pagan worship was largely superseded; churches were established in the temples of the ancient gods. Statues were defaced or destroyed; figures carved on the walls of temples were mutilated. The quarrying of buildings progressed rapidly; limestone went into the kilns; and the villagers moved their houses into the temple areas. The meaning of the hieroglyphs was forgotten and the people wrote their version of the Egyptian language in Greek letters, a writing soon known as Coptic. The power of Amon, predominant for over two thousand years, had reached its end, though a vestige of his great Feast of Opet survives to the present day.

15. Haremhab offering wine to Hathor, Chieftainess of Thebes, painted bas-relief in the tomb of this king, Valley of the Tombs of the Kings.

The Rediscovery of Thebes

THEBES, ONCE THE MISTRESS of Egypt, city of great temples and colourful tombs, was never lost, but it was neglected, ignored and almost forgotten. No Roman long remembered, if any clearly knew, that the great obelisk set up by Constantius in 357 in the Circus Maximus came from Thebes, nor did the people of Constantinople realize that the top of an obelisk, erected by Theodosius some decades later in the Hippodrome, came from the same source. By the time Sixtus v moved the obelisk of Constantius to the Piazza of St John Lateran in 1587, the revival of learning in the Renaissance had directed the attention of scholars to accounts of Greek and Roman travellers who had visited Thebes in her years of decline, and had whetted some curiosity.

In the twelve intervening centuries the fortunes of Egypt had changed. The Copts, the Egyptian Christians, isolated from the Church in the West by the schism at the Council of Chalcedon in 451 and oppressed by Byzantine administrators, welcomed the Moslem conquerors in 640 as liberators. Certain Theban temples had become Christian communities and monasteries; yet these, too, passed away. By the time of the great famine and pestilence which swept the country for seven years around 1065, the result of an unbroken series of low inundations, most had ceased to operate. The Coptic language was superseded by Arabic, and the tongue of the pharaohs remained only in the liturgy of the Church and in some Christian circles. The monks who came from Europe to learn from their brothers in the Thebaid and other pilgrims, among them the Crusaders, had little interest in pagan remains, and there is no record that any came to Thebes. In the thirteenth century Bucardus de Monte Sion mistook the remains of Memphis for those of Thebes, as did others in the following four centuries. None of the Arab travellers who went up the Nile noted the Theban monuments in his account. Yet some knowledge of the location of Thebes remained; a map by the Dutch voyager and cartographer Ortelius, in 1584, placed it correctly.

This map was unknown to the first European visitors of the present millenium who left a record of their journeys up the Nile. The earliest was an anonymous Italian traveller who went from Cairo to Kasr Ibrim in middle Nubia in 1589. The manuscript record of his voyage long lay unnoticed in Italian archives, coming to light only in 1929, so his account had no influence on those who came later. He visited the ancient temples in and about Luxor, but knew not what he beheld, and it is often difficult to identify his descriptions with the extant monuments.[3]

The next known travellers to Luxor, who were equally ignorant of its ancient

16. Painted wooden head of Anubis, detail of figure reclining on gilded shrine, from the tomb of Tutankhamon. *Cairo Museum*

17. Head of the hippopotamus goddess Taweris, on a wooden bed from the tomb of Tutankhamon. *Cairo Museum*

identity, were the Capuchin Fathers Protais and Charles-François d'Orléans, who arrived in 1668. The former wrote a short account of his visit to the temples of Luxor and Karnak. He spent three and a half hours at Karnak, and felt he would need a month or more to see it all. He estimated that one room (the Hypostyle Hall) contained 120 columns, counted seven " needles " (obelisks), three lying broken on the ground (he seems to have included the two pillars before the sanctuary among the four standing ones), and thought that there were more than a thousand figures in half relief on the walls. In a letter from Cairo at the beginning of 1670 he remembered " more than a million statues and figures in bas-relief. In the bas-reliefs on the walls and the pillars all the figures are in bas-relief, and there is not one which is shown frontally ". Of the west bank he learned only by report; he was told of Medinet Habu, with curiosities greater than those of Karnak, of two colossi, male and female, named Tama and Shama,[4] and of statues so well preserved and colours so fresh that it seemed " that the master had not yet washed his hands after his work ". He hoped to return to see them, but died of plague in 1671.

In 1698 Father Vansleb published his own account of travel up the Nile. He did not, however, reach Luxor and his description of it is taken from the writing of Father Protais. Paul Lucas claims to have made a voyage up the Nile as far as the first cataract in 1700. His descriptions are quite fantastic; he claims to have found the ruins of a great city near Assuan which he identified with Thebes. The place he described has never been seen by anyone else. In his accompanying map he places Luxor on the wrong side of the river, and pictures the colossi in the vicinity. On a trip which he did make as far as Esna, in 1714, in the company of the aged Father Charles-François, the hostility of the local inhabitants toward his boat captain made it impossible to stop either at Luxor or across the river at Gurna. The people of Armant took him to the top of a low hill, probably the northern mound of earth left by the builders of Amenhotep III's lake, and pointed out to him the pair of great statues to the north which he thought were columns. He was assured that they were two colossal figures, 60 feet high, called the bull and the cow because they had horns on their heads. Lucas thought they must be Osiris and Isis. He knew from classical writings that Armant was just above Thebes, but he never identified the great structures at Luxor and Karnak, which it is doubtful that he ever saw, with that city.

This identification is to be credited to the Jesuit Father Claude Sicard, who made three or four trips to Upper Egypt in 1707-21, going as far as Assuan. He planned a full account of the antiquities he had visited but he died from the plague in Cairo in 1726; whatever of his manuscript he had finished has not survived. In letters which have been published he identified the temples of Luxor and Karnak with Thebes, but he greatly over-estimated the number of columns in each place. He tells that he visited the colossi and the Memnonion (the Ramesseum) and in the Valley of the Tombs of the Kings counted ten tombs open, with five others in ruins.

All of the early travellers tended to exaggerate the size of the pillars they saw, and their figures vary greatly. Lucas simply added to the account he followed and made them larger still. Charles Perry, who visited Karnak in about 1740, pondered these records and remarked humorously " that these pillars, being planted in a rich fruitful soil, and having taken deep root in the earth, have a sort of vegetable growth, and so increase and lessen their dimensions as the times and seasons vary."

In the winter of 1737-8 two travellers, who wrote extensive accounts and made numerous sketches and plans, visited Thebes. The first was the naval captain Frederick L. Norden, who made the trip under a commission from King Christian IV of Denmark. He was at Luxor from the afternoon of 11th December to the evening of the 12th. The second day he went to the west side, and spent his time examining

18. Wrapped mummy of Amenhotep I, found in the cache of royal mummies in the tomb of Queen Inhapi. *Cairo Museum*

47

the Ptolemaic Pylon at Medinet Habu, the colossi, and the Ramesseum. He believed that the great granite statue lying there was the vocal Memnon.

His notes and his sketches were hurried and he never had a chance to revise this part of his account. Only one drawing was finally engraved by him, a very creditable view of the Ramesseum. One suspects that the engraver who executed the other plates did not do justice to Norden's work. Norden had no knowledge of Greek and little of the classical authors who had written on Thebes. He interpreted what he saw in the light of the interests of his time. Of a scene in the Ramesseum, showing Ramesses II seated under the sacred persea tree while Atum, Sefekh-abu, the goddess of writing, and Thoth write his prenomen on the leaves, Norden writes: "There is an allusion to the fall of Adam and Eve. There is represented a green tree, to the right of which is a man sitting, holding in his right hand some instrument, with which he seems to defend himself against a little oval figure, covered with hieroglyphical characters, that a woman presents to him, while with the other hand he accepts what is presented to him. Behind the man a figure appears standing, the head covered with a mitre, and who stretches out a hand to him." This first detailed description in modern times of a scene on a temple wall is quite creditable, although Norden has reversed the right and left from the viewer's standpoint and has omitted all mention of Thoth; but the description is superior to the accompanying plate. Interestingly, this scene is one of those copied by James Burton ninety years later in the first publication of Egyptian inscriptions which approaches accuracy. Norden's predilection for interpreting scenes in the light of Biblical narrative continued to be shared by others for a century afterwards, and it was only toward the end of the nineteenth century that appeals for funds to finance exploration in Egypt could be based on grounds other than that the results would throw light on the Bible.

Norden was continually molested and threatened by the local inhabitants, and on his return trip from Nubia, when he stopped at Luxor and Karnak on 3rd-4th February 1738, he made his investigation of the temple at Luxor by night when the people were in their houses.

The Danish traveller does not seem then to have met the English clergyman who followed almost on his heels. Richard Pococke reached Karnak on 13th January 1738 and immediately started to explore it. He noted the salient features and made a careful plan of the temple complex. The Temple of Khonsu he found to be occupied by the women's quarters and he was able to visit it only with the special permission of the sheikh. His diagram of the great Hypostyle Hall is completely accurate. In his five days' visit he also made plans of nine of the tombs of the kings of the Nineteenth and Twentieth Dynasties, the Ramesseum, the temple of Deir el-Medineh, and the Luxor Temple. He copied many of the Greek inscriptions on the north colossus of Amenhotep III, which he correctly identified as the vocal Memnon of the Greeks. He visited as well the dark corridors of the tombs of the Saite officials Petamenope and Harwa and made plans of them. His general descriptions show great powers of observation and his plans are the best executed of any until the time of Bonaparte's expedition. He went up river to Assuan and on his return trip, having been passed, unbeknown to him, by Norden, he stopped at the west bank of Thebes from the 5th to the 7th February. The unfriendliness and threats of the local people, which he had experienced on his first visit, persuaded him to move on. He and Norden, who later entered the service of the British government, became members of the first, short-lived, Egyptian Society in London in 1741; one wishes that there were a record of their discussions of their journeys in Egypt.

It was in January 1769 that James Bruce, who was ascending the Nile to Abyssinia, paused for ten days in Luxor. He saw more of Medinet Habu than had his predecessors and marvelled at the depth to which some of the hieroglyphs were cut.

19. Detail of black granite cube statue of Senmut holding on his lap the Princess Neferure, daughter of Hatshepsut. *Cairo Museum*

20

21

He made shrewd observations on the various ways the ancient signs were carved in the stone, some merely scratched, some in bas-relief, some in incised relief, and some in the very deep cutting just mentioned. Bruce kept some sort of a journal of the different hieroglyphs, gathering a total of 514 forms, some variations of others. Not understanding their nature, he decided that they did not represent words, as there were too few, nor an alphabet, as there were too many.[5]

In the Valley of the Tombs of the Kings Bruce visited seven tombs and became greatly interested in the pictures of two harpists in the tomb of Ramesses III. Coming on these scenes late in the day, he and his assistant began sketching them. Night had fallen by the time they had finished and their local guides, never too happy about this visit, deserted them. On their return to the cultivation through the long defile, people on the hills above began to roll rocks down on them; Bruce put an end to this by discharging firearms in the direction from which the sounds came. But he no longer dared to moor his boat on the western bank and at dawn moved to Luxor, where he spent the rest of the visit. Because of his drawings the tomb of Ramesses III became known as " Bruce's Tomb " and some have credited him with either discovering it or clearing it; yet Pococke had made a plan of it when he explored the Valley.

Most of the early travellers to Egypt returned to Europe with souvenirs. Pococke had bought in Cairo a pair of squatting figures in stone, statues of a man and a woman; from inscriptions shown on his plates it is certain that they came from Thebes. One was of a High Priest of Amon. The excellence of the drawings indicates that they were made from the figures themselves. Unfortunately, they cannot now be traced. Bruce reports that a sphinx from the avenues at Karnak had recently been purchased for the collection of the King of Sardinia. This desire for Egyptian antiquities was soon to be quickened.

In 1798 Bonaparte, hoping to control the route to the Orient, invaded Egypt and his armies remained there until 1801. Accompanying his troops was a group of more than a hundred scholars and engineers who excavated and drew, made plans and wrote accounts of the antiquities. Independently attached to the army was Vivant Denon, a sometime diplomat who was an excellent artist and writer. His lively account of his experiences, which included descriptions of a number of visits to Thebes and was illustrated by a few drawings, was published in 1802 and quickly translated into English and German. The popularity of his work has tended to overshadow the great contribution of the French Commission, the publication of which began in 1809. These volumes include two giant folios of plates showing monuments in Thebes. In these there are many valiant attempts to make correct copies of hieroglyphic inscriptions, though in some cases the short inscriptions are the result of the artist's imagination. In the accompanying text the description of the monuments is very extensive. Both the French troops and the British who opposed them brought back to Europe statues, stelae and smaller objects, and made it known that these existed in Egypt in almost inexhaustible supply.

There followed a great scramble to gather as many of them as possible for European museums and private collections. The chief organizers of the various enterprises were men who were or who became consul-generals of the influential European nations, Giovanni Anastasi for Sweden, Bernardino Drovetti for France, and Henry Salt for Great Britain. Through the activities of these men and their agents the early collections of Egyptian antiquities were built up in Turin, the Louvre, the British Museum, Berlin and Leyden. These groups vied with each other for the prize objects, some using bribery and violence to attain their ends. Almost no records were kept, especially as the local population were encouraged to excavate and sell their finds to the Europeans. The Egyptian officials were alternately helpful and hostile. Closed and stubborn monuments were forced open, often with

20. Detail on stele of Intef II, showing three of his dogs, from the court of his tomb. *Cairo Museum*

21. Red Sea fish, painted bas-relief from Punt relief of Hatshepsut in her mortuary temple. Deir el-Bahri.

battering-rams and gunpowder. These methods caused considerable damage and destruction and objects which were not regarded as desirable were frequently shattered deliberately.

One of the most picturesque of this company was Giovanni Belzoni, a giant Italian who had gone to Great Britain in 1803, at the age of twenty-five, to perform as a strong man and conjuror. Twelve years later he went to Egypt, hoping to interest Mohammed Ali in a water-wheel he had invented. Failing in this, he made an agreement with Salt to recover and transport to Cairo the bust of a great statue of Ramesses II lying in his mortuary temple. This building was then called the Memnonion, from the Greek tradition, and the statue was popularly known as the "Young Memnon". Having successfully transported this huge piece of stone to the river bank in August 1816, Belzoni departed up-river for some weeks, to return to Thebes to supervise loading it on to a boat. This he successfully accomplished in mid-November and sent it to Salt along with a number of smaller statues he had collected. This colossal bust is now the largest piece in the Egyptian collection in the British Museum.

While Belzoni had been awaiting the proper conditions for the difficult transfer of the bust from shore to ship, he discovered the tomb of King Ay in the Western Valley, a branch of the Valley of the Tombs of the Kings. The following year, after finding the Western Valley bare of further important antiquities, he and his crew explored the main valley. In October he discovered first of all the tomb of Montu-her-khopeshef, a prince of the late Twentieth Dynasty, then that of Ramesses I. His great find was the tomb of Seti I, the most magnificently decorated in all the Valley. All of these revelations came within less than ten days.

Belzoni, camping with his wife at the mouth of the tomb, set about making wax impressions and colour copies of the scenes on the tomb walls. In this he had the very able help of Dr Alessandro Ricci, whose drawings were somewhat better efforts. The whole collection was later exhibited in London in a building especially built for the purpose. Belzoni recovered the alabaster sarcophagus of Seti I which, rejected by the British Museum, found a home in the Museum of Sir John Soane in Lincoln's Inn Fields, London.

Belzoni excavated widely in the Theban area, showing great ability and keen observation, but he was always cantankerous. He had several quarrels with Salt and became estranged from one of his assistants, Giovanni d'Athanasi, known to that generation of explorers at Thebes as Yanni. At one time Belzoni was assaulted by an agent of Drovetti's in a dispute over prerogatives to dig in Karnak.

Drovetti himself had an adobe hut on top of the First Pylon at Karnak. From there he directed a large gang of men, most of whom were ruffians, in the recovery of antiquities from Karnak and other Theban monuments. Though an able man, he was hostile to all other collectors, even to Champollion.

Various other travellers were collecting and copying; one was William Bankes, in whose copy of an inscription from Philae the English scholar Thomas Young provisionally read the name of Cleopatra in 1821. This came into the hands of the young French linguistic genius, Jean-François Champollion, at the beginning of the following year. He had already made himself proficient in Coptic and was searching for the key to the hieroglyphs. Whether this and other suggestions from Young, and from the Swedish scholar, Jean Akerblad, greatly helped Champollion it is difficult to tell. At the end of September 1822, he announced to the French Academy his decipherment of the hieroglyphic alphabet and two years later published a general account of hieroglyphic writing.

These works became known at once and were made use of by workers in Thebes. In 1825-6 James Burton made copies in which he took great care to show the hieroglyphs in their correct form. He was able to identify by name and position Ramesses II. With him were Robert Hay and Joseph Bonomi, the latter being one of the most accomplished and accurate of the earlier copiests of inscriptions. Unfortunately, most of the copies made by Bonomi and Hay were never published, but they are preserved in the British Museum.

In close association with them was John Gardner Wilkinson, a careful copyist, excavator and interpreter of the inscriptions, who worked in Thebes from 1824 to 1828. His own decipherments of the hieroglyphs, often reached independently of Champollion, convinced him of the correctness of the French scholar's methods, a conclusion in which many of the savants of that generation did not concur. Wilkinson did not have Champollion's flair for the ancient language and his contributions were relatively minor. However, he was the first to place the dynasties of Egypt in correct chronological order and to give the true succession of the kings of the Eighteenth Dynasty. Wilkinson tried to bring some order into the designation of private and royal tombs, assigning them numbers, and in the Valley of the Tombs of the Kings the first twenty numbers used today are, with one exception, his.

Though many travellers had mentioned the painted and carved walls in the tombs of the Egyptian officials in the village of Gurna, none had given them particular attention. This was due in part to the hostility of the inhabitants of the village, many of whom were using these tombs as dwellings. Wilkinson gave his attention to those known and discovered many new ones. From the scenes on their walls he was able to draw up an excellent account of the life and habits of the ancient people. Though some of his conclusions have been superseded, his observations and drawings are still valuable, especially those of scenes which have since been destroyed.

Another traveller well versed in the classical accounts and the new discoveries was the Viennese Anton von Prokesch. Early in 1827 he went quickly up the river into Nubia, making his extended visits on the return journey. He had a great passion for measurement, giving the size of many monuments, even the great pylons, in Viennese feet down to a fraction of an inch. He was able to recognize the names of the rulers of the Eighteenth Dynasty, distinguish the early Ramessides, and knew the names of some of the gods. His account is the first guide to the antiquities of Egypt.

Champollion and his colleague Niccolo Ippolito Rosellini visited Thebes in 1828-9. They spent their days independently copying inscriptions, and at night copied each other's notebooks. This habit caused great arguments when their results were published, Champollion's posthumously, supporters of each accusing the other of plagiarism. Their publications were the first large collections of inscriptional material available.

The greatest copying enterprise ever launched was sent to Egypt in 1842 under the patronage of the King of Prussia, with Richard Lepsius as its leader. He had already made himself proficient in Egyptology and in 1837, when only twenty-seven, had issued a defence of the methods of Champollion which finally convinced most scholars. His party stopped in Luxor for nine days in October 1843, returning thirteen months later for a stay of just over three months, with an additional month beginning the middle of April 1845. By the extensive use of paper squeezes he was able to make many of his copies for publication later in Berlin. From the present day point of view his copies leave much to be desired, but their general excellence was remarkable, as was the great number he was able to collect from Thebes in less than five months of effort there.

Less than a decade after Lepsius, photography was first introduced as a method of recording the monuments. In 1849-51 Maxime du Camp, accompanied by Gustave Flaubert, made paper negatives of several monuments at Thebes, publishing prints from these. Before the end of that decade Francis Frith published prints made from glass negatives. From this time a considerable number of photographers worked in the area and their results are most valuable in showing the conditions of the monuments before modern excavation began.

Up to 1855 the excavations in Thebes had been mere treasure hunts, neither systematic nor scientific. Most of the antiquities were shipped out of the country. The next year there came to Thebes an excavator, Henry Rhind, who protested against such vandalism. This Scotsman saw the need for careful examination and protection of all objects found and for making an exact record of their positions when discovered. He inveighed against the common practice of destroying a monument to obtain one piece. Though his example was not followed and his plea fell largely on deaf ears, there was shortly a change in government policy on the antiquities and the monuments.

In 1858 François-Auguste Mariette, who had come to Egypt in 1850, was appointed Conservator of Egyptian Monuments, the precursor of the Service of Antiquities, and soon founded the Egyptian Museum at Cairo. Excavation was reserved for his department alone and he directed expeditions throughout the country, working through Egyptian assistants. Methods of work were little improved. but some system was introduced and a beginning of the clearing of the Theban monuments was made. Mariette published a valuable book on scenes and inscriptions in Karnak.

Mariette died in 1881 and was succeeded by Gaston Maspero, one of the most intuitive of all Egyptologists. Almost as soon as he came into office he found it necessary to turn his attention to Luxor. Objects had been appearing on the market which had obviously come from royal burials. Enquiry eventually led to the Abd el-Rassul family in Luxor as the vendors of these objects and, after an examination in which torture certainly was used, one confessed the discovery. Some years before, a torrent pouring over the cliffs just south of Deir el-Bahri—the result of one of the rare cloudbursts in the region—uncovered the entrance of a shaft in the crag, and here a member of the family had found a great cache of royal mummies which the priests of Amon had secreted there almost three thousand years before. Emile Brugsch, one of Maspero's assistants, was taken to the tomb, into which he was lowered by rope and quickly had the bodies, their coffins and all the other material in this cache brought forth. Within two weeks of his arrival in Luxor all the mummies were in the Museum in Cairo. As the barge carrying them went northward down the river, people along the banks performed the same ceremonies of mourning as they do for the dead today.

In 1898 Victor Loret, then Director General of Antiquities, found thirteen more mummies, mostly royal, in the tomb of Amenhotep II, including the latter still in his sarcophagus. It was decided to allow the body to remain in its resting place. In the latter part of 1901, while Howard Carter, then Chief Inspector of Antiquities, was temporarily absent from Luxor, thieves broke in and rifled the mummy of the monarch. Carter investigated as soon as the matter was reported. From the measurements and photographs of prints of bare feet and from circumstantial evidence, Carter became convinced that a certain member of the Abd el-Rassul family was guilty, but the local court freed the suspect.[6] The mummy of Amenhotep II was returned to the sarcophagus where it remained until 1939, when the then Chief Inspector of Antiquities, Labib Habachi, took it to Cairo in the berth of a sleeping car.

It is small wonder that the inhabitants of Gurna, who, encouraged by the rapacity of the early collectors, had been robbing tombs for several generations, were little deterred by official regulations. They knew the area well, and dealing in antiquities had been their chief means of livelihood. The appointed guards, when not actually in league with them, were cowed by threats and cajoled by promises of a share in the loot and, in spite of the efforts of the inspectors, the thieves continued

22. Acrobatic dancers, incised relief on red quartzite.

23. Harpist and acrobatic dancers, incised relief on red quartzite.

24. Personification of the temple of Amon in Ipet-esut, incised relief on black granite. Scenes from the sanctuary of the bark of Amon of Hatshepsut.

22

23   24

to cut away at the walls of the tombs and make clandestine excavations. In this they were often encouraged by officials of European museums. The unfortunate result is that much of value has been lost through the clumsy efforts of natives, though they have done no more harm than many early collectors. Even in regular excavations, many smaller pieces, and sometimes larger ones, have been taken by the workmen, a loss which the most careful supervision has been unable to stop entirely.

One of the excavators in Thebes found the local workmen so addicted to stealing the material he unearthed that he soon dismissed them all. This was Flinders Petrie, afterwards knighted, who began excavations in Egypt in 1883 under the auspices of the Egypt Exploration Fund (afterwards the Egypt Exploration Society). He was trained as a surveyor by his father and had received little formal education. In 1880 he surveyed the pyramids at Giza and this won him considerable recognition. He was another to realize the need of saving all objects found, no matter how small or seemingly insignificant, and of making careful descriptions of his excavations. He published his results immediately. To prevent his finds from going on the market he paid fair rewards, *bakshish*, for any objects which might have commercial value. He desired no monetary reward for himself and worked for much of his life for little more than his expenses. Because of this his manner of living was always austere and many tales of his frugality are still related by archaeologists.

It was not until 1898 that Petrie came to Thebes, having as his assistant James Quibell, one of the great number of excavators whom he helped to train. Petrie and his staff lived in the galleries of the old granaries of the Ramesseum. It was at the start of his work that he found the local employees selling antiquities from the excavation to neighbouring dealers, who clustered around the well from which the men drew their water. In one winter Petrie explored the strip of desert edge from the mortuary temple of Amenhotep III to the southern walls of that of Thutmosis III. He discovered a number of truly " lost " temples of which only a few stones and foundation deposits remained. In a tomb of the Thirteenth Dynasty under some of the Ramesseum granaries Quibell came upon a box of fragmentary papyri, once the property of a physician. Though one of the most important archives ever found in Egypt, their condition made their study extremely difficult, and only in 1955 were the last of them made available to scholars. Petrie returned to Thebes again in the winter of 1908-09, this time working north along the desert edge from the causeway of Hatshepsut's temple. Petrie's great care here and elsewhere recovered much evidence that would otherwise have been lost entirely.

Before Petrie made his first excavation at Thebes he had left the Egypt Exploration Fund and founded his own organization. In 1893 the Fund sent the Swiss archaeologist Edouard Naville to begin work on the temple of Deir el-Bahri, Arabic for " Northern Monastery ". It was still covered, to a great extent, by mounds of rubbish and the remains of the Coptic monastery which gave it its name. Some hasty and patchy work had been done by members of Bonaparte's expedition, and by Wilkinson, Lepsius, and Mariette. It was only the last of these who had begun to understand the plan of the temple and who first realized that this structure, and the other temples along the desert edge, were intended for the mortuary services of the rulers who had constructed them.

Naville worked for ten years clearing away the debris, and it was he who erected most of the present roofs over the terraces as a protection for the delicate reliefs. When Naville had completed the clearance and Carter had drawn the scenes, the former transferred his work to the rubble heap at the south, uncovering the remains of the temple of Montuhotep II. By the end of his work in 1907 he had made clear the major parts of both temples as well as uncovering the famous Hathor shrine of Thutmosis III. Yet his methods were not as painstaking as those of Petrie and much more information remained to be found.

25. Column with head of Hathor, shrine of Hathor in the mortuary temple of Hatshepsut. Deir el-Bahri.

Much of this was collected by Herbert Winlock of the Metropolitan Museum in New York and by other members of his team. Winlock had come to Egypt in 1906 with the Museum's new curator of the Egyptian Department, Albert Lythgoe, under whom Winlock had just finished his graduate studies at Harvard. He began the Museum's long period of excavation in the area of Deir el-Bahri in 1911 and continued for twenty years, with an interruption during the First World War.

Winlock took extreme care in all his work, was gifted with a keen eye and a lively but controlled imagination, and above all with infinite patience. He was also a competent philologist. Certainly he and those associated with him took every precaution required by scientific method. When a tomb was discovered, nothing was moved until photographs and other records had been made and the removal of the finds was never hurried.

It was just such care that led to the discovery and preservation of the group of models from the Eleventh Dynasty tomb of Meket-re. The thorough examination of the tomb, already explored by others, revealed a small lower chamber where these models were deposited. The photography and planning of every detail of the objects where they lay enabled Winlock to restore parts which had been broken off by bits of rock falling from the ceiling during the four thousand years the wooden figures had lain there. These were restored to almost the same condition they were in when placed in the tomb: the finest group of models found in Egypt, showing life on the estate of a prominent official of the realm.

Under Winlock's supervision most of the area about the two Deir el-Bahri temples was dug to bed rock, and also the quarry of Hatshepsut, where the workmen of Thutmosis III had dumped the statuary snatched from the temple of his late co-regent and smashed it. The Service of Antiquities had appointed Émile Baraize to conserve Hatshepsut's temple. He and Winlock cooperated fully and thus many of the fragments were restored to their original position. When Winlock returned to New York in the spring of 1931 to become the Director of the Metropolitan Museum, Ambrose Lansing and William Hayes, following his methods, continued work until 1936. Since the war the photography had been done by Harry Burton, often under the most difficult conditions. This dean of archaeological photographers also took pictures of the scenes in a great many private tombs, and continued this work until his death in 1940.

The exploration of Deir el-Bahri is still unfinished. In 1962 Lazek Dabrowski, sent by the government of Poland to continue the work of consolidation in cooperation with the Service of Antiquities, uncovered a building of Thutmosis III above the southern part of Hatshepsut's temple. This was perhaps dedicated to Amon.

Two years after Naville began work on Deir el-Bahri, the Service of Antiquities put Georges Legrain in charge of the clearance and consolidation of Karnak. While the main walls and columns were always visible, much of the temple complex had the appearance of a vast rubbish dump, with pits and mounds where the treasure seekers of the century past had dug for loot, so Legrain began a programme to clear all the rubble and strengthen the structure.

Already two of Bonaparte's engineers had noted that one column on the north side of the Hypostyle Hall was leaning dangerously, and that the foundations of many other columns were precarious. They warned that the columns might collapse and bring down the whole structure in ruin. It was a century after their observations that the dire prediction was partially fulfilled. In the night of 3rd October 1899, the leaning column fell, bringing ten others down with it. The roar of this collapse was heard in Luxor more than a mile and a half away.

Legrain then had the task of rebuilding these fallen pillars and reinforcing the foundations of those still standing. Earth ramps were built, up which the workmen pulled the column drums and architrave blocks, following the methods used

26. The obelisks of Hatshepsut (near) and Thutmosis I (far), with tatue of Amon erected by Tutankhamon in left foreground. Karnak.

in the original construction. The foundations of the standing columns were removed, half at a time, and solid piers made of burned brick were built in their place.

Legrain also began the removal of the core and the foundations of the Third Pylon of which almost all of the blocks had come from earlier buildings. There was found an almost complete limestone shrine of Sesostris I and an alabaster shrine of Amenhotep I and Thutmosis I, now re-erected. In addition to many other blocks there were a great number from the central sanctuary of Hatshepsut. Approximately half of this building has been recovered.

In 1903, clearing the court north of the Seventh Pylon, the northernmost on the north-south axis, Legrain came upon a cache containing 751 stone statues and stelae, more than 17,000 bronze pieces, mostly figures of Osiris, and numerous other objects. There had been many statues of wood, but these had disintegrated. Legrain dug down forty-six feet, using thirty-two shadufs to bail out the water, and never reached bottom. The latest dated objects found make it evident that the deposit was made in the Ptolemaic period, after 300 B. C. It was a *favissa*, where the priests placed temple furniture no longer in use, similar to the *genizah* of the synagogue. Karnak had undergone a general house-cleaning under the early Ptolemies.

Legrain's efforts were halted by his death in 1917; of the great work on Karnak which he had outlined only a small part was finished, and was published twelve years later. The preservation of the temples was continued by two successors, Maurice Pillet and Henri Chevrier. In recent years Egyptian engineers and architects have taken over the conservation of Karnak, and the work is still continuing.

Of the hundreds of other Egyptologists who contributed to the preservation of the ancient buildings and the copying of the records, only a few can be mentioned. The French were active in Deir el-Medineh, the Montu temple at Karnak, and other sites until political difficulties between Egypt and France a few years ago brought work to a halt. The Service of Antiquities has had excellent men directing the clearance and consolidation of various monuments; Georges Daressy, an Egyptologist who was capable but often hasty, and Alexandre Barsanti worked at the removal of debris from Medinet Habu. The latter, because of his zeal in filling in the holes in temple walls, earned, among the Arabs, the nickname of Bar-cementi, " Son of cement ".

In 1897 the German Academy called upon Adolf Erman to collect materials for a hieroglyphic dictionary. His colleagues and students filled many notebooks with their copies of inscriptions; for the Theban temples and tombs the burden of this work fell on Kurt Sethe. James Henry Breasted, of the University of Chicago, did most of his copying in other parts of Egypt. As a result of his experiences he became convinced that the publication of accurate copies was a prime necessity for the pursuance of inquiries into the history and civilization of ancient Egypt. When, with the aid of John D. Rockefeller, Jr., he founded the Oriental Institute in 1919 and as soon as possible began to carry out his ambition, he chose Medinet Habu as the place to begin. An architectural survey of the area has been completed and the Epigraphic Survey has published facsimile drawings, with some photographs and colour reproductions, of the Mortuary Temple of Ramesses III and other Theban structures of this ruler.

The tomb chapels of the officials have received the meticulous attention of Norman Davies and his wife, whose copies in line drawings and exact colour facsimiles, published by the Metropolitan Museum, the Egyptian Exploration Society, and the University of Chicago, have made available some of the vast library of records which the carved and painted tombs contain.

The greatest public fame came to another archaeologist who through his skill, insight and patience discovered and preserved the most spectacular treasure which has survived from the ancient world. This man was Howard Carter. He was first

27. Tutankhamon, standing on reed float, spearing hippopotamus, from the king's tomb. *Cairo Museum*

of all an artist, not yet quite nineteen when he came to Egypt at the beginning of 1892 to assist Percy Newberry in copying tombs in Middle Egypt and to aid Petrie in the excavation of El-Amarna. He went on to work with Naville in the autumn of 1893, making delicate drawings of the walls of Hatshepsut's temple at Deir el-Bahri. Late in 1899 Maspero appointed him Chief Inspector of Antiquities for Upper Egypt, in which capacity he began the systematic protection of the Theban private tombs.

At his suggestion the American, Theodore Davis, began to excavate in the Valley of the Tombs of the Kings in 1902, with Carter closely supervising the work the first year. In the next year he was transferred to Sakkarah, where he soon ran into trouble defending the guards and the antiquities against a group of drunken Europeans. Their consul demanded an apology from Carter and, rather than give it, he resigned from the Service. For some years he devoted himself to water-colours of Egyptian scenery and assisted Davis with paintings of the objects this excavator had found.

Lord Carnarvon had come to Egypt in 1903 for reasons of health and became fascinated by the antiquities. In 1907, without previous experience, he started to excavate in the Theban necropolis, at a site where the authorities thought he would do the least harm. Though his results were almost negative, his enthusiasm was undiminished. Maspero insisted that he associate himself with an expert in excavation, if he were to continue, and recommended Carter. For five years the two worked together at the lower end of Hatshepsut's causeway, making several important discoveries.

For some time Carter had been fascinated by the Valley of the Tombs of the Kings. Each excavator, from Belzoni onward, believed that he had exhausted the valley. Davis had found a number of hitherto unknown tombs, among them a very small one which contained some fragments bearing the name of Tutankhamon. He was convinced that this king had been buried there and that these pieces had been overlooked by the robbers who had despoiled the grave. He also found at a spot near the tomb of Ramesses VI a cache of pottery jars, sealed, with hieratic inscriptions on their shoulders. Since they seemed to contain rubbish, he was not interested in them and eventually turned them over to Winlock, who took them to New York where he examined them carefully. He discovered that they contained the sweepings of the debris left after the funeral of Tutankhamon; they had been buried, as was customary, somewhere outside the actual tomb. Davis, however, showed no further curiosity; in 1912 he wrote: " I fear that the Valley of the Tombs is now exhausted ", and soon relinquished his concession.

Carter, the better archaeologist, recognized what the jars and their contents signified and was certain that the fragments with the names of Tutankhamon had been stolen from the king's tomb and left where found by the thieves, perhaps when they were about to be apprehended. He finally persuaded Carnarvon to take up the concession but the outbreak of the First World War prevented any intensive search for several years. On brief leaves from his war work in Cairo Carter did make several contributions to the knowledge of royal burials at Thebes.

It was in the autumn of 1917 that the systematic examination of the Valley began. For five winters Carter dug down to the bedrock with scant reward. The first area explored was a triangle formed by the entrances of the tombs of Ramesses II, Merenptah, and Ramesses VI. Near the entrance of the latter some ancient workmen's huts were found; to excavate them would have barred that popular tomb to visitors. Moreover, such rude shelters would hardly have been built over the entrance to a royal tomb. Otherwise all that was forthcoming was a group of thirteen alabaster jars which, from the names thereon, seem to have been gifts of Merenptah at the time he buried his father. Other areas were cleared to virgin soil with little result.

28. Gold mask which covered the head of the mummy of Tutankhamon.
Cairo Museum

29. Red granite statue of the god Khonsu, found in his temple at Karnak. Probably from the reign of Tutankhamon.
Cairo Museum

29

Discouraged, Carnarvon decided that the season of 1922-3 would be the last. On 1st November Carter started to work, spending the first three days uncovering all the ancient huts, making plans, and clearing them away. The workmen usually started their day of digging before Carter arrived; when he approached on the morning of 4th November he noticed that no work was in progress. When he came up the men announced that a step had been found, thirteen feet below the present level of the valley.[7] Further examination showed that this was, indeed, the beginning of a stairway. It was not until early the next afternoon that the debris could be cleared enough to show the upper edges of the stair-well. Once this was delineated, the rubbish within was rapidly removed, and at sunset the top of a sealed doorway was brought into view.

Carter knew that Carnarvon must be present before further work was undertaken and so, after filling the pit and placing an adequate guard, he cabled his employer the news. Carter had noted that the seals he saw were those of the necropolis officials; when the whole doorway was cleared on 24th November, with Carnarvon present, it became evident that this area had once been opened and then closed and resealed. The undisturbed section of the doorway bore the seals of Tutankhamon. Whatever lay beyond, it was not completely intact. When the stones blocking the passage were removed, the excavators were confronted by a blocked corridor sloping downwards at some considerable angle. Thirty feet further on a second sealed doorway loomed before them.

In the three weeks between the finding of the step and the clearing of the passage, Carter often had misgivings. Scraps found on the lower steps, and later in the passage, led him to suspect that the sealed chamber before him was not a tomb, but a cache in which royal furniture saved from El-Amarna had been placed. The evidence of the " breaking and entering " also caused great concern as to the amount of damage the ancient thieves had done. It was on the afternoon of 26th November that Carter, with Carnarvon and his daughter, Lady Evelyn Herbert, at his side, broke open a corner of the second sealed doorway, put through a lighted candle to test the purity of the air and by its dim light saw a little of the treasure which has so astonished the world.

It was a discovery for which no one was prepared; many gave help but multitudes hindered, even if unintentionally. The Metropolitan Museum offered its staff in Egypt and Burton took charge of all the photography. Other scholars and experts made themselves available as needed. A laboratory was set up in another tomb. Carter moved as rapidly as adequate precautions for the protection of the objects allowed. But there were constant delays and discords. Carnarvon had given the London *Times* exclusive rights for news and picture coverage, thinking thus to eliminate the trouble that great gatherings of the press would bring. All other papers, and their correspondents who sat upon the walls about the tomb entrance, resented this deeply and the Egyptian press was especially bitter at being denied news of a great national discovery. As a result, the excavators received unfriendly treatment in many publications. Multitudes of visitors arrived with urgent letters of introduction; many were from the Egyptian government and could not be denied. Not only did these people take up time, but they endangered the relics, for any touch or mis-step could cause damage. Even the dampness from breath and perspiration, increased by each one who entered, could do serious harm.

All this pressure, combined with jealousies from without, made both Carter and Carnarvon irascible. Questions of policy brought about a sharp disagreement between them and they were reconciled only on Carnarvon's deathbed. An unattended insect bite on his cheek became infected, and before the seriousness of it was realized, the poison had so worked through Carnarvon's frail and tired body that no cure was possible. With his death the newspapers gave great publicity to the supposed

30. Red granite statues
of kings north of the west tower
of the Seventh Pylon
at Karnak. From the left,
two of Thutmosis III,
usurped by Ramesses II, two
of Thirteenth Dynasty kings,
and one of Amenhotep II.

31. The vulture goddess Nekhbet.

32. The " sacred eye " amulet,
with the snake goddess
of Lower Egypt
and the vulture goddess
of Upper Egypt.

Both pectorals of gold,
with inlays of stone, glass,
and frit paste, found
on the mummy of Tutankhamon.
Cairo Museum

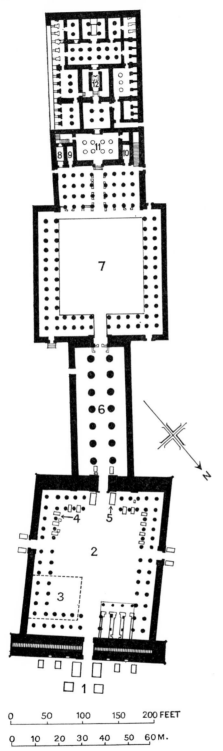

LUXOR TEMPLE

1 Obelisk, statues, and pylon of Ramesses II
2 Court of Ramesses II
3 Mosque of Abu-'l-Haggag
4 " Striding " statue of Ramesses II
5 Statue of Ramesses II, " The Sun of the Rulers "
6 Corridor decorated by Tutankhamon
7 Court of Amenhotep III
8 Original sanctuary for the bark of Khonsu
9 Sanctuary for the bark of Mut
10 Later Sanctuary for the bark of Khonsu
11 Chapel of the Roman Legion
12 Sanctuary for the bark of Amon built by Alexander

curse,[8] a stupidity against which Carter futilely voiced his anger. The Egyptian government quarrelled with Carter over the terms of the concession and forbade his work, thus spoiling some of the delicate material in the process of treatment. Eventually a political change enabled him to return to the tomb. It was ten years after the discovery that he discharged his duties by the final clearance and preservation of the objects from Tutankhamon's burial.

Unfortunately, this great collection of funerary furniture has never been carefully studied and a full inventory of the finds has only recently been published. With each passing year the possibility of an adequate treatment becomes less. This, alas, has been the fate of too many objects found in Thebes and, indeed, in many archaeological enterprises. The thrill of excavation being over, too few are willing to undertake the tedious work of careful examination of the material found and the completion of a full published report. So, too, with the standing monuments; many temples and tombs are still unpublished and an unpublished record is an unknown one, even though it has been in full public view for generations.

Is there more to be discovered in Thebes? Certainly there are many possibilities and almost every Egyptologist has his own dreams as to where he would like to search. The rubble at the foot and on the sides of the western hills may still cover some brilliantly painted or choicely carved tomb chapel, though one may expect the burial to have been robbed. Certainly the Second, Ninth, and Tenth Pylons at Karnak have in their cores and foundations many blocks from earlier buildings. Perhaps some day a combination of luck and care will bring to man's attention another great treasure. If this happens, may it be hoped that it will receive more careful publication than such wonders have been given in the past.

The Abode of the King of the Gods

Waset is the pattern for every city.
Both the flood and the earth were in her from the beginning of time.
The sands came to delimit her soil,
To create her ground upon the mound when earth came into being.
Then mankind came into being within her,
To found every city in her true name, (The City),
Since all are called " city "
After the example of Waset.

So begins the tenth canto of a " thousand " [9] canto poem in praise of Amon, " the King of the Gods ", and of Thebes, " the Mistress of Every City ". Composed in Ramesside times, it collected together the threads of various traditions and dogmas and wove them into a tapestry which showed Thebes as the capital of the world and Amon as the universal god. He it was who existed at the beginning, from whom even the primordial gods sprang. To him all nations sent tribute and all peoples paid obeisance. As master of the heavens and the underworld, Amon sustained men in both life and death.

His home was in Ipet-esut, Karnak. The first European travellers who saw the temples of Thebes were certain that they were the palaces of its ancient kings. They were only a little wrong; they were the dwellings of its ancient gods. The royal palaces, like the humble homes, were made of mud brick, but the abodes of the great gods were made of stone, to endure for all eternity. In Karnak Amon possessed the largest temple ever erected, already being built, when the poem was written, for almost a millenium. Its pylons reached toward the sky. Its great Hypostyle Hall seemed, in its gloom, to extend almost as far as the priests within could see. In its sanctuary Amon was served daily with food and drink. On the many lesser feast days he was paraded about its precincts and during the great feasts left his home to visit other temples and gods.

About the halls of Karnak were shrines of other deities. Crowding the halls and courts were statues of past rulers, ranging in size from smaller than life to colossal, and those of the chief officials who had worshipped Amon and found favour with their royal masters. All these made their home with Amon that his favours might be poured out upon them.

The great temple of Amon and its adjuncts grew through a period of more than two thousand years. The earliest extant traces of building date to about 2000 B. C.;

69

the first temple of Amon must have been centuries earlier. There were constant replacements, additions, and changes in plan. The continuing deterioration and destruction of the structures which were standing at the beginning of our era, with all else, give an impression that all is confusion. The archaeologists' work of investigation, clearance, and consolidation, still continuing, has brought some order out of the chaos which confronted the first visitors. However, it may never be possible to determine the position of buildings of which only fragmentary evidence survives, nor the exact date of all the buildings now remaining.

The structures now standing show the growth and expansion of the power of Amon; in the beginning his domain was more simple. Yet the nature of the temple was the same, the house of the god where his priests might serve him. On a mound safely above the waters of the annual inundation stood the town, and in its midst a primitive shrine, its mud walls strengthened with reeds, and within it the archaic statue of Amon.

While no traces of the early shrines have been discovered, a suggestion of the one of the Eleventh Dynasty is found in the oldest non-mortuary temple in the district. On a mountain top, about a quarter of a mile above the cultivation, and a little north of the entrance of the Valley of the Tombs of the Kings, Montuhotep III erected a mud brick enclosure, 70 by 82 feet in its external dimensions. At the front, oriented toward the river, was the earliest known pylon, once surmounted by a limestone crenellation, a unique feature. At the rear of the enclosure was a mud brick chapel, 33 feet square, and within it a hall and three shrine rooms, the whole probably roofed with palm trunks. The jambs and the lintels of the doorways were of stone; the walls and floor were plastered with clay whitened with powdered limestone or gypsum. It was a building similar to this that Intef II filled with libation vases honouring some god, perhaps Amon.

Within this chapel were found fragments of a limestone naos dedicated to Horus and with an inscription giving the earliest occurrence of the name of the temple of Amon at Karnak, Ipet-esut, " the (Most) Esteemed of Places ". Perhaps it was the first part of this name, which, with the prefixed article, was pronounced something like *Taype* in the early part of the last millenium B. C., that sounded like Thebes (*Thaybai*) to Greek ears.

The Twelfth Dynasty temple of Amon at Karnak occupied an area behind the present sanctuary of the bark about 135 feet square. Of the original structure there remain only the granite sills of three successive doorways, each barely four feet wide, and behind these an alabaster pedestal of Senusert I on which once stood a black granite naos housing the statue of Amon. Wilkinson reported " polygonal columns " of Senusert nearby; these have disappeared. An inscription on the jamb of a doorway found there dated to the twentieth year of this king, *c.* 1950 B. C., relates that at this time " his majesty was dwelling in Waset celebrating the feasts of Amon ". Since the name and the figure of Amon on this jamb and on the naos had been erased during the Amarna period and later restored, it is certain that these parts of the Twelfth Dynasty temple were still in existence and in place in Ramesside times.

This mention of Waset is the earliest known occurrence of the name of the city in which Ipet-esut was situated. As the temple complex grew, the residence area of the ordinary people was pushed farther from the river. Throughout the whole history of pharaonic Egypt it was only this temple and the houses and buildings about it which were included in the city of Waset.

Somewhere in Karnak Senusert I erected a large limestone building on the occasion of his first jubilee. Of this parts of an architrave and several pillars have been found. One of the pillars has at its front, and of one piece with it, a statue of the king more than fifteen feet high. The king is in the garb of Osiris, his arms crossed over his chest, holding the symbol of life in each hand (Plate 9).

33. Head of Ipuia,
mother of the vizier Ramose,
in the tomb chapel of the latter.
Reign of Amenhotep III.
Theban Tomb No. 55

34. Ramesses II receiving emblems
of office from Amon,
attended by Mut and Khonsu.
Original raised relief
altered to incised relief.
Inner south wall of the great
Hypostyle Hall, Karnak.

34

While there are only fragments of this great structure extant, one small building has been preserved almost complete. From the foundation and core of the Third Pylon Henri Chevrier, engineer in charge of the work in Karnak from 1926 to 1956, recovered the pieces, often badly shattered, and in the grounds north of the First Court he reconstructed this limestone shrine. It is the finest small building which has come down from Egyptian antiquity.

This shrine is well proportioned, 21½ feet square and 16½ feet high, the base and combined architrave and roof each about 46 inches high, with sixteen columns, two by three feet in the end rows and two feet square in the other two rows. Between the outer columns, except at the entrances at either end, is a parapet with rounded top 30 inches high and 18 inches wide, aligned with the outer edge of the pillars. On either end a ramp, with parapets, leads up to the platform. In the centre was a pedestal for the bark of Amon, now replaced by one of slightly later date.

The scenes on the sides of the pillars show Senusert accomplishing various ritual acts before a god, most often Amon in one of his aspects. As noted, Amon appears in the forms and with the epithets which were to be traditional throughout the active life of Karnak. In the Greek period "Amon-re, King of the Gods", was transcribed as *Amonrasonter*, and his name in the ithyphallic representation, Kamutef, "Bull of his mother", that is, "self begotten", as *Kamephis*, both representing the then current Egyptian pronunciation of the names. On the southern side of the base of the shrine is a list of the nomes of Upper Egypt, giving pertinent data about them, including their chief gods, their principal cities, and their length.[10] The hieroglyphs and the figures were carved in great detail, showing, for instance, the feathers of the birds and the scales of the snakes (Plate 14 and back end papers).

The building originally was erected in an enclosure called "The High Lookout of Kheper-ka-re" (the prenomen of Senusert I, and the shrine was named "The Throne of Horus, Son of the White and Red Crowns". The occasion for the building was also the king's first jubilee, but it was not here that the jubilee drama took place. Rather it was a way station used in festival processions. The bark of Amon, on the shoulders of the priests, was carried in at one end and set on the pedestal. After fitting ceremonies, it was carried out the other end to the next station.

The jubilee feast celebrated the renewal of kingship on the thirtieth anniversary of the king's accession to the throne, either independently, or, as in the case of Senusert I, as coregent. In the distant past this period was the limit of the king's reign, after which he was slain and his successor placed on the throne. After the first jubilee the festival was celebrated regularly as long as the king lived, usually at intervals of three years.

The only informative description of this festival is given in the tomb chapel of the Steward of Queen Tiy, Kheruef, which tells of the first and third jubilees of Amenhotep III in the thirtieth and thirty-seventh years of his reign. In a scene of the first jubilee Amenhotep, wearing a special robe for the occasion and accompanied by Queen Tiy, is towed in a bark which, according to religious tradition, carried the sun through the underworld at night. So the king symbolically passed through the underworld like the sun and at the end of the passage was, like the sun, reborn.

Thus in the jubilee the king ceremonially died and rose again. In his "death" he was identified with Osiris, the legendary king of Egypt who was treacherously slain by his brother Set who dismembered his body and threw the pieces into the river. His sister-wife, the queen Isis, gathered up the members, bound them together with strips of linen, and revivified her royal husband. Then she conceived by him a son, Horus, who became his father's heir. Osiris, having died, could not

35. Figures of the Overseer of Royal Horses, Maiy, and his wife Werel, in the tomb chapel of the vizier Ramose. *Theban Tomb No. 55*

continue in the realm of the living, but became the living king of the underworld. Following this tradition each deceased king became Osiris and each succeeding king Horus.. In the jubilee feast the king became, for a time, Osiris, so that it is often impossible to distinguish statues of him garbed for the occasion from those which would appear in the courts of his mortuary temple.

The buildings of the later kings of the Twelfth Dynasty are known only from a few fragments. Since to describe the buildings of the New Kingdom in chronological order would be confusing and sometimes impossible, the description henceforth will continue generally by location.

The modern approach to Karnak is by a road coming from the river. The road follows the course of the ancient canal which once came to the quay. This quay, elevated above the avenue leading to the main entrance of the temple, is reached by a ramp on the temple side and on the west corners once had stairways leading down to the water. Seti II erected 12 foot obelisks at the east corners of the platform. On the west face, now covered, the heights of inundations are recorded from the middle of the tenth to the beginning of the seventh centuries B. C. The highest Nile recorded occurs in the sixth year of Taharka, when it rose 33 inches above the present pavement of the Hypostyle Hall. This is approximately the height of the crest of the inundation in 1946, when it overflowed the bank between Karnak and Luxor. Before the drainage canal was built about Karnak in 1925-6, the infiltration water might rise as much as a metre in the Hypostyle Hall in the latter part of October.[11]

In Ramesside times it was from the temple quay that some of the river journeys of Amon began. He was joined by other gods in their barks, which came by way of the communicating canals leading from their temples.

Between the quay and the First Pylon the dromos is lined on either side by crio-sphinxes. Their ram's heads identify them with Amon, who, though usually shown with human features, had a ram's head on the prow and stern of his bark. Once this avenue led to the Second Pylon, but when other structures were erected before it some of the sphinxes were moved to either side of the First Court, where they still remain crowded together (Plate 57).

These crio-sphinxes received their final inscriptions from the High Priest Pinodjem I, who usurped them from Ramesses II, who in turn had usurped them from a predecessor. They could not have been set in their present position any earlier than the reign of Haremhab who erected the Second Pylon. After Pinodjem became king his queen, Henuttawy, commemorated the time " when Pinodjem I brought the crio-sphinxes to the House of Amon ".

The unfinished First Pylon has a base 370 feet long and 48 feet wide. The south tower is just over 100 feet high, about three-quarters of its intended height. In the front face of each tower are four niches for flagpoles which, if the usual proportions were maintained, would have been about 165 feet tall.

In the gateway of the First Pylon there are indications that the great wooden doors were burned as they stood open, and the same is true in the gateway of the Second Pylon. This destruction must have taken place in the first half of the Ptolemaic period. The lintel of the gateway of the First Pylon was in place before the construction halted; a fragment of it has been found. The platform it made and the tops of the pylons were reached by an internal stairway, access to which is through a doorway at the west end of the north wall of the First Court.[12]

The First Pylon, the great and brick temenos wall about the temple of Amon and all the gateways through it, except the Tenth Pylon, were built by Nekhtnebef. Mud bricks stamped with his name have been found in the wall; he decorated the eastern gateway and the small one before the temple of Ipet. The First Pylon closes the First Court on its west side, the north and south walls of which were built by

36. The hawk, Horus, with sun-disc on his head, pectoral of gold with inlaid stones, from the tomb of Tutankhamon.
Cairo Museum

37. Bracelet surmounted with scarab, gold with inlaid stones, from tomb of Tutankhamon.
Cairo Museum

38   39

Shoshenk I, who originally planned the pylon also. In his twenty-first year he ordered the opening of the quarry at Gebel el-Silsila to get sandstone " to build a
very great pylon which is similar to ' Illuminating the City ', and to erect its doors
of millions of cubits, to make a Festival Hall in the house of his father Amon-re,
King of the Gods, surrounding it with statues and columns." The structure was
named " The Mansion of Shoshenk I in Waset ".

Shoshenk's order was to make his pylon a copy of the Second which had the name,
" Illuminating Waset ". This is a typical example of the ancient Egyptian approach to architecture and, indeed, to all facets of their culture. They believed
that all proper forms of building, art, literature, care for the gods and the dead
were laid down by the gods in remote antiquity and that the way to improve and
perfect them was not by creating new forms but by making larger and more osten-
tatious copies of the old. They did not succeed in keeping to this norm, but because of their attempts to do so there is an apparent sameness in Egyptian antiquities which sometimes becomes monotonous. There is no difference in form, for
instance, between the mud brick pylon of Montuhotep III and the great sandstone
pylons at Karnak.

As Shoshenk did not realize his plan, neither did Nekhtnebef nor his successors
complete it. Bonaparte's expedition found, lying on the earthen ramps leading
to the pylon, blocks waiting to be moved into place. These ramps and building
platforms have, for the most part, been cleared away in the past seventy-five years.
Only a vestige of the platform east of the south tower remains. Up the ramps every
block of stone was pulled, the platforms becoming higher and the ramps longer and
steeper with each successive course.

Just such ramps, of tamped earth between mud brick retaining walls, are shown
in the tomb chapel of a Vizier of Thutmosis III, Rekhmire. In building the temple
of Amon of that period, after each successive course of stone was in place the building was filled with earth to the highest point reached and the blocks for the next
course hauled up the ramp and over the platform thus made. When the walls were
completed and the roof slabs in position, the interior was " excavated " and the
walls dressed as the earth was dug out.

The court of Shoshenk I, four-fifths as deep as wide, covers about two acres. Within
it, at the north west, was enclosed a way station of Seti II, with three chapels for
Mut, Amon and Khonsu, and at the south east the front of a much larger way
station of Ramesses III (Plate 62). On the central axis of the court Taharka erected
a kiosk with ten columns, of which only one, which is 69 feet high, is completely
preserved. The campaniform capital derives its shape from the blossom of the papyrus reed. Stone architraves once rested on the abaci, while the roof was
of wood. Side doorways toward the front give effect of a transept and an inverse
cruciform shape to the ground plan. The remains of a pedestal found within the
kiosk show that it, too, functioned as a way station.

The largest of the way stations, built by Ramesses III, is a fully developed small
temple. Before this building was cleared the debris came half to two-thirds of the
way up the walls. Dark streaks on these show the approximate upper limit of the
soil before it was removed. The corrosive salts in the damp earth have, through
the centuries, eaten away some of the surface of the stone and the reliefs are thus
considerably damaged, often obscured, and still deteriorating, as in most of the temples in Egypt. This is one compelling reason for making facsimile copies of the
records on the walls. Yet few Theban temples have been given much attention.
This way station of Ramesses III is the first of which a complete record has been
published.[13]

While it will be impossible to give more than passing notice to most of the reliefs
on the temple walls, their nature needs to be understood. They fall into two gen-

38. Head of acrobatic dancer.

39. Hands of Amenhotep III
and Queen Tiy.
Both in the tomb chapel
of the Steward
of Queen Tiy, Kheruef.
Reigns of Amenhotep III
and Amenhotep IV.
Theban Tomb No. 192

eral classes, historical records, especially accounts of conquests, and religious scenes showing the great feasts, the coronation ceremonies of the king, and episodes in the daily and festival rituals. To the Egyptian the division was not so clear, as everything happened under divine direction, as it did for the writers of the Hebrew scriptures. These scenes are not, as the pictures in medieval churches, to show worshippers the appearance of the chief elements of their faith. Indeed, the temples had no congregation, and it is doubtful that any but the priests visited the inner parts of the temples. For the Egyptians religious representations were an external auxiliary to and a substitute for the actual cult. When the decoration of a temple was completed, the priests moved along the walls and " opened the mouth " of each figure; that is, through magical arts they brought each representation to life. Henceforth for all time, even though the actual ceremonies should fail, the ones on the wall would continue.

The belief that these figures were alive had much to do with the deliberate disfigurement they suffered. The god Set, popular in the Nineteenth and Twentieth Dynasties, sometime later fell into disfavour as the legend of his murder of Osiris and of his struggle with Horus was taken more seriously. His figure on the walls was then hacked out, to " kill " him. Certain birds and animals shown in the hieroglyphs were considered unlucky and were effaced. In early times no hieroglyph showing a whole living creature appeared in a tomb chamber, lest such a creature might harm the dead. When Christianity became the religion of the people, the belief that the figures on the walls were alive did not disappear. It was thought that they were demons and must therefore be eradicated. Prudery operated in the case of the ithyphallic Amon and the male organ was hacked out. Moslems, with religious taboos against images inherited from the Hebrews, sometimes continued the work of defacement, but most of it seems to have been done before their ascendancy.

Another type of defacement found on the walls of Theban temples are vertical gouges, often covering large areas. These were made by persons collecting the stone dust from the sacred buildings for magical potions and charms. This superstitious practice began as early as the end of the Twentieth Dynasty. Similar gouges appear on the outer walls of medieval cathedrals in Europe.

The drab, damaged walls of the Karnak temples belie their pristine condition. When the sculptors had finished their work, the walls were thinly washed with gypsum plaster and the representations painted. Many of the details of the hieroglyphs, the sacred furniture, the dress and features of the figures were shown only in colour. Often the painter added objects which the sculptor had not carved. In the few cases where the paint is still preserved the covering dust has dimmed it. Originally the representations were brilliantly coloured and the rest of the wall white. The whole might seem garish to the modern viewer.

In the account of Ramesses III of his way station in Karnak he tells Amon, " I made for you a mysterious horizon in your city Waset, in front of your forecourt, O Lord of Gods, being the temple of Ramesses III in the estate of Amon, to remain as long as the heaven bears the sun. I built it; I sheathed it with sandstone, hanging great doors of fine gold. I filled its treasuries with offerings which my hands brought, to present them to your face as daily fare ". On the western architrave of the forecourt Ramesses relates that he " made an excellent monument [14] for him who begot him, a great holy place on sacred ground, in front of Ipet-esut and " Illuminating Waset ". When Amon rests therein his heart is glad, and the ennead in his retinue is overjoyed to see the fine and pure monument of Ramesses III."

The towers of the pylon are 33 feet each in length, barely larger than the mud brick pylons before the mountain top shrine of Montuhotep III. On the face of each is the traditional scene of the king smiting his enemies, whose locks he grasps

40. Burial chamber of Tutankhamon, with red quartzite sarcophagus and second coffin, which contains the king's mummy. The main scene shown on the wall depicts Tutankhamon and his ka, spiritual double, embracing Osiris, the god of the underworld.

41. Bust of Akhenaten, from one of the colossi found at the site of the king's temple at Karnak. *Cairo Museum*

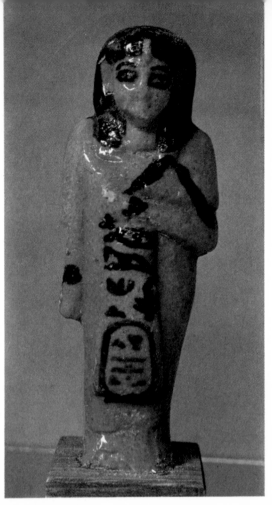

43

44

in one hand. The prototype appears on the ceremonial slate papette of Narmer at the dawn of Egyptian history.

The forecourt has a colonnade on both sides and across the end, each pillar fronted by a statue of the king in Osirian garb. Though less well proportioned than the corresponding statue of Senusert I, the conception is the same. While Senusert had the " life " hieroglyph in each hand, Ramesses carries the crook and the flail.[15] The pylon, viewed from within, is similar in shape to the hieroglyph for " horizon ", the sun rising over a valley between two hills. It is this common conception which is referred to in the quotation above, following the Egyptian thinking which saw a cosmological pattern in much of its cult.

The plan of the temple is similar to that of the dwelling of a wealthy Egyptian. The court and raised portico of the temple correspond to the public reception area, and have a forerunner in the models found in the tomb of Meket-re, eight hundred years earlier, where there is a court and porch, the roof of the latter supported by four rows of columns. The hypostyle hall of the temple, behind the portico, corresponds to the family living quarters of a private house. In temples which had a resident deity, the god was paraded in such a hall during festivals, but we have no means of knowing what part of the cult took place in this hall.

At the rear are the chapels for the barks, similar to the sleeping rooms of a house. The bark of Amon rested in the central chapel, that for Khonsu was on the right and for Mut on the left. The side walls of these chapels show the respective barks. On the prows of each are the symbols of the god, a ram's head, with a broad jewelled collar about the neck for Amon, a hawk head surmounted by the crescent and darkened disc of the new moon for Khonsu, and a woman's head crowned with the double crown of Egypt for Mut.

When Shoshenk I built the great court, he left a portal between Ramesses III's temple and the Second Pylon. On the south side of the wall, east of the portal, he listed the communities he had occupied in his Palestine campaign. Following the traditional style, each name had around it an oval, representing a crenellated fortification, topped by a bust of a typical inhabitant of the land. In the early days of Egyptology, when the discipline was less developed, it was common to make fanciful identifications of the names with Biblical records. One place name, which transliterates the Hebrew *Yad-hammelek*, " Hand of the King ", was thought to read, " Judah, the King ", and the figure above said to be the actual portrait of Rehoboam. For many years the list was neglected, but with a recent publication of a new and accurate copy, it became recognized that this is a list of actual places, and that the first five lines give the route of Shoshenk's army.[16]

The craftsmen of the king used a novel means of emphasizing the figure of the king. The wall was covered with a thick coat of plaster, which was cut away from all but the royal figure, leaving the king in bold bas-relief. Unfortunately, the plaster now has completely disappeared; only tool marks, visible in the raking light of the morning sun, outline the area where the relief once stood.

On the north side of the portal the architrave and pillars were decorated by Shoshenk, the only ones in the court bearing his name. On the north and west walls are the annals of Prince Osorkon telling of his accomplishments as High Priest of Amon. One passage mentions an eclipse of the moon.

The Second Pylon stood at the eastern end of the court of Shoshenk I. To understand the history of this pylon and the great Hypostyle Hall behind, a start must be made with the Third Pylon, built by Amenhotep III. At his accession the temple of Amon had as its front the Fourth Pylon, erected by Thutmosis I. His porch and pair of obelisks stood before it, while a few yards to the west was a pair of obelisks of Thutmosis III.

Of his pylon Amenhotep said: " The king added a monument for Amon, making

42. Canopic jar found
in the so-called " Tomb of Tiy ",
Valley of the Tombs of the Kings.
Cairo Museum

43. Faience ushebti figure
from the burial
of Queen Henuttawi,
wife of Pinodjem I.
Cairo Museum

44. Glazed faience hippopotamus.
Middle Kingdom.
Cairo Museum

for him a very great doorway before the face of Amon-re, King of the Gods, embellished with gold throughout. (On its door) the sacred ram-headed image, inlaid with lapis lazuli, is embellished with gold and precious stones; the like will never be done (again). A stele of lapis lazuli stands on either side. Its pylon reaches to the sky like the four pillars of heaven; the flagpoles thereof, embellished with electrum, gleam brighter than the sky."

The gateway itself was wider, in its passage, than the distance between the obelisks of Thutmosis III. The front edges of these were incorporated into the pylon itself so that the shafts were, at their bases, flush with the face of the pylon. There may have been some obstruction which prevented Amenhotep III from building his pylon farther to the west, perhaps another structure he did not wish to demolish.

In the tomb chapel of Nefer-hotep, Chief Scribe of Amon in the reign of Ay, there is a cross section of the temple of Amon as it was at that time. Like most ancient Egyptian plans, it shows only the principal features. Notable are the Third and Fourth pylons with an obelisk between. Before the Third is a short tree-lined avenue which terminates at a basin at the end of a canal leading to the river.

A few years after this picture was painted Haremhab began the Second Pylon, faithfully copying the details of the Third to the eight flagpole niches and the vestibule before the gateway, but making it slightly larger.

While no name for the Third Pylon has survived, there were two for the Second. The more popular one was " Illuminating Waset " but a picture in the court of the temple of Khonsu gives a second, " Amon Rejoices ".

As Amenhotep III had used stone from the dismantled temples and shrines of his predecessors for the foundations and core of his pylon, so Haremhab utilized blocks from constructions of Akenaten and from a temple of Tutankhamon and Ay. The former were quite small, averaging a little less than a foot square by two feet in length. Only a fraction of the blocks so re-used have been recovered in the work of clearing and consolidation; [17] many more are still within the mass of the pylon.

The inner ends of the towers were built on the fill dumped in the basin mentioned above. This caused some instability, and in the Ptolemaic period it was necessary to consolidate the ends of the towers. The extensiveness of this work is shown by a graffito with the name of a Greek workman cut into an architrave of Tutankhamon which was incorporated in the fabric, about level with the platform over the gateway and some yards in from the south end of the north tower. When the first European visitors arrived the ends of the towers were again in imminent danger of collapse and for the first half of the present century great timbers, placed by Legrain, prevented the final destruction. Recently this part of the structure was dismantled, and after the inner stones had been removed, the shell was reconstructed.

One of the features of the Hypostyle Hall which was built between the Second and Third Pylons is the central double row of columns with campaniform capitals (Plate 53), the same height as, but more massive than, the columns of the Kiosk of Taharka. A similar row of columns, decorated by Tutankhamon, stands in front of the temple at Luxor built by Amenhotep III, and it has been suggested that both colonnades were built by the latter king. However, they are not shown in the picture in the tomb chapel of Neferhotep. The engineers consolidating the Hypostyle Hall found, under the adjoining rows of columns supporting the clerestory on either side of the central aisle, foundations of walls, suggesting that the colonnade was once part of a long, narrow hall, as at Luxor. But similar foundations have been discovered under other columns and it is probable that other great columns were not erected as part of a separate plan.

Be that as it may, the Hypostyle Hall was conceived and built after the death of Haremhab. The north and south walls start from the ends of the two pylons,

45. Red granite pillars before
the sanctuary of the bark
of Amon, Karnak,
with heraldic flowers,
the papyrus blossom
of Lower Egypt (left) and
the " lily " of Upper Egypt (right).
Reign of Thutmosis III.

while for the east wall the Third Pylon was faced with new blocks, except that the
niches for the flagpoles were left open almost to the top. The width of the hall is
the same as that of the First Court, 330 feet, and the area enclosed one and a quarter
acres. To support the stone roof slabs there was erected a forest of columns with
bud capitals representing the unopened papyrus flower. On each side of the hall
there are seven rows of nine columns each, except that in the rows which support
the clerestory there are two less, the walls of the vestibule of the Third Pylon oc-
cupying the rest of the space. The architraves did not rest immediately on the
capitals but on the intervening abaci.

With the twelve taller central columns there are 134 in the hall, the largest constructed until modern times, but the multitude of columns makes the space seem
much smaller than it is. The smaller columns are 42½ feet high and 27½ feet in
circumference, while the central columns are 33 feet in circumference. It has been
said that, were it not for the abacus, 125 men could stand on a capital of a central
column, but no one has been brave enough to test this hypothesis.

The columns were built of half drums, the bases, with rounded sides, being larger
than the columns. The east sides of the eastern pair of great columns have lost
their original surfaces, and the small blocks fitted in for repair were never dressed.
The damage was caused when the doors of the vestibule, standing closed, were
burned, probably at the same time that the doors of the first two pylons were fired.

The inscriptions of Haremhab on the Second Pylon were not long left undisturbed.
In the vestibule his cartouches were usurped in turn by Ramesses I and Ramesses II;
they overlooked only a small group of cartouches of the builder on an altar pictured
high on the west wall of the south wing. The east faces of the Second Pylon, which
became the west wall of the Hypostyle Hall, were redressed, and only some parts
of scenes on the north tower, cut deeply, now remain. One was a great representation of the river procession of the bark of Amon copied from one in a similar position on the Third Pylon.

When first seen by modern travellers, the upper part of the west face of the Second Pylon had collapsed and great heaps of stone, now cleared away, lay piled
before each tower. Legrain believed that this destruction was too great to have
been caused by the earthquake of A. D. 27, and suggested that it was caused by
mining with gunpowder in recent centuries.

Before each wing of the vestibule stood a colossus of Ramesses II; it was under
the north one that the stele of Kamose was found. To the west of it there is a
great granite statue of Pinodjem I as High Priest, re-erected a few years ago, though
the rediscovered fragments were known to Belzoni. On the feet of the priest stands
a short figure of Queen Henuttawy.

It may be that the plan of the Hypostyle Hall was conceived by Ramesses I, since
there are a few scenes with his name high on the north side of the west wall. But
even these could have been made in his honour by his son, Seti I. The hall was not
a part of Ipet-esut proper, but was always described as standing before it. Though
roofed, it was called a " court " by both Seti I and Ramesses III. The structure,
of " the finest sandstone ", was named, " Seti I is blessed in the domain of Amon ".
The king relates that he " built a monument in the domain of Amon, making for
his creator a great holy precinct of Ipet-esut, that Amon might rest within it, a place
where the Lord of Gods might appear in his New Year Festival. It was surrounded
(within) with campaniform and bud-topped columns, (the former) inlaid with electrum." The king's " heart was happy to make the monument for his father Amon,
since he had given him victory " over his enemies.

When the great doorways at either end of the nave, those at the ends of the transverse aisle, and the small ones at either end of the Third Pylon were closed, the only
natural lighting in the vast hall was through the gratings of the clerestory windows,

46. Mourning women, wall
painting from the burial scene
in the tomb chapel
of the vizier Ramose.
Reign of Amenhotep III.
Theban Tomb No. 55

47. Mourning women,
wall-painting in the tomb chapel
of the Overseer
of Egyptian Granaries, Minnakht.
Reign of Thutmosis III.
Theban Tomb No. 87

the small openings at the top of the uncovered flagpole niches at the east, and small openings in the roof. The dimness of the hall added to the sense of awe which surrounded the religious processions.

On the outer north wall Seti I commemorated the victories which Amon had given him. To the east are shown the campaigns against Syria and Canaan. The way through the southern desert of Canaan is marked by fortified waterholes, always a necessity when the Egyptians campaigned to the north. The king, in his chariot, drives some prisoners before him, while others, manacled, are pulled along by ropes attached to the chariot. As the king approaches the boundary of Egypt, marked by the crocodile-infested " dividing canal ", near the fortress of Tjel, crowds of Egyptians on the other side hail the victorious ruler.

To the west of the doorway are shown the wars against Kadesh and against the Libyans. In the upper west corner appears the fortress city, " Kadesh, in the land of Amor ", with the dying defenders about it, one falling from the battlements. Below the fortress is an exquisite vignette of a terrified cowherd driving his cattle into the hills, and, as he looks behind him, raising his hand as if to ward off the fierce onslaught of the Egyptians.

These reliefs show the Egyptian artist at his best. The valour and might of the king, the mettle of his horses, the inability of the enemy to withstand his attack, and the dejection of his captives, all are convincingly portrayed (Plate 61). It was only a just retribution for their unholy rebellion that those of the enemy who lived through the battles, and the wealth of their lands, should be brought back and dedicated to the temple of Amon.

Such prisoners, through the years of the Egyptian empire, built the temples and palaces. The picture in Rekhmire's tomb chapel shows Syrians at such labour. Others became slaves of officials; on the walls of the tomb chapels of the Eighteenth Dynasty they are shown at work in the fields, Negroes as well as Syrians and Libyans. Their lot did not differ much from that of native Egyptian peasants whose work on the land was arduous and who might be conscripted into the royal labour corps.

In the Nineteenth Dynasty it was customary to place the supervision of construction under the Chief of the Medjay, the internal security forces. One such commander, Iwny, was " Overseer of Works in the House of Amon " and may have helped erect the Hypostyle Hall. Another, Hatiay, whose father lived long enough to become Steward of the Ramesseum, says that it was he " who erected the great columns in the House of Amon ". Amenemone, who at one time in his career was Overseer of Works in the Ramesseum, is mentioned in a letter as being in charge of soldiers and *Apiru* who brought stone for a pylon of Ramesses II. These *Apiru* were akin to, if not identical with, the Hebrews; it was such as these that Seti captured in his campaign against the Bedouins in southern Canaan.

The decoration of the interior walls, begun by Ramesses I or Seti I, was in bas-relief. In some scenes, notably on the north wall, there were extensive alterations of the figures, especially those of the king. Apparently inspectors decided that the proportions, as originally carved, were wrong, but it is now difficult to tell which version was the earlier.

All of the north half and part of the south half of the hall was decorated by Seti, and Ramesses II at first continued carving his reliefs in the same style. However, early in his reign he ordered all the reliefs so far executed in the south half of the hall, including those of his father, whose cartouches he usurped, to be changed to incised relief. The work was done by cutting back inside the edges of the bas-relief, and in many scenes the outlines of the original can be seen (Plates 34 and 59). The walls as yet undecorated were finished in the new style.

48. Black granite statue group of the Mayor of Thebes, Sennefer, his wife Senetnay, and their daughter Mutneferet. Reign of Amenhotep II. *Cairo Museum*

48

The reason for the change is not evident. Up to the time of Ramesses II it was customary, in limestone and sandstone buildings, to decorate the exterior walls in incised relief and the interior walls in bas-relief. Now all were of the former sort. This certainly was quicker and simpler, requiring the cutting of the figures and hieroglyphs into the stone instead of cutting the background away from them. Incised relief, too, may have been easier to see in the dim light of the interiors, but in their original state the visibility of the reliefs depended on their colours.

The river barks of the gods are prominently displayed on the walls of the hall, the place of honour being given to User-hat-Amon, " Splendid is the prow of Amon ". Over the representation of the one carved by Seti I the thanks of Amon contain a play on the names of the Second Pylon, " My son Seti, my heart is happy with your monument in Waset. I am pleased that you have made my heart *joyous*, ...that you have *illuminated* Ipet-esut with eternal work ". The Egyptians were fond of such word play, but their puns, usually humorous, lose their effect in translation. In the similar scene carved by Ramesses II, the river issues from under the feet of the enthroned Amon. The usual god of the First Cataract, where the river was believed to spring from a secret cavern, was Khnum, also ram-headed. This representation shows the increasing tendency to identify Amon with many of the major gods.

Also shown by both rulers is the procession of the barks of Amon, Mut, and Khonsu during festivals. Mounted on long poles, they are carried on the shoulders of the priests. In the scene which owes its final version to Ramesses II these priests wear masks with hawk and jackal heads, representing the " Souls of Pe and Nekhen ", the primordial spirits of the ancient religious centres of Lower and Upper Egypt (Plate 59).

Such processions were frequent, not only for the great feasts but also for lunar festivals, among others. At the time of Thutmosis III there were fifty-four regularly appointed festivals. During these the bark of Amon was paraded in the halls and outside the temple, resting for ceremonies in the way stations. On these occasions the bark of Amon could be seen by the public, not only outside the temple, but also within the Hypostyle Hall. Ramesses II speaks of it as " a place where the populace extols the name of his majesty " and " within which " Amon " is mannifest to the populace ".

At least as early as the Nineteenth Dynasty these processions could be the occasion for the consultation of the god. On such an occasion in the Twentieth Dynasty, the office of Scribe of the Storehouses of the Estate of Amon fell vacant through death. During the celebration of a lunar festival the officiating priest asked Amon if he were willing to consider the matter of a new appointment, and the god nodded in assent. Then the classes of temple priests were read to Amon, and he selected the Inspectors of Divine Offerings. To be sure that the god had been rightly understood, he was asked if it was this class of priests he had indicated, and he gave an affirmative answer. Then, as the procession continued, the names of those in this group were read out, and the god came to a stop at one name. Again the god was asked if he was understood correctly, and again he nodded in the affirmative. The priest selected for the office was the son of the former incumbent, whose forefathers had held the same office. It was the natural choice, but it had to be submitted to Amon for his affirmation that the appointment corresponded to his desire. By similar means Amon selected Nebwenenef from among all the high officials of the government to be his High Priest at the beginning of the reign of Ramesses II.

Other questions were also answered by oracle. In a case of a theft the list of villagers was read to the god who selected one as the culprit. This man protested his innocence, and appealed to other gods, with the same result. The alleged thief

49. Daughters of the owner of the tomb, and girl harpist, wall-painting in the tomb chapel of the Accountant of the Granary of Amon, Djeserkareseneb. Reign of Thutmosis IV. *Theban Tomb No. 38*

93

never confronted the oracular images himself, but had the question submitted through attending priests.

In this instance one suspects fraud or collusion on the part of the priests. Yet the Egyptians were essentially a devout people, believing that their destinies were divinely guided, seeking the divine will, asking divine approval of their actions, and hoping for divine guarantees of their welfare alive and dead.

These oracles were not, like the Greek, enigmatic, but a straightforward indication of the god's desire and a forthright declaration of his word. There were various ways of his making a selection or answering in the affirmative or negative by some motion or halting of the bark.

To what extent the priests who carried the bark were parties to its movements in oracular decision it is impossible to say. They could have felt a common compulsion which was quite unconscious. A parallel exists in modern Moslem funerary practice. The wrapped body is placed on a bier with poles and supported on the shoulders of mourners who carry the deceased to the cemetery. Usually the procession of men chanting religious songs proceeds without event, but sometimes the bearers feel the body becoming heavier until they are finally unable to carry it any farther.

In a recent funeral procession in Luxor this happened and the pallbearers retraced their steps for some considerable distance three times before they could pass the point where the corpse first resisted the trip to the burial ground. Local tradition says that such resistance may be because the man has been wicked and wishes to delay judgment. On the other hand, the Moslem cemetery of Luxor lies about a mosque in which is buried a local saint who, it is related, chose this spot by refusing to allow his body to be carried farther. There is also the opposite effect, when the corpse becomes so light that the bearers feel compelled to run, " flying " with their burden.

The ancient Egyptian term for the public procession of the bark of the god was " divine arrival ". In a fragmentary ghost story of the Nineteenth Dynasty a spirit appeals to the High Priest to restore his ruined tomb. The ghost says of himself, " when I was living on earth, I was overseer of the Treasury of King Rahotep and Lieutenant Commander of the Army. I was in front of the people when the gods arrived." Some of the conspirators against Ramesses III took advantage of such a " divine arrival " and the crowd it attracted to slip into the harem precinct at Medinet Habu.

Various scenes relating to the coronation of kings are on the walls of the hall, but the order of occurrence varies. There is the baptism of the king prior to his induction, where two of the four celebrating gods are shown pouring water over the royal figure. The streams are symbolically represented by the alternating hieroglyphs for life and dominion, or by the first alone. Two gods, usually Atum and Montu, introduce the king into the temple where he is crowned by Amon, Mut, and Khonsu. Again, the king kneels beneath the sacred persea tree of Heliopolis, on the leaves of which Thoth inscribes his name.

In the final ceremony Ramesses II appears within the shrine, kneeling before Amon to receive the crook and the flail, emblems of his office, while Mut and Khonsu add their blessing (Plate 34). Outside the shrine stands Thoth writing the royal titulary and addressing the king: " Lo, I am acting at the command of your father, the King of Gods. I have confirmed your life records to cover millions of years and hundreds of thousands of jubilees. I am causing your lifetime to continue like the heavens; as long as Re shall exist, you shall exist. I am causing the whole South to bow in obeisance and the North to tremble before your power. I am placing the fear of you in all foreign lands and the dread of you in the hearts of their princes."

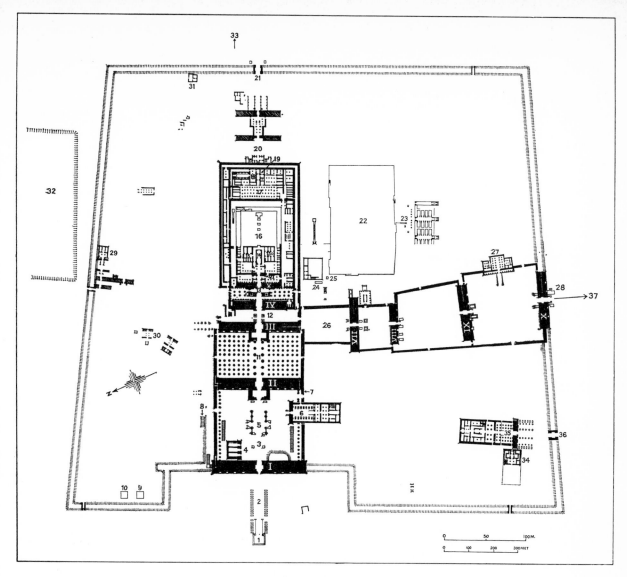

KARNAK, THE TEMENOS OF AMON

One series of scenes, at the north end of the east wall, shows some of the episodes in the daily cult. From these and other scenes, and from papyri giving parallel texts, a general picture of the daily activities in the temple can be constructed.

The golden image of Amon, which travelled about in the shrine on his bark, had its home in the granite naos of Senusert I. The statue itself was less than one quarter human size. When the officiating priest, acting in the name of the king, approached the shrine in the morning he found the doors closed and sealed. Chanting the proper spells, he broke the seal, withdrew the bolt, and opened the doors. The god's meal was prepared in his presence while he savoured the sweet odours. For each stage there was a proper incantation, for lighting the fire, putting on the incense, fanning the fire, placing the spit with the roast, and basting the roast with beer. Other spells accompanied the preparation of the bread, cake, wine, and milk, and for arranging the fruit and flowers. These offerings were purified by water and incense. When all was ready, the meal was presented as a gift from the king, and laid out before the god. With further libation and censing the god was brought to his meal.

When the repast was finished, incantations made certain that the god would be sustained by the food of which he had partaken. When the food had been removed, the doors of the shrine were closed and fastened, and a priest, dragging behind him the branch of a bush, erased the footprints of the servitors.

This, however, was not the end of the temple service. The offerings then reverted to the statues of the former kings and officials which crowded the temple halls. By the end of the Twentieth Dynasty there were thousands of these about. Many still standing in Ptolemaic times were removed and buried in the court to the north of the Seventh Pylon. Most of the Egyptian statues in the museums about the world once stood in temples and tombs, embodying the spirits of the persons they represented, so that they might enjoy the blessing of the god and the sustenance provided through the favour of the reigning monarch.

The cult image of the god was regularly washed and clothed, anointed with perfumed oils, and garlanded. Such concern for the welfare of the god brought in return the god's concern for the welfare of Egypt, for its king, and through him for the land and those who lived on it.

The priests serving the temples were held to strict rules of ritual purity. Daily they had to shave their whole bodies, twice daily and twice nightly they washed in the temple lake, or if the temple had no lake, with water brought in basins. It mattered not whether the weather was hot or cold, the sky cloudy or sunny.

The lesser priests were divided into four phylae, each taking turns in monthly service. It was possible for some to be promoted through the ranks. Bekenkhonsu, whose long career corresponded roughly to the reign of Ramesses II, spent four years as a "purified one", the most humble rank of the priesthood, twelve years as a "god's father", then was Third Prophet of Amon for fifteen years and Second Prophet for twelve. At the end of this career he served as First Prophet of Amon, that is, as High Priest, for twenty-seven years.

Few High Priests, however, came up through the ranks in such a manner. Nebwenenef came from an outside priesthood. Amenemhat, elevated to the highest office in the reign of Amenhotep II or Thutmosis IV, was, until the age of 54, still an ordinary priest, whose special charge was the care of Amon's sandals and the overseeing of the temple domestics. Then he became a "god's father" and only achieved the high priesthood some years later. Shortly after the death of Ramesses III the office of High Priest of Amon became hereditary. The office remained in the hands of one family, that of Herihor and his descendents, from the end of the Twentieth Dynasty through the Twenty-first.

On the south outer wall of the Hypostyle Hall Ramesses II tells of his northern

50. Serving girls and a guest at a banquet, wall-painting in the tomb chapel of Djeserkareseneb. Reign of Thutmosis IV. *Theban Tomb No. 38*

51. Guests at a banquet, wall-painting in the tomb chapel of the Astronomer of Amon, Nakht. Reign of Thutmosis III. *Theban Tomb No. 52*

50 · 51

campaigns, and continues on the walls which extend to the Tenth Pylon. Close to the beginning of this extension is the Egyptian version of the treaty between the Hittite king Hatusili and Ramesses II in the twenty-first year of the latter's reign. The treaty provides for external peace, for mutual aid if either is attacked, for the extradition of offenders of one country who have fled to the other, and a guarantee of humane treatment for the fugitives who are returned. The gods of the two countries, Hatti and Egypt, are called upon as witnesses. The treaty remained in force as long as the kingdom of Hatti existed.

The Eighteenth Dynasty temple of Amon, Ipet-esut proper, began with the Fourth Pylon. The pylons and halls of this earlier temple are now in ruin. There was, throughout the period of their use, frequent alteration and repair from the time of Thutmosis I, who removed most of the buildings of his father, Amenhotep I, down to the Ptolemaic period.

In its original condition Ipet-esut was a thing of splendour. The inscriptions speak of the extensive use of gold and electrum and of precious stones, especially lapis-lazuli, in its decoration. These riches have long since been stripped away; in some cases they may not actually have existed, but were only simulated in paint. However, the pyramidal points of the obelisks of Thutmosis I were covered with electrum, the upper half of the obelisks of Hatshepsut just beyond them were plated with gold, and the pair east of the temple were sheathed with gold throughout. The top of an obelisk of Thutmosis III, lying north-east of the Third Pylon, has holes drilled in the granite for the attachment of the metal.

The constructions of Thutmosis I were under the supervision of Ineni, who served Amenhotep I in the same capacity, and who lived on in semi-retirement into the reign of Hatshepsut and Thutmosis III. To transport from Assuan the two granite obelisks he eventually erected before the Fourth pylon he built a barge 208 feet long and 60 feet in the beam. He says that the Fourth and Fifth Pylons were built of limestone; in fact this was the material of the facing blocks only, and the cores were made of sandstone. In the four niches in the front of the foremost pylon were set flagpoles of Lebanon fir hewn for the purpose, their tips covered with electrum.

The gateway of the Fourth Pylon also was "plated with electrum". This and the two successive pylons, the last built by Thutmosis III, had similar names, "Amon, Mighty of Prestige", "Amon, Great of Prestige", and "Amon, Senior in Prestige". The word for "prestige" was a homonym of the word for "ram's head", the symbol of Amon.

In the passageway of the Fourth Pylon there has been set a granite stele of Amenhotep II, found in the Third Pylon. Here this king appears in his chariot shooting with bow and arrow at an upright wooden target and at a copper ingot. This public display of his strength and skill is thus described: "A great slab of native copper through which the king shot, being three fingers in thickness. The 'Great of Strength' (Amenhotep himself) pierced it with many arrows, which he made come out of this slab three hand breadths." And since he was divine, who could dispute that Amenhotep was strong enough to shoot arrows through a copper block more than two inches thick so that the shafts protruded almost nine inches at the back?

Between his two pylons Thutmosis I erected a hall, with statues of himself in jubilee attire along the walls, and with a wooden roof supported by a row of seven wooden columns. It was in the northern wing of this hall that the boy who was to become Thutmosis III was serving as an acolyte when, during a festival procession, the bark of Amon stopped before him, and the god led the youth to the Station of the King, thus proclaiming Amon's choice of the future ruler.

In the fifteenth year of her reign, and in celebration of her first jubilee, Hatshepsut began the quarrying of the two great obelisks which she introduced into the hall.

52. Head of red quartzite statue of Tutankhamon, usurped by Ay and then by Haremhab, found in the mortuary temple of these kings. *Cairo Museum*

99

If the jubilee celebrated a thirtieth anniversary, it must have been that of her appointment as ruler which she claimed had been made by her father Thutmosis I.

The problems of quarrying and erecting the obelisks have intrigued many. An unfinished obelisk lying in the Assuan quarry gives the answer to the first problem. Three of the sides of this shaft, about 125 feet long, were freed from the native rock by pulverizing the stone around it with hammer blows from diorite boulders. As the work was proceeding on the underside, a crack divided the shaft, and it was abandoned. For the erection the most probable hypothesis is that a mound with approaching ramp was erected over the base of the obelisk. In the centre was a funnel filled with sand. When the shaft had been dragged, butt first, to the top of the mound and placed in a predetermined position, the sand was withdrawn, and the obelisk settled on to the base, where it was held by a slot as it was pulled upright.

The northern obelisk of Hatshepsut, still standing, is eight and a half feet square at the base and 97 feet high (Plate 26). Sometime after Hatshepsut's death the two obelisks became offensive to Thutmosis III who sheathed them with sandstone blocks up to the roof of the hall.

Starting from the Fifth Pylon Thutmosis I built a court surrounding the Middle Kingdom temple, jubilee figures of the king along the inner wall, and on all four inner sides an " august colonnade (of sixteen sided columns) which makes the Two Lands festive with its beauty ". From the Fourth Pylon another wall surrounded all Ipet-esut, with rooms against the south wall, and before them a corridor which led to another building to the east of the Middle Kingdom temple.

In front of that temple Hatshepsut erected a suite of rooms and in front of it her sanctuary of the bark of Amon. Its base was of black granite and above these were seven uniform courses of red quartzite, one register of reliefs to each course. In these she commemorated her actual coronation in the second year of her regency, showing the ceremonies with musicians and acrobatic dancers (Plates 22 and 23); on the black granite course were recorded the nomes of Egypt, Theban temples, and other geographical features (Plate 24). The great festivals of Opet and the Valley were shown on upper courses, with Thutmosis III given equal prominence with the queen. Since the two obelisks she erected in the hall of her father are mentioned, this sanctuary was not earlier than her fifteenth year of reign.[18]

After her death Thutmosis III was first occupied, in the twenty-second year of his reign, with a military campaign, and only on his return did he begin his own building operations. He first turned his attention to the earlier building reached by the corridor of his grandfather, to the east of which Hatshepsut had erected her first pair of obelisks.

He says that he found this building in a ruinous condition, the soil almost hiding the walls which were within a mud brick enclosure. To " extend this temple (Ipet-esut) ", he purified the area, " exorcized its evil, removed the debris which had mounted to the town quarter and levelled off the place where the walls had been to build upon it " his Festival Hall. He swore that he began this building anew, for " he would not work upon the monument of another ". He protests: " My majesty has spoken these things truthfully so that all people may know. My majesty detests falsehood; it is not in me to weave tall stories."

This Festival Hall was named " Menkheperre (the prenomen of Thutmosis III), Blessed Through Monuments ". In a room at the entry was a list of the earlier rulers of Egypt; the building commemorated them and the first jubilee festival of Thutmosis III, the latest occupant of the eternal throne, and was, like the mortuary temples, called a " Mansion of Millions of Years."

The " Central Hall ", on the west side of the building, has the roof supported by square columns about the sides and two rows of round ones down the centre. These latter took their design from the tent poles like those used in the kiosk of the jubilee festival. When the Christian faith superseded the religion of Amon this hall became a Christian church and traces of painted portraits of the saints can still be seen on the round columns. At the north end of this hall were three chapels, perhaps for the Theban Triad,[19] and behind them a second story chapel to Re, open to the sky.

To the east, within the building, was a chapel which in later years Alexander the Great took over as his own. Actually, it is probable that he himself was ignorant of this, and that this and adjoining rooms were decorated in his name by the priests who followed the ancient tradition that it was always the king who built the temples and made offerings to the gods.

In the north-east section of the Festival Hall are two rooms, the remaining walls of which show "every exotic plant and every beautiful flower which was in 'God's Land'[20] and which his majesty brought back when his majesty journeyed to Upper Retenu (Syria) to subdue the northern countries, as his father Amon had commanded, who put them under his sandals from today onward for a million years. His majesty said, 'I swear, as Re loves me and as Amon praises me, all these truly exist; there is not a word of exaggeration here.' It came about through the power of his majesty that the fertile soil (of Egypt) brought them forth as its produce."

Well might Thutmosis protest the veracity of his picture, as the identification of many of the plants, animals and birds has defied naturalists. Part of the difficulty lies in our ignorance of the flora and fauna of Syria over three thousand years ago, and part in our inability to see form through the eyes of the Egyptian artist.

It was probably after the end of his campaigns, in his forty-second year, that Thutmosis remodelled the court of Thutmosis I, building small rooms where there had been a colonnade. Before Hatshepsut's sanctuary he built the Sixth Pylon, on the towers of which he listed the places he had captured in Syria and Nubia. In his reconstruction he covered some of the reliefs and inscriptions of Hatshepsut, saving them from his later destruction of her records.

At the time he built the pylon the sanctuary of Hatshepsut still stood, and indeed, he claimed it as his own. He did decorate the upper course which Hatshepsut had left blank. A few years later he began to remove her figure and name, but before he had gone far he decided to erect his own sanctuary.

This, built of red granite slabs, he placed somewhat to the rear of Hatshepsut's sanctuary, cutting away the middle rooms of the suite she had built in front of the Middle Kingdom temple. In the remaining rooms on the southern side he erased her cartouches, replacing them with those of his father and himself. In the northern rooms he erased her figure, replacing it by representations of offerings. The ambulatory about his sanctuary he faced with new blocks, and on the walls so created placed a long account of his military campaigns and his gifts to Amon.[21] More than a millenium later Philip Arrhidaeus "found the bark room of Amon falling into ruin, a construction of the time of Thutmosis III. His majesty built it anew of granite." This sanctuary has stood up well through the past two thousand years and much of the colour remains on the reliefs.

Before his sanctuary Thutmosis III erected two square granite pillars, bearing, on their sides, the heraldic flowers of the two parts of Egypt, the papyrus bloom for the Delta and the lily for the Nile Valley (Plate 45). At the north side of the vestibule before the sanctuary, perhaps as a sign of reconciliation after the Amarna schism, Tutankhamon erected red quartzite statues, one of Amon and one of Amonet. The features of Amon resemble those of the official portrait of the king, a phenomenon common in other reigns.

Toward the end of his reign Thutmosis III built a new enclosure wall about his enlarged Ipet-esut, removing the eastern obelisks of Hatshepsut to do so. To replace the building he had removed two decades or more earlier when he built the Festival Hall, he constructed against the eastern face of the wall, in the centre, a chapel, Amon's "proper place of the ear, the shrine therein of a single block of stone". The lower part of this alabaster shrine is still *in situ* and seated within are a pair of statues, identified at the end of the Twentieth Dynasty as Amon and Amonet of the "Hearing Ear".

Thutmosis had commissioned to stand before this chapel "a single obelisk (to be erected in) the Upper Court of the temple, near to Ipet-esut, the very first time of erecting a single obelisk in Waset". While the sculptors were finishing the decoration in their atelier on the south side of Karnak, the king died and the shaft lay there for thirty-five years until found by Thutmosis IV. He ordered it set up in the place originally intended, "the Upper Gateway of Ipet-esut opposite Waset".[22]

Here the people of the city just outside the gate might come in and offer their prayers to Amon. One of the tomb chapels of an Eighteenth Dynasty official pictures a statue named "Thutmosis III (or IV) who hears prayer". Under Ramesses II the venerable High Priest, Bekenkhonsu, extended the chapel, telling that he made "a chapel (named) 'Ramesses II who hears prayer' in the Upper Gateway of the House of Amon" and "erected obelisks in it". This entrance became known as the "Great Door of Beki". Taharka and Nekhtnebef made further additions, the latter building his eastern gateway just behind the obelisks of Ramesses II. Finally, "Ptolemy VIII who hears prayer" redecorated the frame of an inner doorway. The conclusion can legitimately be drawn that there was an identification here of the king and Amon, both officially and in the minds of the Thebans who prayed in the chapel.

To the south of Amon's temple Thutmosis III "dug for him (Amon) the Southern Lake" more than two-thirds the size of the temple itself. In this lake the priests performed, four times daily, their required ablutions. On it swam geese and ducks of which great numbers were needed for the temple offerings. The fowl-yard was south of the lake; their covered runway from the yard to the lake can still be seen. At the south-west corner of the lake, by a ruined chapel of Taharka, now lies the upper part of the fallen southern obelisk of Hatshepsut. Nearby is a monument to the sacred scarab, the god Khoperi, one of the manifestations of the sun, commissioned by Amenhotep III.[23]

Also on the Southern Lake, at the west, was the apartment of the High Priest of Amon. The original structure was built in the time of Senusert I; it was completely reconstructed toward the end of the Twentieth Dynasty. Adjacent to it were the temple kitchens where the baked foods, beer and sweetmeats were prepared. Rebuilt at the end of the Nineteenth Dynasty, no trace now remains. The knowledge of these buildings comes from inscriptions of the High Priests on the nearby walls of the southern approach to the temple of Amon.

This southern approach, with four pylons and courts between, is a puzzle. While the Ninth and Tenth Pylons, the southernmost, are in line with the avenue going to the temple of Mut, the axis of the Seventh and Eighth Pylons is not; nor is it at right angles to the main axis of the temple of Amon nor on the line of the processional avenue going to Luxor.

Amenhotep I relates that he built a pylon with a limestone doorway twenty cubits high (about thirty-four feet). Thutmosis III tells that he "found the Southern Pylon built of mud brick" and certainly claimed that he rebuilt it of stone. This was the present Eighth Pylon, actually built by Hatshepsut. To the south of it still stand two red quartzite seated colossi of Thutmosis II and a limestone seated colossus of Amenhotep I, repaired by Thutmosis III in his forty-second and twenty-second years respectively. Those who complain about the megalomania of Ramesses II as shown by his great colossi have forgotten that such large statues were common from the very beginning of the Eighteenth Dynasty.

The extant decoration of the Eighth Pylon is a good example of the changing

53. Central columns
and clerestory windows,
great Hypostyle hall of the temple
of Amon, Karnak.
Reign of Seti I.

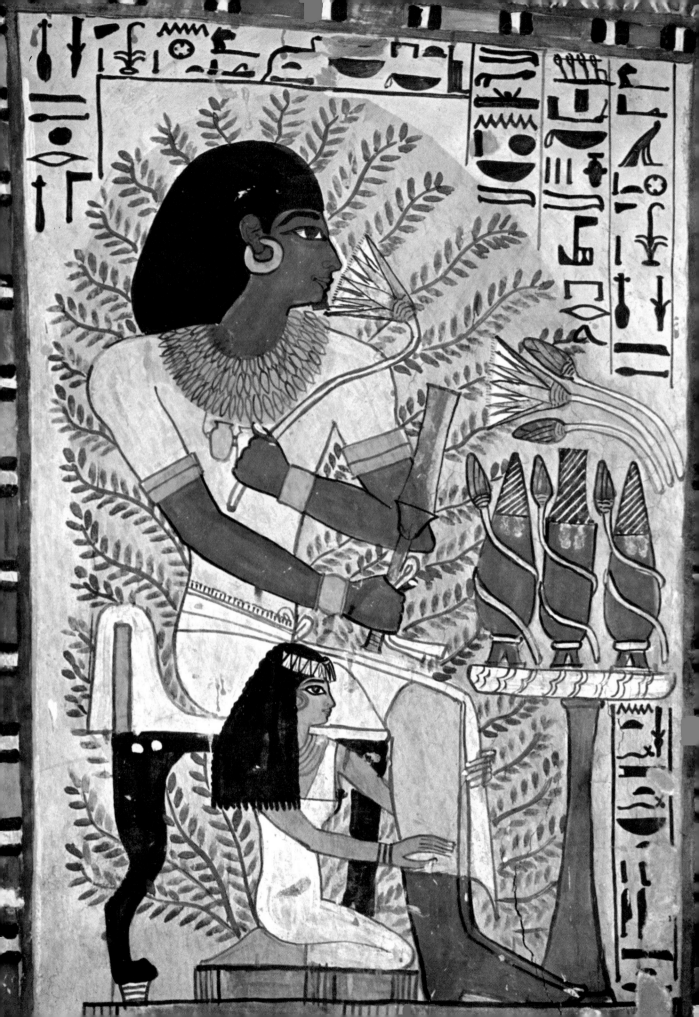

and usurpation of inscriptions. Originally decorated by Hatshepsut, Thutmosis III replaced her cartouches with those of his grandfather, his father and himself. Amenhotep II had scenes of his triumph over his enemies engraved on the south faces of the towers. Akhenaten erased the figures and names of Amon and other gods; Seti I took the occasion of their restoration to place his name in many of the cartouches. Ramesses II redecorated the passageway in the gate, and Ramesses III added scenes on the north face of the west tower.

It has been conjectured that north of the Eighth Pylon, to which it gave entrance, was a temple built by Amenhotep I or a predecessor, subsequently removed by Thutmosis III or Amenhotep III. The front, according to this theory, was in the court where, in the third or second century B. C., the great cache of statues was buried. Parts of a shrine, copied by Amenhotep I from the now reconstructed one of Senusert I, and other fragments of buildings of the early Eighteenth Dynasty have been found, but none can be identified with certainty as belonging to this hypothetical building.

The Seventh Pylon, larger than the Eighth, has on both sides lists of northern and southern places conquered by Thutmosis III. At the north, at either side of the doorway, are a number of statues of kings, two on each side of Thutmosis III, with one of the three others on the west representing a Sebekhotep of the Thirteenth Dynasty (Plate 30). Nearby, at the east, was found the remarkable seated statue of Amenhotep, son of Hapu, celebrating his eightieth birthday.

Before the Seventh Pylon Thutmosis III placed two colossal statues of himself and his second pair of obelisks; it is the top of one of these which now stands in Istanbul. To the south-east this king erected an alabaster shrine in a peripteral setting, a way station celebrating his second jubilee. It replaced an alabaster shrine begun by Amenhotep I and finished by Thutmosis I which was named " Amon, Enduring of Monuments ". This shrine was shown in one of the scenes in the sanctuary of Hatshepsut. The discarded blocks were re-used in the Third Pylon and have now been re-erected near the limestone shrine of Senusert I.

The remaining pylons, the Ninth and Tenth, owe their final construction to Haremhab. In the northern one he used blocks from earlier, dismantled buildings, including some from a temple of Amenhotep III and some from the later temple of Akhenaten. The southern one was planned and begun by Amenhotep III. In the completion Haremhab used in the core large blocks from an early temple of Akhenaten, erected before he adopted the Amarna style, showing the king adoring Re-Harakhty, the traditional sun god.

To the south of this pylon Amenhotep erected a colossal standing figure of himself, sculptured from the 69 foot block of red quartzite that Amenhotep, son of Hapu, had brought up river to Thebes. At the north of the pylon, on either side of the doorway, are two large standing statues which Ramesses II usurped from a predecessor. At the base of the eastern one were found, sitting side by side, four statues, about life size, of scribes, two representing Amenhotep, son of Hapu, and two of Paramessu, son of Seti. The latter was the chief deputy of Haremhab; on the death of this king he succeeded to the throne as Ramesses I.

Walls between the ends of the pylons made courts between each. On the east of the court between the southernmost pylons was a chapel of Amenhotep II commemorating his second jubilee, also a way station for the bark of Amon. On the west wall of this court and on both walls of the court between the Eighth and Ninth Pylons were once representations of the procession of Amon in the Feast of Opet.

It was down this processional way, through the gateway of the four southern pylons, that the bark of Amon was carried by the priests when the god began his journey to the Luxor temple. As Amon passed through the last of these he went out of his own abode and left Ipet-esut behind him.

54. The Mayor of Thebes, Sennefer, and his second wife Meryt sitting under the persea tree, wall-painting on a pillar in the burial chamber. Reign of Amenhotep II. Theban Tomb No. 96

The Lords of Thebes

AMON WAS KNOWN as the " Ruler of Thebes ", but only the other deities who lived in the various temples and shrines which were in the city of Waset were the " Lords of Thebes ". Within the three areas now enclosed by the temenos walls of Nekhtneb-ef there are great vacant tracts; earlier these were filled with the houses of the inhabitants. When Thutmosis III inspected the building east of the main temple of Amon he found that the debris " mounted to the town quarter ".

In the summer of 1126 B. C., at the beginning of the investigation of the violation of the tombs of the ancient kings, to be related in the next chapter, certain officials met in public " by the side of the house of Ptah, Lord of Waset ". Ptah, whose home was in Memphis, was one of the three great national gods and was therefore honoured in Thebes. The other, besides Amon, was Re of Heliopolis, who was so completely identified with Amon that he had shrine rooms but no temple in the Southern City. Following his inspection of Theban temples, Thutmosis related: " My majesty found this temple (of Ptah) built of mud brick, the columns wooden, its door-frame of wood, and falling into ruin. My majesty ordered the stretching of the cord [24] on this temple anew, the erection with sandstone, the walls about it of mud brick, of enduring and eternal workmanship. Then my majesty erected for it doors of real cedar of the High Terraces (Lebanon), bound with Asiatic copper, new (doors) at the front of the mansion of Ptah bearing the name of my majesty. There never had been done for him (Ptah) a similar thing previous to (the time of) my majesty ".

Thutmosis further described the building as the " temple of Ptah South-of-His-Wall (i. e., of Memphis) in Waset, which is in the processional circuit of my father Amon-re, Lord of the Thrones of the Two Lands, in which his desire is centred at the time of his annually observed festival processions, when he proceeds to the Treasury of the Head of the South ". Thutmosis decreed that, on such occasions, increased offerings be made to Amon when he rested in the temple of Ptah and that, when Amon was satisfied, part of the offerings revert to the priests and part to a statue of Thutmosis himself, the latter to revert to Ptah when the royal statue had taken its fill.

Nekhtnebef included the temple within the temenos of Amon, the wall of which is just to the north. A paved street went from the gateway in the wall just north of the dromos of the temple to the north doorway of the Hypostyle Hall; to the south of the street are three chapels built in the Twenty-fifth and Twenty-sixth Dynasties. The dromos has six gateways of the Ethiopian and Ptolemaic periods;

between the last two was a porch, the room supported by four columns with campaniform capitals bearing multiflorous designs, buds and flowers, sculptured about the exterior.

The pylon, of which the last gateway is a part, is about 48 feet wide; the temple extends 54 feet behind its face. Within each tower of the pylon is a porter's lodge. Beyond is a shallow court and a portico, in the walls of which are niches which once contained statues. In front of the doorway is a pedestal of Thutmosis III on which rested the bark of Amon during his visits.

Within the temple are three rooms, the northern one for Ptah and the southern one for Hathor, Chieftainess of Thebes. In the latter room there stands a statue with a lioness's head, surmounted by a disc, a representation of Sekhmet, at Memphis the consort of Ptah.

This statue is illuminated only by the light which comes from the original hole in the roof directly above it and gives it a weird appearance. Visitors are often startled at the apparition-like form which confronts them when they enter the room through the door in the opposite end and even when their eyes have become accustomed to the gloom, the figure does not lose its almost hypnotic fascination. Through the years a number of stories have been told about this statue. Half a century ago the villagers of Karnak were convinced that she was an ogress who prowled at night, seizing children, and on one occasion the villagers physically assaulted the statue. It is said that visitors have become hysterical in its presence and some of them have sworn that they have seen Sekhmet's arm, which holds a long-stemmed lotus blossom, move toward them.

A Ptolemaic relief on the north wall of the court shows the king making offerings to Ptah, to Hathor and to " Imhotep, son of Ptah, the beneficent god who comes to the one who calls him, giving life to all people ". Imhotep, the architect and adviser of Djoser, builder of the Step Pyramid at Sakkara, became a god of medicine, identified by the Greeks with Asclepios. With him became associated Amenhotep, son of Hapu, and on the rear wall of the temple a graffito shows the two side by side. At the time of Ptolemy VIII Euergetes II an inner room was added to the sanctuary at Deir el-Bahri and dedicated to these two gods of healing. Graffiti on the walls show that the sanctuary was very popular with the sick and infirm.

Within the temenos of Amon are a number of small chapels and shrines, mostly of the first half of the second millenium B. C. The one most deserving of notice is consecrated to Osiris, Ruler of Eternity. It is situated against the inner side of the eastern temenos wall, half way between the eastern gate and the northern corner. The earlier part of the building, consisting of two lateral rooms, was constructed by the God's Wife of Amon, Shepenwepet I; on the walls she appears with her father, Osorkon III and her brother, Takelot III.

There are many unusual features in the decoration. At the left of the original façade are carved eight doorways, one inside the other and each slightly recessed behind the next larger. In the upper part of the narrow opening of the last is a niche. This unique representation attempted to show the view through a series of gateways along the dromos, court and halls to the naos where the statue of the god resided, much as one sees in the temple of Ptah. Since no space is shown between the doorways and all have a common base level, true perspective is not attained. However, this is a noteworthy attempt to give a spatial conception, a thing seldom, if ever, seen elsewhere in Egyptian art.

There is an unusual variety of decorative detail, especially in certain items of dress. While a single lion tail, attached to the back of the belt, is an ancient element of costume of both the king and some gods, here Osorkon wears two and Takelot three. Shepenwepet wears an interesting assortment of crowns, in one instance two double crowns front to front.

107

The original court before this chapel had walls of mud brick; Amenartis I replaced these with walls of stone. Access to it is through " the great gateway of the God's Wife, the Adorer of the God, Amenartis, adored of the populace, in the house of her father Osiris, Ruler of Eternity ". Other doorways incorporating the term " adored of the populace " are known from extant monuments or from records; perhaps through such gates the common people were admitted to the court of the temple. But in the temple of Edfu of the Ptolemaic period the people were required to worship from outside the gate of the court.

The reliefs of Amenartis are less ornate and the outlines more definite than those of her predecessor. Many find this style, introduced under the Sudanese pharaohs, more pleasing, feeling that the ornateness which had been increasing since the end of the Twentieth Dynasty shows decadence.

Outside the later temenos of Amon were two major temples about which Nekhtnebef or another pharaoh of the latter part of the first millenium B. C. built mud brick temenos walls. To the north, with only a broad avenue between the precincts, is the temenos of Montu.

Montu was the god of the Theban nome, with ancient temples at Medamud, Armant and Tod. It has been presumed, without confirming evidence, that he had a contemporary temple at Thebes. The earliest temple there so far identified was built by Amenhotep III,[25] named, from the Horus name of the king, " Appearing in Truth ".[26]

The front of the temple, now in ruin, was about 1000 feet to the north of the centre of the Festival Hall of Thutmosis III. Amenhotep enlarged his original temple by doubling its length, making extensive alteration in so doing. The final dimensions were approximately 175 feet in length and 90 feet in width. Two granite obelisks were set before the entrance hall. Additions were made by Ramesses II, the Sudanese rulers and the Ptolemys. Euergetes I decorated the great north gateway into the temenos which Nekhtnebef had erected.

Behind the temple of Montu, and adjoining it, was a small temple of Maat whose name means " Truth ". The ancient Egyptian conception of truth included justice, order and genuineness. In the reign of Ramesses IV a priest of this temple, Merimaat, appeared before Amon during the latter part of the month-long Feast of Opet to ask for an oracular decision, but the rest of the account is lost. Appearing on the stele relating the incident are the barks of the Theban Triad and also a portable naos of Maat carried by a priest. From this and a similar representation it is certain that this goddess played some part in oracles.

Under Ramesses IX the temple of Maat was used as a place of examination of the tomb robbers and a temporary repository for the loot recovered from the thieves.

The temples within the temenos of Montu have only the lower courses remaining and those within the temenos of Mut are in the same condition. Even the Ptolemaic gateway has only the lower parts preserved. This lies at the southern end of the 1100 foot sphinx avenue erected between the Tenth Pylon of the temple of Amon and the Mut precinct by Haremhab. Some 270 feet farther to the south is the front of the temple of Mut, Lady of Isheru, erected by Amenhotep III, replacing one built by Hatshepsut. In later times Isheru was identified with the U-shaped lake which lay about the temple on three sides.

Amenhotep's temple to Mut was about the same size as the second stage of the one he erected to Montu. In and about it have been found many black granite seated statues of Sekhmet made by Amenhotep III. Some have the names of later rulers. The least damaged of these statues were removed by the early exploiters of antiquities and scattered about the world.

Sekhmet has already been met in the temple of Ptah. She was associated with

55. Men piling up grain preparatory to threshing.

56. Wild birds being hunted in the papyrus swamp. Both details of wall-paintings in the tomb chapel of Supervisor of Royal Fields, Menna. Reign of Thutmosis IV. *Theban Tomb No. 69*

fire, war and pestilence. The inscriptions often mention her desiccating breath. In a poem to Mut on the Ptolemaic gateway there are ten lines which begin: " The awe of Mut is in all countries ". Two lines tell that she caused fever and desiccation, but another says that " she gives the breath of life to her admirers ". Here seems to be an identification of Sekhmet and Mut, but the statues bear the name of the former only.

The remains of a text in a small room in the temple give an account of the great number of buildings, barks, statues and other monuments restored or made anew in Thebes by Montuemhat. Though the extant part of the inscription does not mention the Assyrian invasion, the depredations of which Ashurbanipal boasts, then recent, must have been more responsible for the sad state of the sacred objects than the ravages of time, the neglect of the priests or the spoliation of the impious.

Fine figures of the God Bes are carved on the inner faces of the engaged columns of the Ptolemaic porch before the ruined pylon of the temple. He is shown here, as usual, as a bandy-legged dwarf, in full face wearing a feathered headdress, with an animal tail attached to the back of his belt showing between his legs. Usually he was a gentle household spirit having connections with music and dancing and closely associated with child birth.

To the west of the temple lake are the remains of a temple of Mut built by Ramesses III, in size close to that of Amenhotep III's. None of the fragmentary scenes and inscriptions is of great interest. A third temple, again similar in size and no better preserved, is in the north-western corner of the temenos. On the north wall of the first court is a famous scene of the circumcision of a boy, one of a series concerned with a royal birth. There is no conclusive evidence by which this temple may be dated, nor can we tell to what deity it was dedicated.

Whereas only the lower courses of the temples in the sacred precincts of Montu and Mut have survived and the blocks of their upper walls have disappeared entirely, stones from the walls of the temple of Amenhotep IV-Akhenaten were known long before there was any knowledge of the location of the building. The traces of this temple, dedicated to the Aten, the physical disc of the sun, were discovered by accident in 1925 during the construction of the drainage canal about Karnak. It lay 300 feet to the east of the eastern gateway of the temenos of Amon and extended to the north of the main axis. Excavations were carried on sporadically for thirty years after the first discovery, but little information has been published about the extent of the temple. The few published photographs give the impression that it was at least as large as the temples built by Akhenaten's father Amenhotep III for Montu and Mut.

It is not possible to determine whether the temple whose large blocks were re-used in the Tenth Pylon was enlarged at a later date or whether the remains which have been discovered belong to a new structure. The alterations in the texts inscribed on the large blocks show that the building with reliefs in traditional style continued to stand after the new Amarna style had been introduced.

In reliefs, the Amarna style treats the human figure with greater freedom and is characterized by certain distortions amounting almost to caricature. The iconography is markedly different; Akhenaten, his chief queen Nefertiti and their daughters are frequently shown, usually blessed by the sun, represented by a disc from which extend life-giving rays terminating in little hands. A wide variety of scenes of domestic life are depicted, similar in theme to those found in the private tomb chapels of the Eighteenth Dynasty. As already noted, the blocks on which the relief appear are small and so far no complete scene has been reconstructed.

The reliefs from Amarna have made familiar the figure of the king, showing him with a thin face, long jaw with thick lips and a large head. In the torso the hips and thighs are unusually developed. The excavations of the temple of the Aten at

57. Crio-sphinxes moved in antiquity into the south-west corner of the First Court of the temple of Amon at Karnak.

Thebes uncovered colossal figures of Akhenaten, arms crossed on chest, his hands carrying the crook and flail, in which the physical peculiarites shown in the reliefs are emphasized (Plate 41). One of them shows him nude but with no indication of sexual organs. This statue especially, along with the other statues and reliefs depicting Akhenaten, has been the subject of much speculation which is closely bound up with aspects of a skeleton discovered in the Valley of the Tombs of the Kings.

In 1907 Theodore Davis found a tomb just south of that of Ramesses IX, only a few yards across the narrow valley from the spot where the tomb of Tutankhamon was uncovered fifteen years later. Though the entrance was still sealed, there was great confusion in the single room. The coffin in the corner had the mummy half out of it, and scattered about were parts of a shrine originally intended to cover it, various funerary objects, and in the corners " magical bricks " of mud. Two of these latter were inscribed and one clearly bore the prenomen of Akhenaten. The wooden shrine, carved in the Amarna style and covered with gold, had been made for his mother Tiy by Akhenaten, though his figure had been effaced. Other objects bore Tiy's name. On the coffin the royal cartouches were empty, the original name having been cut out, and changes had been made in the text by putting in new gold plates. A uraeus had been added to the head, and similar additions had been made to the heads on the stoppers of the canopic jars (Plate 42).

There was no evidence of robbery, though there is still disagreement as to whether there had been an earlier burial which was removed at the time when the burial found by the excavators was made. It would seem that the interment had taken place in haste and with considerable carelessness. However, some of the disorder could have been caused by water coming in through a crack in the roof in sufficient quantity to float the shrine and coffin, both of wood, and to deposit some of the mud. This, too, would have accounted for the decomposition of the mummy, of which little more than the skeleton was left, and that in poor condition.

Davis believed that he had found the burial of Queen Tiy; Weigall, then Chief Inspector of Antiquities at Luxor, who was in charge of the excavation, believed that the reworked inscriptions indicated that this was the body of Akhenaten. Maspero, who was present for the clearance, warned against premature conclusions. Present, helping in all the work, was an American artist, Joseph Lindon Smith. He made extensive notes but it was half a century later that these were finally edited by his wife and published after his death in 1950.

There happened to be touring in the Valley two American physicians, one of whom was an obstetrician, and these were invited to examine the bones. They declared that the pelvis was so roomy that the deceased must have been a woman. Davis was elated. The bones were coated with paraffin wax by Weigall, placed into a basket by Lindon Smith, and the basket sealed by Maspero. In Cairo this was delivered to Dr G. Elliot Smith, the Professor of Anatomy at the School of Medicine in Cairo. He had had wide experience in examining ancient Egyptian skeletal remains, and a decade and a half later co-authored a book on Egyptian mummies.

Without knowing the source of the skeleton, Dr Smith examined it and declared it to be that of a young man about 25 or 26 years old, whose skull showed that he had suffered from some degree of hydrocephalus. In answer to a question he said that the person, if he had been normal, could not have been more than two or three years older than this.

Davis, disappointed, published the tomb as that of Tiy. Weigall, in 1922, published an article in support of his belief that the burial was that of Akhenaten. In 1926 Elliot Smith published a further report, considering the skeleton in the light of contemporary portraits of Akhenaten which many had long considered to show feminine characteristics. He came to the conclusion that if the pharaoh was suffering from a disease known as Froelich's syndrome, union of the epiphyses might be so delayed that even if he were 36 years old at the time of death, the condition of the bones might be that of a man of 22 or 23. He also stated that hydrocephalus and the overgrowth of the mandible which he had noted could be associated with such a disease.

There the matter rested for another five years, when Professor D. E. Derry, Elliot Smith's successor at the Medical School, re-examined the skeleton at the request of Reginald Engelbach, Chief Keeper of the Egyptian Museum in Cairo, giving special attention to the skull. He concluded that the man was about 23 years old at death, that there was no sign of hydrocephalus, and that the skull closely resembled that of Tutankhamon. Influenced by Engelbach's conclusion that the coffin had been used finally for Smenkhkare, he concluded that the body it contained was actually of this obscure associate of Akhenaten.

The problem was not reopened until 1957, when the late Sir Alan Gardiner came to the conclusion, in a published article, that the changes in the text of the coffin were due, not to its usurpation by another person, but to changes in the personal relationships of the royal family at Amarna. He stated that the body buried in the coffin was one that the friends of the lately deceased king had rescued from the final chaos at Amarna, believing it to be his. Two years later, after Cyril Aldred of the Royal Scottish Museum had called to his attention certain discrepancies in this position, he accepted Aldred's contention that the original owner of the coffin was one of the Amarna princesses, but maintained his belief, supported by Aldred, that the body was supposed to have been that of Akhenaten.

In 1961 H. W. Fairman of the University of Liverpool and Aldred continued the discussion in further articles on the subject. On only one thing were the scholars agreed: that the princess for whom the coffin had originally been made was Meritaten, the eldest daughter of Akhenaten and Nefertiti, whom Akhenaten later married. Fairman followed Engelbach's identification of the body as that of Smenkhkare. Aldred followed the earlier identification of the body as that of Akhenaten. He returned to the anatomical observations of Elliot Smith and Derry and asked Dr A. T. Sanderson, pathologist at the University of Glasgow, to comment on these in the light of the colossi of Akhenaten found at Karnak, especially the one showing the king in the nude.

Dr Sanderson concluded that Akhenaten had suffered from an endrocrine abnormality which would have made him sexually and physically immature, and would have caused the feminine characteristics shown on the mandible and the possible abnormalities of the skull. These conclusions led Aldred to ask whether it would have been possible for Akhenaten to have fathered the daughters ascribed to him.

In early December 1963 Fairman was able to have the skeleton examined by a team of British and Egyptian anatomists and radiologists. From a clinical investigation, including X-rays of both the cranium and the mandible, they concluded that the skeleton was that of a male of 19 or 20 years of age, with no abnormalities of the cranium, with a normal mandible, and with no feminine characteristics of the pelvis.[27]

When the evidence is published and studied by other anatomists it should be possible to come to a final conclusion, but with the data now in hand the identification of the skeleton as that of Akhenaten appears to be ruled out. There still remains the possibility that it is that of Smenkhkare, an opinion shared by many Egyptologists since the publication of Engelbach's study. Certainly it will no longer be possible to refer to this skeleton in accounting for the peculiar physique of Akhenaten shown on the Karnak colossi and on certain reliefs. Though these peculiarities may be due to some physical abnormality, the true explanation may lie in the different aesthetic conventions of the period. At times their emphasis on "truth" in art seems to have led them almost to caricature. Questions of religious or cultural symbolism may also be involved which are not now entirely within our comprehension.

After the restoration of the ancient deities the temple erected by Akhenaten was dismantled, a retribution on Akhenaten, who had shown his hostility to Amon and the gods, destroying their images and names. Two major temples within the temenos of Amon as enclosed by Nekhtnebef, at the south-western corner, had not yet been built in their present form when Amon returned to his temple.

The westernmost was the later, the temple of Ipet-(Ta)weris, a hippopotamus goddess who was the protector of pregnant women (Plate 91). The narrow gateway in front of it was built by Nekhtnebef, while the decoration of the temple, so far as preserved, dates from the reigns of Ptolemy VIII Euergetes II, Ptolemy XII Neos Dionysos, and Caesar Augustus. It was under the rule of the last that the exterior reliefs were executed. These include, round the base on the north and south, personifications of the nomes, the figure of the chief deity of each, and the personification of the arable lands and the back districts of each nome. On the east side are similar personifications of the produce of the land and manifestations of the inundation.

In many of the personifications the figure is that of a Hapi. Hapi is the ancient word for Nile and both these words refer, not to the river itself, but properly to the annual inundation whose water and fertile silt ensures the agricultural richness of the land. The figure of Hapi has pendulous breasts, often a roll of flesh about the lower chest, and a rounded abdomen; there is always a beard on his chin. Though this figure has often been called androgynous, it is actually that of a very obese male, symbolizing the good living which the flood makes possible. Nomes and temples are often personified by such figures, as on the sanctuary of Hatshepsut, but on the temple of Ipet the nomes are all female figures.

The temple of Ipet was built immediately to the west of the temple of Khonsu, the child in the Theban triad. The latter structure, about 240 feet in length and 96 feet wide behind the pylon, was begun by Ramesses III, replacing one of the Eighteenth Dynasty in front of which Amenhotep III placed a long avenue of criosphinxes. This avenue was later interrupted about 150 feet in front of the temple by a gateway built by Nekhtnebef but not decorated until the reign of Ptolemy III Euergetes I.

In the temple itself most of the stone blocks used in construction were re-used from earlier buildings. Often parts of scenes and inscriptions from these blocks, not cleanly dressed anew, intrude into the later relief. Ramesses III began the construction in the latter years of his reign and the decoration of five rooms off the second hypostyle hall were due to him. Ramesses IV continued the work and the rest of the decoration in the rooms behind the first hypostyle hall was carried out in his reign. In most of these rooms the figures are in a bas-relief so low and with the change in level so gradual that the sculptor seems to have moulded rather than cut the edges. In contrast, the majority of the inscriptions are in low incised relief. The second hypostyle hall was redecorated under Caesar Augustus and the walls of the ambulatory about the sanctuary have all of the carving in incised relief.

As would be expected, this part of the temple has Khonsu as the prominent god. Usually he is shown as a standing, swaddled child with sidelock on his head (Plate 29). Often he is crowned with the crescent new moon bearing the disc of the darkened moon, a phenomenon regularly observed in the clear skies of Egypt. He also is shown with a hawk's head, the emblem which was mounted on the prow and stern of his bark. In the rear of the temple there is a syncretism in form with other gods, and Khonsu appears as a human-headed god with the plumed crown of Amon, as a hawk-headed figure with the crown usually worn by Montu, and with the figure and emblems of Osiris.

58. Offering bearer, wall-painting in the tomb chapel of the Astronomer of Amon, Nakht. Reign of Thutmosis III. *Theban Tomb No. 52*

59. Ramesses III censing the bark of Amon, original bas-relief changed to incised relief, inner south wall of the great Hypostyle Hall of the Temple of Amon, Karnak.

In later times, as may be seen on the Ptolemaic gateway, there was a proliferation of the names of Khonsu. Within the temple his full name was Khonsu-in-Thebes Neferhotep, the latter term an old name meaning " gracious ", borne by humans and applied to several gods. As a moon god he was identified with Thoth, the ibis-headed deity from Ashmunein, whose association with the moon was ancient. The baboon, in certain aspects of its nature, was sacred to Thoth and statues of baboons identified with all the moon gods still remain in the first hypostyle hall (Plate 63).

Part or all of the temple was named Benenet, also written Benbenet. Particularly identified with this name is Hathor of Benenet, who is crowned with a naos in which are one or two uraei, and from which sprout flowers. Also associated with Benenet was a manifestation of the god known as Khonsu the Counsellor.

When Champollion and Rosellini were exploring Thebes they found, in a destroyed temple outside the south-eastern corner of the temenos of Amon, a stele with an apocryphal story, set in the time of Ramesses II, and written in the Ptolemaic period as propaganda for Khonsu, telling of the taking of the statue of Khonsu the Counsellor to a foreign land.

The story begins during the yearly visit of Ramesses to Naharin (north-east Syria) to receive tribute from the rulers of distant countries. The king of Bakhtan (probably Bactria) presented his eldest daughter Neferure to the pharaoh. Her beauty found favour with Ramesses who made her his queen and returned with her to Egypt.

In the twenty-third year of Ramesses' reign a messenger from the ruler of Bakhtan arrived in Thebes, interrupting the king during his celebration of the Feast of Opet. Besides gifts to the queen, the envoy bore a message that her younger sister, the princess Bentresh, was grievously ill, and a request that Ramesses send a physician to treat her. After consultation with his learned men and courtiers, Ramesses sent the physician Thutemhat.

The messenger and the physician reached Bakhtan after a seventeen months' journey. The princess was found to be possessed by a demon, against which some one would have to do battle. The ruler sent another message to Ramesses asking that a god be sent to deal with this demon. When the pharaoh heard this, he consulted Khonsu-in-Thebes Neferhotep, and the god advised him to send Khonsu the Counsellor, who could combat strange maladies.

The god came to Bakhtan, was welcomed by the king and court, and healed Bentresh. Khonsu the Counsellor then had to contend with the possessing spirit, whom he had pacified with the celebration of a feast and great offerings to them both. The ruler of Bakhtan decided to keep the god with him and for forty-five months made no move to return him to Egypt. Then in a nightmare the ruler saw the god as a hawk flying toward Egypt. Showering him with gifts, the chief of Bakhtan sent the god back to Egypt. When he arrived after his long journey, he returned to the temple of Khonsu-in-Thebes Neferhotep, where most of the gifts were deposited, and Khonsu the Counsellor returned to his own shrine.

In the temple of Khonsu there is no room which is shown, by its decoration, to be a treasury where such gifts might be stored. However, in the upper left corner of the south wall of the room off the west side of the second hypostyle hall, there is an opening into a hidden cupboard which extends into the wall of the ambulatory behind the sanctuary. Originally, the opening was covered by a panel over which the wall decoration continued. Some have taken the view that this cupboard was used by a priest who would speak when the god was delivering an oracle. Apart from the fact that there is no record among the many oracular texts of such an enunciation by a god, and that there is no peep hole in the wall through which the priest could have received signals, this view implies a chicanery which nowhere

60. Men bearing offerings for the deceased, wall-painting in the tomb chapel of the Overseer of Egyptian Granaries, Minnakht. Reign of Thutmosis III. *Theban Tomb No. 87*

appears in the records. It seems more likely that this cupboard was a treasury where the valuable possessions of the god might be kept hidden away near his presence, and it was here that the compiler of the tale thought the treasure sent from Bakhtan would have been laid away.

Another form of Khonsu was associated with Amon of Opet, the ithyphallic form of the god whose temple is in modern Luxor. This Khonsu appears in the temple only once, in the reliefs of Ramesses IV. A farmer attached to the lands of Khonsu of Amon of Opet was interrogated about the robberies of the Royal Tombs. In the reign of Nekhtharheb, the last of the native rulers, Ahmes, a priest who also served in Ipet-esut, was prophet of Khonsu-Amenopet (by this time the genitives had been elided) in Iou-akhes, the name of the walled enclosure in which the temple of Khonsu stood. Ahmes says that he was responsible for the redecoration of the doorways from the court into the first hypostyle hall and from that hall into the ambulatory. If he completed the decoration, which is of one style, he lived into the reign of Ptolemy I.

In the second of the redecorated doorways the new relief followed the old in part, and here the name of Herihor appears in cartouches, the only place in this hall where he is designated king. It would seem that work on the temple of Khonsu came to a standstill with the death of Ramesses IV, and was not resumed until Herihor became High Priest of Amon. It may be that he found the structure of the temple unfinished, as the columns of the court, re-used from another temple, have been thought to come from the mortuary temple of Tutankhamon-Ay-Haremhab, which was still standing in the latter years of Ramesses III.

Herihor changed the theme of the decoration and Amon predominates in the scenes, perhaps because of Herihor's position. On the walls of the first hypostyle hall the king, Ramesses XI, is generally shown officiating in the cult, but on each wall Herihor shows himself at least once in the position of officiant. The work is all of one piece, and credit for the decoration of the hall must go to the High Priest.

In the court the political situation has changed. All the pillars, architraves and walls, except that of the pylon, show Herihor as priest-king. His title, High Priest of Amon, was enclosed in a cartouche as his prenomen. The pylon is the best preserved of any large temple in pharaonic Egypt: both towers are complete, as is also the porch above the doorway. The decoration of the pylon was executed by Herihor's immediate successors in the office of High Priest.

In the left, or eastern, half of the court, the relief is incised, while on the opposite side the walls have low, almost moulded, bas-relief similar to that in the rear rooms of the temple. This dichotomy may have been inspired by the similar decoration of the Hypostyle Hall of Amon's temple, where there is bas-relief on the left and incised relief on the right. All the decoration shows incipient signs of the elaboration of design which was more developed in the older part of the small temple of Osiris, Ruler of Eternity, already mentioned.

One of the best known scenes on the walls of the court is on the east side, near the south end. Here is shown the Second Pylon of Amon's temple, the four flag-poles on either side, each named after a goddess, with streamers flying at the tips, while over the gateway Herihor says that it is a structure " which he made as a monument for his father Amon-re, King of the Gods, renewing for him ' Illuminating Thebes ', the name of which is ' Amon is Joyous ', and embellishing for him the temple of Khonsu-in-Thebes Neferhotep, for eternity."

On the west wall, in the lower register, is a representation of the river barks of the Theban Triad, each bearing the smaller temple bark, being towed to the Luxor Temple in the Feast of Opet. Now damaged and begrimed, the original colourfulness of this river procession cannot be seen by the viewer on the ground. The sails of the towing ships had a coloured chequer board pattern; streamers festooned the yards, and in the rigging were members of the crew. Gaily decorated small boats went alongside the river bark of Amon, while along the banks some laid hold of the ropes, Sudanese dancers performed, and troops marched in escort. An inscription, painted on the poles of the shrine on the barge and carved on the face of the architrave above the columns in front of the wall, says that for Amon Herihor "hewed his river bark from cedar of Lebanon, ornamented with gold throughout its length".

Many kings had built river barks for Amon from Syrian timber, but only in this instance is anything known about its procurement. Early in 1089 Herihor sent Wenamon, an official from the temple of Amon at Karnak, to the Lebanon to bring back this timber; when he returned, at least a year and a half later, he dictated an account of his journey to a scribe who set it down on three sheets of papyrus. This report passed into the archives of the High Priests, and the first two sheets have been preserved. The account, free from official jargon and remarkably frank, is written in a lively, conversational style and is an important social and historical document.

Wenamon arrived in Byblos with neither credentials nor funds, the first having been left with the governor at Tanis and the second stolen by a sailor who deserted Wenamon's ship at Dor. However, he appropriated a similar amount of treasure from a ship of Dor which was in the harbour at Byblos. Then he waited a month without being able to obtain an interview with Tjeker-baal, its prince. As he was preparing to return to Egypt, a retainer of the prince fell into an ecstatic trance at a temple service and prophesied that Wenamon was an envoy of Amon whose statue he carried with him.

Tjeker-baal summoned Wenamon and in a long conversation told him that in the past the Egyptian kings had sent an abundance of produce in exchange for the timber, and denied that he was under any obligation to Egypt. Moreover, he claimed that the benefits of Egyptian civilization, Amon's gift, already had passed over to Syria, and Egypt was now of little importance. Wenamon defended Amon's power, and asked that a letter be sent to the governor at Tanis requesting trade goods in payment for the timber.

The letter was dispatched, and when the goods arrived, the trees were felled, and in the spring of 1088 the logs were ready for shipment. As Wenamon was preparing to leave, ships from Dor came to arrest him for the appropriation of the treasure the summer before. Tjeker-baal would not allow them to harm the envoy of Amon while he was in Syria, but insisted that Wenamon put to sea with his cargo. A storm blew him to Cyprus where the people sought to kill him. He reached the palace of the princess, and she offered him asylum. Here the extant manuscript breaks off, and nothing is known of what further adventures befell Wenamon before he delivered the timber to Thebes.

So Herihor built a new river bark for Amon, User-hat-Amon, and the god was carried on it at the Feast of Opet and the other feasts where Amon required water transport. While for the Feast of the Valley Amon certainly boarded his bark at the western quay of Karnak, it is uncertain where he went on board for his journey to Southern Opet, now known as the Luxor Temple. Scenes on Hatshepsut's sanctuary show the bark stopping at six way stations during this journey, and while the river bark is never shown there, the start of Amon's procession is described as "setting out in peace to Southern Opet in his annual river procession".

The priests carried Amon's bark south along the avenue through the southern pylons and to the first station named "The Dais of Amon opposite Per-hen", just north of the later gateway into the temenos of Mut. Here the god paused in a peripteral sanctuary behind which were rooms for other gods,[28] one for the ithyphallic Amon, whose chief shrine was Per-hen, "the Temple of Jubilation",[29] 300 feet to the east.   Later the rear of the way station was altered to include a second sanctuary, conjecturally for the bark of Mut, who here joined her consort for the feast.   Possibly the river barks were waiting on the "Jubilation Canal" nearby and proceeded along it to be joined by the bark of Khonsu coming along an intercepting canal 300 yards to the west.

It was to this point, where the canals joined, that later Nekhtnebef built a broad avenue lined with human-headed sphinxes straight from before the Luxor Temple. Clément Robichon, the excavator of the temple of Montu, once suggested that this avenue was built along a filled canal, and that it was on this canal, and not on the river, that the water procession of the Feast of Opet took place.   This theory is attractive, especially as it is certain that by the end of the Twentieth Dynasty the canals would have no water in them at the beginning of the feast.[30]

Whether by canal or by river, User-hat-Amon bore the temple bark of Amon to Luxor, stopping at four way stations, whose position between Karnak and Luxor is not known.   Finally, before proceeding to the sanctuary in the temple itself, it came to rest in the sixth station, later rebuilt by Ramesses II and incorporated in the First Court, his addition to the Temple of Luxor.

The main incidents of the Feast of Opet, with the procession from temple to temple, but with no mention of the way stations, were shown on the inner walls of the long columned hall which Amenhotep III added in front of his temple.   Left unfinished during the reign of Akhenaten, the inner walls were decorated by Tut-ankhamon, who honoured Amenhotep III by picturing statues of him behind the cabins on the river barks.

Haremhab, who thought Tutankhamon tainted by his Amarna association, put his own name in the cartouches of the latter and Seti I later put his name in some. The whole depiction of the feast is, in a way, the celebration of Amon's return to power after his brief eclipse.

At the beginning of the story, on the west wall, the barks of the Theban gods are in their sanctuaries, as is the bark of the reigning ruler.   Then, after the proper offerings by the king, they are mounted on the shoulders of the priests and carried through the incense laden air, out from their temples.   At the water's edge the river bark of each of the gods is waiting, attached to a towing barge with oarsmen at their posts and sails set, ready to pull the gods upstream to Southern Opet.

Along the banks trumpeters herald their coming; Sudanese with African drums beat out the rhythm for wild dances of their fellows.   More sedately Egyptian wo-men shake their musical rattles and men beat together their curved ivory wands. The local people crowd for the honour of laying hold of the tow ropes to help along the barks, and others prostrate themselves to pay obeisance to the gods in their public appearance.   Escorting troops, standards held high, march along the par-allel road, while a charioteer holds his majesty's span and chariot ready for the king's use when he disembarks from User-Hat-Amon.

In the court of the Luxor Temple young girls, clad only in loin cloths, perform acrobatic dances.   Within the abattoirs butchers have already dismembered the fatted cattle, and the choice meats are being brought for the enjoyment of the vis-iting gods.   When the day comes for the return journey, the same sort of cele-bration accompanies the gods as they go home to Waset.

It is not only in the magical procession on the walls that the memory of Amon's feast is preserved.   Within the court of Ramesses II was built a church which fell into disuse as Islam made its many converts.   When the missionary who tradi-tion says introduced the faith of the prophet to Luxor, Abu-el-Haggag, died, he was buried in the mosque which rose within the walls of the church.   To this day, on the last days of the waxing moon before the great feast of Ramadan, this Moslem saint is honoured in Luxor by family feasts and public performances of music, horse-

61. Seti I driving foreign captives before him, north outer wall of the great Hypostyle Hall of the temple of Amon, Karnak.

62. The first Court of the temple of Amon at Karnak, looking south-east, with way-station of Ramesses III at the centre right and the Eighth, Ninth, and Tenth Pylons in the background.

manship and other celebrations dear to the people. On the day of the full moon a parade circles the great block which holds the ancient temple and the modern mosque. Troops march at its head; the local boys' band plays its best; gaily arrayed horses proudly bear their riders and camels carry the emblems of the faith. The chief participants in the procession are two boats with brightly coloured sails, set on wheels and pulled by horses, in which sit the fortunate children who, for a small coin, have the joy of riding in the boats of Abu-el-Haggag.

Moslem tradition tells that Abu-el-Haggag, sailing on a ship across the Red Sea on his pilgrimage to Mecca, stilled the storm which threatened to destroy the ship by his prayers to Allah. But the real origin of the boats is the Feast of Opet, still surviving more than a millenium and a half after Amon had been supplanted.

The origins of Southern Opet are lost in antiquity. Gone are all traces of the temple of Hatshepsut and those earlier. Hieroglyphs on temple walls record that here Amon had his primeval seat. The word " Opet " was a designation of royal harem quarters and this has led to the mistranslation of the temple name as " The Southern Harem ". But the primary meaning of the word denotes the private quarters in a palace where the women kept to themselves, and in a temple the innermost sanctuary. Thus the correct translation should be " The Southern Sanctuary ".

The Luxor Temple, from the rear of Amenhotep's building to the front of the pylon of Ramesses II, extends 840 feet parallel to and not far from the river. When Ramesses built his court, he slanted the axis to meet the processional avenue (or canal?) to Karnak. On the bases of the sphinxes with which Nekhtnebef lined this long avenue he relates that he planted trees and flowers along the way; the burned brick water channels of his gardens still remain. The mound of medieval Luxor which covered the avenue is being cleared away and soon visitors will be able once more to walk along part of this ancient processional way.

In front of his pylon Ramesses II erected two obelisks and, behind them, two colossal seated figures of himself (Plate 70). Two standing statues of the king, about as tall as the seated colossi, guarded the front of each tower. The western obelisk was presented to France and erected in the Place de la Concorde in 1836.

On the front of the towers of the pylon are scenes of the battle of Ramesses at Kadesh on the Orontes in Syria. At the left of the west tower the king receives the reports of his scouts and to the right is the scene of the Egyptian camp as it is overrun by the attackers. On the east tower is the battle before Kadesh, in which Ramesses, surprised and surrounded, fights his way clear and with the aid of reinforcements turns defeat into victory. Below the scenes are texts telling about the battle, copies of which appear on all the temples of Ramesses II.

Between the pillars within the court are standing statues of Ramesses II. One of the finest, in the south-eastern corner, shows the king striding, his left shoulder thrown forward (Plate 77). By his side is a small statue of his queen Nefertari, the loveliest of the representations of her in the court. Two more seated colossi of Ramesses II are at the entrance to the long columned hall.

The left colossus before the pylon and the right one in the court have identifying names, the former " Ruler of the Two Lands ", and the latter, " Re (the sun) of the Rulers " (Plate 69). It is a curious fact that above the doorway of the small temple at Abu Simbel, on either side of his cartouches, where it was customary to note that the king is beloved of a god, he is beloved of these two statues. There were other statues of " Re of the Rulers " at Abu Simbel, the Ramesseum and in his delta residence; the latter is known to have had its own priesthood. Similar practices are known in regard to statues of Amenhotep III; the southern colossus of Memnon was named " Ruler of Rulers " and offerings were made to it.

On the lower western wall of the court is a parade of fatted oxen, some branded for the Feast of Opet and some with the byre where they were stabled. All are

63. The first hypostyle hall of the temple of Khonsu, Karnak, with baboon sacred to the moon in the foreground. Reign of Ramesses XI and the high priesthood of Herihor.

127

gaily decorated, a number having heads of foreigners mounted at the base of their horns, on the tips of which are hands in the attitude of praise to the god (Plate 76). As the procession turns the corner on to the southern wall it is led by the sons of Ramesses II, their precedence according to their birth. All are about to enter the pylon of the temple, the façade shown with flagpoles, obelisks and colossi all in their places.

The court of Amenhotep III is about 165 feet square, with a double row of cluster columns at the front and sides. To the south is the vestibule with thirty-two similar columns in four transverse rows. This forecourt of the temple of Amenhotep III is aesthetically one of the most pleasing architectural units in the area (Plate 75).

Behind the vestibule were rooms for the barks of the visiting gods. To the east of centre were sanctuaries for Mut and Khonsu; in the reign of Ramesses II the latter was moved to a room west of the central doorway. The reliefs in this chamber suggest that it originally was used as a shrine for Amon of Opet.

The central doorway gave access to an eight columned hall, with another wide doorway in the opposite wall. When the Romans made the Luxor Temple the centre of a *castrum*, the southern doorway was blocked with an apse. Before this was a canopy resting on four pillars, two of which still remain; under this canopy once stood a statue of the emperor. Painted on the walls of the apse were the figures of the two Augusti and the two Caesars of the end of the third century A. D., parts of which are still visible. This hall was the sanctuary of the imperial cult and the *sacellum* for the standards of the Roman legion whose heroes were shown on the painted plaster surface covering the pharaonic reliefs. It was in this very sanctuary that Diocletian and Maximin Daia commanded Christians to make sacrifices to the divine emperor.[31] In the vestibule, just short of the doorway, is a pedestal bearing the name of the emperor Constantine, another relic of the Roman camp.

The pillars which supported the roof of this hall when the bark of Amon was carried through it were removed by the Romans, who used the drums to raise the level of the floor. In recent years a low doorway has been cut through the apse so that it is again possible to follow the processional way, stepping down to the floor of the four columned hall beyond.

The walls of the anteroom of the sanctuary and, indeed, all of the decorated walls of Amenhotep's temple clearly show the great fury with which the servants of Akhenaten carried out the orders of the Amarna heretic. The objects of their destruction were the names and figures of all gods, their barks and the priests bearing them, the ka, or " double ", of the king, the name of Amenhotep within the cartouche because it incorporated the hated name of Amon, and various lines of inscription, the content of which remains uncertain even after careful examination.[32] The figures and some of the names were crudely restored, but it is evident that those doing the restoration not only made mistakes, but often were at a loss to know what the original inscriptions said. It is surprising that this temple which continued to be the centre of the greatest festival of Thebes and which was the scene of the coronation of Haremhab was allowed to remain in such a deplorable state of disrepair.

On the south side of the anteroom is the doorway to the sanctuary of the bark of the visiting Amon of Karnak. In the wall dividing the two rooms, above the doorway, is a narrow space large enough to hold a man, visible because the northern part of the lintel has fallen. That this was not just a hole left accidentally by the builders but a deliberate part of the construction is proved by a small chamber at either end. These were once covered by removable slabs, now gone, and in the walls of the eastern chamber are hand and toe holds cut into the dressed stone surface. The question again arises, as in connection with the hidden chamber in the temple of

64. Food offerings for Osiris, wall-painting in the tomb chapel of the High Priest of Thutmosis I, Userhat. Reign of Seti I. *Theban Tomb No. 51*

Khonsu, whether the chambers and passage were used by a priest speaking for the god on oracular occasions or whether they were used as a treasury for the most sacred objects of the temple. They were well placed for the former purpose, but it remains to be demonstrated that the inner part of the temple was visited by any but the priests.

In the sanctuary the original four columns were removed in the reign of Alexander the Great and a shrine for the bark of Amon erected in their place. Three registers of reliefs on each outer side wall show Alexander making offerings to Amon depicted alternately in his clothed and ithyphallic forms. At the time of the prudish mutilation of the ithyphallic figures a considerable amount of debris had accumulated about the shrine, as the lack of this disfigurement on the lower registers shows. Near this shrine was found a statue of a pharaoh from the Greek period; though often identified as Alexander it probably represents an early Ptolemy (Plate 92).

It may have been at the time of Alexander that a doorway was broken through the back of the sanctuary into the twelve columned transverse hall, the central feature of the rear portion of the temple. The doorway at the north end of the east wall of the sanctuary is Roman. Originally the only access to the side and rear rooms of the temple was through a doorway in the west wall of the anteroom and a small outside doorway on the west. It was this back part of the present temple which was truly a private area, the real meaning of the word " Opet ".

The eastern wall of the rear part of the temple was destroyed no later than the middle of the first millenium B. C. The room lying to the east of the antechamber, originally accessible only through the side rooms and transverse hall, is now easily entered. On the wall at the west is the legend of the divine origin of Amenhotep III.

This legend had been used earlier in reference to Hatshepsut and was used again by Ramesses II. All accounts were brutally defaced or destroyed. In the Luxor Temple the story begins with Queen Mutemwia being embraced by Hathor. After a conversation between Amon and Thutmosis IV, Amon, in the guise of the king, enters the queen's chamber and meets Mutemwia. Then Khnum, on instructions from Amon, moulds the figures of the royal child and his ka on a potter's wheel. Afterwards the queen is led into the birth room where, assisted by various deities and genial spirits, she sits on the birth stool and delivers the child. The infant Amenhotep is brought to Amon, who cradles him in his arms and blesses him with a kiss. In the nursery the royal child is suckled by Hathor, both in her human and bovine form, and cared for by attending deities. Finally the figures of the child and his ka are presented to Amon who proclaims Amenhotep as the future king.

Along the inside of the outer side walls of the rear rooms were cupboard-like niches, with floors raised about 30 inches above the floor of the rooms. While they may have been for statues of other gods, it is more likely that they were store chambers. In the central room south of the transverse hall the raised platform between the two rear pillars was the base of the great naos which housed the statue of Amon of Opet. He was an ithyphallic figure, identical in form with Min and Kamutef as manifestations of Amon.

In the reign of Ramesses II this Amon made a trip outside his private rooms every ten days. At this time he may have gone only as far as a building which then lay between the temple and the river. However, this building may have been the first way station for a journey which is first recorded at the beginning of the Twenty-first Dynasty, when these journeys took Amon of Opet to Medinet Habu, where there was another ancient shrine of Amon. In these journeys Amon of Opet, and in the annual Feast of the Valley, Amon of Karnak, paid visits to the Lords of the West, the earlier kings whose mortuary temples lay across the river in Western Thebes.

65. Head of alabaster statue of Seti I from the Karnak cache. The hands and lower limbs of this statue were made separately and fastened together, the eyes and brows were inlaid, and the crown was a separate piece. *Cairo Museum*

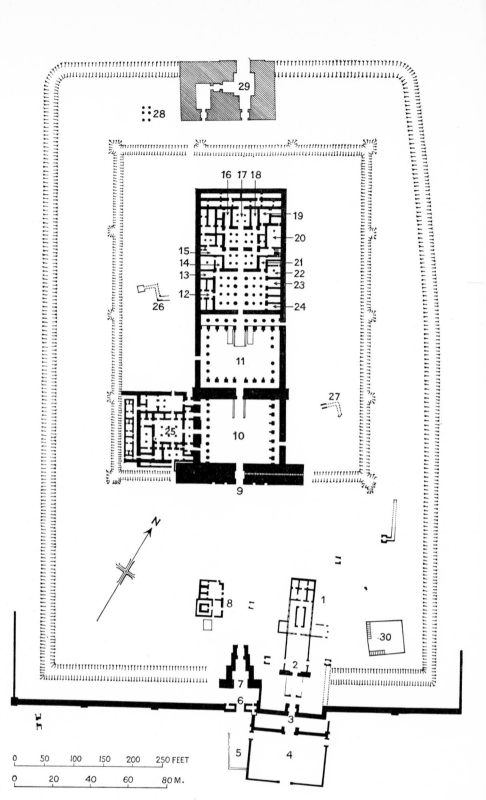

0   50   100   150   200   250 FEET

0   20   40   60   80 M.

The Lords of the West

On a morning in the middle of August 1126 B. C., a commission of investigation set out from Medinet Habu. The annual inundation was well advanced, filling the canals and beginning to flood the fields. The water evaporating under the hot sun added an uncomfortable amount of humidity to the air. Yet however uncomfortable the day, the task could not be put off. Paser, mayor of Thebes, had charged that certain tombs of the kings, and many of bygone officials, had been violated. The accusation reflected on the person and staff of Pawerao, mayor of Western Thebes and head of the security police who guarded the cemetery. He, in turn, drew up a list of several men said to be engaged in tomb robbery, to be used when the time seemed right. As the senior official of the necropolis he had been made head of the commission of inspectors.

In the cool of the morning the group climbed the mountain by the path behind Deir el-Medineh to visit, high up on the south end of the Valley of the Tombs of the Kings, " the horizon of eternity of King Djeserkare, Son of Re, Amenhotep (I), which measures 120 cubits (about 200 feet) in depth from its stele called ' The High Trace ', north of the chapel of Amenhotep of-the-Garden ". If the charges of Paser proved true, this violation would be especially heinous, as Amenhotep I, with Ahmose-Nefertare, his mother, was the patron god of the necropolis workers. The inspectors found the tomb untouched.[33]

Following the mountain path and descending near the entry of the road to the Valley of the Tombs of the Kings into the hills, the inspectors then went to " the pyramid tomb of the Son of Re, Ini the Elder (Intef II), which is north of the chapel of Amenhotep-of-the-Open-Court, from which the pyramid has been removed, but before which the stele still remains, the figure of the king standing on the stele with his dog, Behhek, between his legs ". This tomb was found intact.

Going south along Dra Abu-el-Naga, two tombs of Seventeenth Dynasty rulers were examined; into each thieves had tried, without success, to force an entrance, so they were noted as still intact. The next tomb, of Sekhemre-Shedtawy Sebekemsaf, was found violated, entry having been forced from a chamber of an adjoining private tomb chapel, and completely despoiled. Four more royal tombs in this line were inspected; then the commission turned into the valley to inspect that of Montuhotep II; all were found undamaged.

After this two of four tombs of the female singers of the chapel of Divine Adorers of Amon were found violated. Then the commission examined " the tombs and burial chambers on the West of Thebes in which rest the august ancestors, the citizenesses and citizens of Egypt. It was found that thieves had despoiled them all. They had displaced the owners of their coffins and sarcophagi so that they were abandoned on the open ground, stealing their funerary equipment which had been given to them, along with the gold, silver and furnishings of their coffins."

That afternoon the commission placed its report in the hands of the vizier and governor of Thebes, Khamuas, and his court, and Pawerao presented his list of thieves. Four of these were immediately apprehended, imprisoned and questioned. In supplementary documents recording their confessions is that of Amenpanefer, a stonemason of the temple of Amon.[34]

" I was serving under Ramessesnakht, the High Priest of Amon, King of the Gods, with other fellow stonemasons, and I became an habitual tomb robber along with the stonemason Merenptah, of Medinet Habu. Now in the thirteenth year of Pharaoh our Lord I joined with (seven other workmen) and went to rob tombs according to the manner we habitually practised. We found the tomb of King Sekhemre-Shedtawy, Son of Re, Sebekemsaf, which was not like the pyramid tombs of the officials we usually went to rob. We took our copper tools and broke through the pyramid of the king at its rear chamber. We found its deep shaft and took lighted tapers in our hands and descended. We demolished the dry wall we found blocking the passage. We found this god laid out at the back of his burial place, and by his side we found the burial place of Queen Nubkhaas, his queen, guarded and protected by plaster and hidden by a dry wall. We broke through this also and found her resting in the same manner. We opened their sarcophagi and their inner coffins in which they lay. We found the august mummy of the king provided with a scimitar, a great number of amulets and golden jewels on his neck, and his head-mask of gold upon him. The august mummy of this king was overlaid with gold throughout, his coffins plated with gold and silver within and without, and set with precious stones."

The thieves stripped the valuables from the mummies and coffins, then set them on fire to collect any overlooked gold and to destroy the evidence. Twenty deben of gold fell to each of the eight thieves. Some days later Amenpanefer was arrested and imprisoned at the headquarters of the mayor of Thebes, then escaped by bribing the scribe of the harbour with his share of the loot. His companions divided their shares with him. After that, he confessed, " I and the thieves associated with me have continued up to the present in the same manner to rob the tombs of the officials and the people of the land who rest in the West of Thebes. Great numbers of men in this area rob them as well and they are all companions (in guilt)."

During the examination, which continued into the morning, Amenpanefer confessed to robbing the tomb of the Third Prophet of Amon, Tjanefer, and many others not named. The vizier Khamuas decided to investigate matters himself. Accompanied by a palace official, he took with him the apprehended thieves, and also the coppersmith Peikhar, son of Khari, whose names indicate Syrian ancestry. The mayor of Thebes accused him and several fellow craftsmen, all workers at Medinet Habu, of robbing the tomb of Queen Isis in the Valley of the Queens just behind that temple.

The vizier first visited the empty tomb of Sebekemsaf and heard again the story of the miscreants at the scene of their crime. Then Peikhar was blindfolded and taken to the Valley of the Queens where, two years before, he and others had been found loitering about the tombs. Under compulsion he had recently confessed to entering the tomb of Isis, but when the blindfold was removed he could not identify the spot. After an extensive examination the vizier was convinced of the innocence of Peikhar. It was found that all the tombs in this valley had intact seals.

It is obvious that there was personal enmity between Paser, mayor of Thebes,

66. Head of a fragmentary limestone statue of a queen, found at the Ramesseum. *Cairo Museum*

and Pawerao, mayor of Western Thebes. Now only one of the royal tombs listed as violated by the former was actually found despoiled and the apprehension of the thieves was due to Pawerao, not to Paser, though one thief had been arrested and imprisoned and had then bribed his way to freedom, all while under Paser's jurisdiction. That afternoon the vizier himself, apparently a partisan of Pawerao, brought the people of the necropolis area, inspectors, police and workmen, to Thebes for a triumphal demonstration.

In the evening Paser, smarting from this affront, met several of the men from the necropolis near the temple of Ptah and quarrelled with them. He boasted that two scribes of the necropolis had informed him of five grave charges and that he was writing a report to Pharaoh. Pawerao was standing in the background and the next day wrote a full account of the quarrel to the vizier. The point of the complaint is that the scribes should have reported the charges directly to the vizier Khamuas himself.

The next day a court of eight Theban officials, headed by Khamuas and including Paser, heard the charges against Peikhar. The vizier testified that he had found no basis for these charges. The court found Paser wrong in his accusation; in reality, it was trying one of its own members, whom it found guilty of slander or worse.

A day later Amenpanefer and his companions so far apprehended were turned over to the High Priest of Amon by the same court and warrants were issued for the others. The punishment of all was to be set by Pharaoh; it almost certainly was the supreme one, death by impalement. Pawerao continued in office for several years, but nothing more is heard of Paser, who may have suffered from his ill-advised accusations.

Ill-advised as the accusations may have been under the circumstances, the investigations they set off revealed a serious state of affairs in the necropolis. It is certain that the burials were no longer safe. The few houses along the edge of the necropolis were in the areas of the temples of Seti i, Ramesses ii and Ramesses iii, and could have been observed easily. Systematic policing should have kept out unauthorized persons, and it is difficult to understand how the destruction discovered by the commission could have been going on unknown to the authorities.

The royal tombs inspected in 1126, with the exception of that of Amenhotep i, belonged to dynasties anterior to the Eighteenth. The kings of that and the succeeding two dynasties were buried in the Valley of the Tombs of the Kings. Of the despoliation of these tombs there is little record. The tomb of Tutankhamon was broken into a few years after the burial and almost immediately resealed. About the same time the tomb of Thutmosis iv was surreptitiously entered and Haremhab ordered the reclosing of the tomb in the eighth year of his reign, 1341 B. C.

While Wenamon was in the Lebanon obtaining wood for the new river bark of Amon in 1089, at home Herihor attended to the reburial of Ramesses i, Seti i, and Ramesses ii. About a hundred years later their bodies, put into wooden coffins, were transferred to the tomb of Queen Inhapi, in the cliff south of Deir el-Bahri. There the mummy of Amenhotep i, the patron of the necropolis, carefully and lovingly rewrapped for the second time (Plate 18), had been laid some time earlier. These and the other mummies so reburied remained untouched until found by a member of the Abd el-Rassul family at Gurna about A. D. 1875.

Thus by the beginning of the first millenium B. C. all attempts to protect the royal cemeteries at Thebes were abandoned. Yet a century and a half earlier the mummies of the rulers of the Eleventh and Seventeenth Dynasties rested safely in their chambers, as did most of those of their successors. In a span of a thousand years it was only during the period after the death of Tutankhamon, when the uncertainty of succession and the administrative confusion inherited from the Amarna

67. Vignettes and texts from the third division of the " Book of Gates ", painted bas-relief, tomb of Seti i, Valley of the Tombs of the Kings.

episode caused a brief relaxation of the usual vigilance, that the royal burials were endangered.

The royal cemeteries previous to the New Kingdom were in open areas. The earlier kings of the Eleventh Dynasty chose a cemetery site at the edge of the western desert north of the present road to the Valley of the Tombs of the Kings. Here the Intefs cut courts into the rock about 200 feet wide and 20 feet deep at the western end, where they made the entrances to the burial chambers of the royal family. Whether the mud brick pyramids were in the court or on the desert surface above the tomb chambers is not known. The excavation of these tombs, now occupied by local families, was made before careful records were kept and no plans of them ever have been made. In the central of the three most prominent courts Maspero found parts of the stele of Intef II seen by the inspectors in 1126 B. C. Five dogs were shown on this stele; Behhek, whose Libyan name is translated "Oryx" on the stele, is the uppermost of three shown under the king's skirt (Plate 20).

Several workers in the royal necropolis in the Nineteenth and Twentieth Dynasties have left, in their tombs, lists of the "Lords of the West", the deceased kings buried in the Theban Necropolis. The earliest mentioned is Montuhotep II who united all Egypt under his rule. A simple court tomb like those of his forefathers was not adequate to honour the ruler of so great a kingdom. He chose instead to build his mortuary temple and tombs for himself and his family on a site against the cliff at the head of a valley almost opposite the temple of Amon across the river. This area became known as "Opposite the Face of Her Lord" and the name was extended to the whole necropolis. Until overshadowed by the mortuary temple of Hatshepsut half a millenium later it remained the only major structure on the west side of the river.

The bed of the valley was levelled off for the forecourt and a platform left which was about 15 feet high and 200 feet wide. On it Montuhotep erected his temple, the front an almost square structure slightly higher than the platform on which it stood. It had a double row of square columns about it on three sides, and within the walls three rows of round columns about a central core 65 feet square, the base of a pyramid whose apex is estimated to have risen 85 feet above the level of the court. Only fragments of the delicate painted reliefs on limestone were found by the excavators; these show both religious and secular subjects, including a battle, the river bark of Amon and other ships, and various animals and birds.[35]

Along the rear walls of this building were chapels dedicated to the favourites of the royal harem. From the burial chambers under the floor behind these chapels came the finely decorated limestone sarcophagi of Queens Ashait and Kauit, now in the Cairo Museum. These show a variety of domestic scenes, including one of Queen Kauit with her hairdresser. Within the sarcophagus of Ashait was a wooden coffin, astronomical calculations on the under side of its lid, and on the sides of the interior parts of the great mass of religious material of the Middle Kingdom known as the Coffin Texts. These texts lie midway between the Pyramid Texts, from which they draw material, and the New Kingdom Book of the Dead, to which they make contributions.

On this coffin is an old poem to the winds, the text already corrupt, but still of considerable charm.

> *These winds are given to me by these maidens.*
> *It is the north wind who encircles the Aegean isles,*
> *Who stretches out her arms to the ends of the Two Lands*
> *Who at night with regularity brings the effects of her concern.*
> *A living wind is the north wind; through her I am made to live.*

These winds are given to me by these maidens.
It is the east wind who opens the windows of heaven,
    Who traces the beautiful path of Re, along which he rises.
— Re grasps my arm, setting me in the rush-bearing meadows,
    Where I graze like Apis bull, where I gorge like Set —
A living wind is the east wind; through her I am made to live.

These winds are given to me by these maidens.
A brother of the desert is the west wind,
    An offspring of desolation,
    Living on only one portion,
    No second helping in his land.
A living wind is the west wind; through him I am made to live.

These winds are given to me by these maidens.
The south wind is a living wind,
    (coming from) the southern Nubians,
    Bringing the life-supporting waters.
A living wind is the south wind; through him I am made to live.

Who were the maidens who gave the winds? The text gives no answer to this question. The lines about the meadow of rushes, a part of the geography of the underworld, clearly are an interpolation; they are retained to show how secular poetry was given a funerary reference.

Behind the pyramid-centred square of the temple was a hall about the width of the pyramid and twice as long. The rear half had a forest of pillars supporting the roof and a central chapel against the back wall. The front was an open court surrounded by a portico, in the middle of which was the entrance to a sloping passageway which descended 500 feet to a granite-lined tomb chamber ending in an alabaster naos. Unrifled though the tomb may have been in 1126 B. C., the excavators found only bits of wooden models from the burial of the king.

Naville discovered the ruins of this temple unexpectedly in the early winter of 1903. On an evening at the beginning of January 1900, Howard Carter, riding across what later proved to be the court of the temple, was thrown from his horse when its front legs sank into the sand.[36] Examination showed a hole and after excavation a sloping passage was found. Some way down was a blocked, sealed doorway and 500 feet from the entrance was a chamber with an empty wooden coffin and a large linen-wrapped mass. The linen was unwound to reveal a great squarish painted statue of Montuhotep II shown seated, wrapped in the white robe of the jubilee celebration and wearing the red crown (Plate 1).

Stretching from the court to the edge of cultivation was a causeway and at its lower end the basin of a canal from the river. On the morning of the new moon in the tenth month of the civil year the bark of Amon left Karnak and was ferried across to the western bank. On a high point on the cliff south of the temple the priests kept watch for the first appearance of the god, and while waiting scratched their names on the rocks. As the bark proceeded up the avenue it stopped at appointed stations for ceremonies. At the threshold of the temple the bark, too large to negotiate the turns between the pillars, was set down and the god taken by the priests to the rear chapel for the feast.

This celebration became known as the " Feast of the Valley ".[37] In the New Kingdom the bark of Amon visited the mortuary temple of the contemporary ruler. There was a reversion of offerings from this feast to the tombs of the various Theban officials often illustrated on the walls of the tomb chapels. It was during a celebration of this feast that the conspirators against Ramesses III took advantage of the crowd it attracted to slip into the harem quarters at Medinet Habu.

The Twelfth Dynasty rulers, though resident in the north, continued their support of the feast and of Montuhotep's temple; Senusert III added to its offerings and in it set up a number of statues of himself. Following this dynasty there is a gap in the records until the Seventeenth Dynasty. In 1126 it was reported that the burials of its principal rulers, along the foot of Dra Abu-el-Naga, with but one exception were intact.

They did not remain so for long. Though the accounts of the modern recovery of the coffins and the funerary equipment of some of the kings and queens of this period are obscure, it is evident that in ancient times the mummies had been removed from their original burial places and secreted nearby in groups. The chapels of these tombs have disappeared and of the steep mud brick pyramids, about 25 feet square, few traces remain.

Ahmose, the conqueror of the Hyksos, built the last royal pyramid tomb. His son Amenhotep I had his tomb quarried into the cliffs of the valley behind Montuhotep's temple-tomb; his choice of position set the pattern for the next four and a half centuries. With the exception of Akhenaten, all the rulers until the end of the Twentieth Dynasty were interred in this valley, while their mortuary temples were strung out along the edge of the cultivation from south of the Intef cemetery to Medinet Habu.

Ineni, who may have built the tomb of Amenhotep I, says that for Thutmosis I he " saw to the quarrying of the tomb of his majesty all alone, none seeing, none hearing ", boasting that he had the sole responsibility for the construction rather than that it was done in secrecy. The tomb was situated at the end of the valley dominated by the peak 1300 feet above the Nile alluvium. This peak is now known as el-Gurn, " The Horn ", giving its name to the village of Gurna.

The rulers of the Eighteenth Dynasty tried to place their tombs as far as possible from those of their predecessors and Amenhotep III abandoned the main valley, building his tomb in the western branch. Ay went to the end of that branch for his burial place. His predecessor, Tutankhamon, was buried in a hastily constructed tomb in the narrow floor of the main valley across from the slightly earlier burial of the young man who may have been Smenkhkare.

Haremhab and the first five kings of the Nineteenth Dynasty had their tombs in the near vicinity and their dynastic successors placed theirs near that of Thutmosis I. Setnakht, who began the Twentieth Dynasty, abandoned the tomb he had begun in the central area when it ran into that of Amenmose, and usurped that of Tausert. Ramesses III started a tomb slightly to the north of the central spot, near the burial of the parents of Queen Tiy; finding the stone of poor quality, he took the one his father had begun, turned aside from the break through, and extended the passage. Some of his successors built in the vicinity, some slightly farther north. The tomb of Ramesses XI was left unfinished and neither the tomb nor the mummy of Herihor has ever been discovered.

The first three kings bearing the name Thutmosis had burial chambers with rounded ends, like cartouches, approached by descending passages and stairways. In the passage Thutmosis III added a deep well, the doorway in the far wall being closed, plastered over, and decorated. This ruse to mislead robbers, copied in the larger tombs until the reign of Seti I, was unsuccessful in protecting the burial of the kings.

Hatshepsut had a very steep passage and stairs which descended 200 feet in about twice that length, and a rectangular sarcophagus chamber, a shape retained from Amenhotep II onward. Seti I introduced a vaulted sarcophagus chamber, continued

68. Queen Nefertari, wife of Ramesses II, in attitude of worship, painted bas-relief, in the queen's tomb, Valley of the Tombs of the Queens.

69. Colossus of Ramesses II, named " Re of the Rulers ", in the first court of the Luxor temple and colonnade decorated by Tutankhamon.

140

by many succeeding rulers down to Ramesses III. The steep descending passages were no longer used after Merenptah and had been abandoned by Ramesses II.

The number of rooms and divisions in the passageways varied, as did the number of small storage rooms off the sarcophagus chambers. Under the floor of the sarcophagus chamber of Seti I, whose tomb was the largest and most complex, Belzoni found a further descending passage which he traced 300 feet before the collapsing stone made it too dangerous to go farther. Recent excavators, speculating on the existence of treasure beyond, have not been able to penetrate even to this distance.

The walls of the sarcophagus room of Thutmosis I were plastered and decorated with a painted composition entitled " The Writings of the Secret Chamber ", better known by its subtitle " The Book of What is in the Underworld ". The texts were written in cursive hieroglyphic and the scenes were made up of sketch figures. From this tomb only a few fragments remain; the fullest versions are in the tombs of Thutmosis III and Amenhotep II. They appear on a buff-coloured background, as if a vast, ancient papyrus had been unrolled on the wall. That the walls had indeed been copied from a papyrus is indicated by the number of times losses through damage to the original source are indicated by the words, " found destroyed ". In later versions such gaps were ignored and this practice, with other errors, led to very corrupt texts.

The walls of the well and anteroom to the burial chamber of Thutmosis IV were decorated with conventional paintings of the king with funerary deities. Tutankhamon and Ay had only short extracts of the standard text, but added some funerary scenes, and the latter showed himself and his queen fowling in the marshes, like scenes in contemporary private tomb chapels.

Haremhab first introduced parts of " The Book of Gates ". With Seti I there began the use of many other texts, filling the walls and ceilings of all rooms and passageways. On the vault of his sarcophagus chamber Seti showed the night sky, the most recognizable constellation being Ursa Major, shown as a man driving a bull, but still known by its old name " Adze " (Plate 88). Throughout the dynasty most of the tombs had on the walls of the entrance halls " The Litany of Re ". Ramesses VI, whose tomb, along with that of Seti I, is the best preserved and the most prolific in the number of compositions, had on the entrance halls " The Book of Caverns " and " The Book of Gates ", then large extracts of " What is in the Underworld " and shorter selections of other mortuary texts. On the ceilings were two copies of " The Book of Day " and " The Book of Night ", as well as several astronomical maps. He and his next two successors entered on ceilings parts of bi-monthly astronomical observations made almost 400 years earlier.[38]

The study of the royal funerary texts is a discipline on which few Egyptologists have made themselves authorities. The texts use the pattern of the course of the sun through the heavens to explain the pattern of life. The sun is born in the morning, ages as it travels westward, and dies in the evening, to pass through the underworld at night, where it is regenerated and brings regeneration, to be born again the next day. Even when one begins to understand the text the symbolism is strange and often contradictory. The texts include reflections on the human condition, observations on the courses of the heavenly bodies, and bizarre legends about the geography, dangers and pleasures of the underworld.

On the pillars of his sarcophagus chamber Amenhotep II was shown embraced by a god or goddess, as was Seti I in similar scenes. The ability of artists to draw, freehand, long lines, often curved, with a sureness and evenness, is outstanding (Plate 87). Most of the decoration in the tomb of Seti was in bas-relief, following the style first introduced by Haremhab. In the tomb of that ruler, where the work was left unfinished, the whole sequence is clear. The first outline draughtsman, guided only by his copy and by divisions he had ruled on the wall, sketched in red

70. Gateway in First Pylon of the Luxor temple, with colossi and obelisk, all erected by Ramesses II. Valley of the Tombs of the Queens.

71. The vulture goddess Nekhbet, over a doorway.

72. The god Harakhti and the goddess Hathor.

Both painted bas-reliefs in the tomb of Queen Nefertari, wife of Ramesses II.

145

the rough outline of the text and vignettes. A second draughtsman went over the whole in black, adjusting positions and shapes. Then the sculptor began his work, painstakingly cutting away the background so that the signs and figures stood out. Only in the well and anteroom was work in the tomb of Haremhab completed and the walls painted; here the scenes of the king with various deities are among the finest in the royal tombs (Plate 15).

The use of this delicate bas-relief reached its highest point in the tomb of Seti I, who used a great variety of colour on his walls (Plate 67). Though Ramesses II in other monuments changed from bas-relief to incised relief, in the royal tombs the change was only made under his son Merenptah. This was a great artistic loss, but since these reliefs were never intended to be seen by humans after the burial the Egyptians saw the aesthetic aspect of the work as secondary.

Though the great mass of treasure found in the tomb of Tutankhamon staggers the imagination, the nature of the contents had been heralded by other discoveries. The collection found in the tomb of Iouia and Thouia, the parents of Queen Tiy, consisting of a chariot, excellent furniture and a wide variety of funerary equipment, showed the richness of the burial of royal relatives. The standard-bearer Maiherpri, who lived about the time of Thutmosis III and who was educated in the royal school, was buried with a blue glazed bowl (Plate 78) which is an excellent example of a number of such objects. His blue glass bottle, with supplementary colours laid on (Plate 90), is one of the earliest examples of its type, which was commissioned by royalty. Fragments of royal funerary furniture, discarded by the robbers, were found in other tombs and the second coffin of Thutmosis III, stripped of its precious metal, was used for his reburial.

Little of the material from Tutankhamon's tomb has been properly described and published. Many scholars believe that some of it was originally made for Smenkhkare. Some of the treasure belonged to the palace furniture of Tutankhamon. The throne, on which the cabinet-maker used coloured stone, glass, glaze and precious metal in an elaborate mosaic picture of Tutankhamon served by his queen Ankhesenamon, had come from Amarna, as the presence on it of the blessing disk of Aten shows; surely it had been prepared for another.

The painted chest was Tutankhamon's own. On its four panels it shows the boy-king's dreams of himself as a mighty warrior against the Syrian and Nubian enemies of Egypt and as a hunter of lions and desert game. In each panel the central figure is the same, Tutankhamon standing in his chariot springing his bow while the plunging span delivers him into the midst of the field of action. Inside the chest were outgrown garments worn when he first came to the throne at about the age of ten.

Some of the jewelry must have been worn in life. Of the many bracelets a choice one is the golden band on which was mounted a scarab, its back of lapis lazuli (Plate 37). Among the great variety of ornaments were hawk (Plate 36), vulture (Plate 31), and wadjet-eye (Plate 32) pectorals, the last representing the sound eye of Horus, elaborated by the serpent and the vulture, the early goddesses of the delta and the Nile valley. The latter two, with other pectorals, were found on the mummy of the king. Some were made to be worn, but others were only protective charms for the deceased king.

In the tomb were chariots, bows and arrows, an iron dagger in a gold sheath, walking sticks, fans, chairs, footstools, game boards, a scribal outfit and much more which the king may have used in life. Alabaster vases and carvings abounded, some beautiful, others rather garish for modern taste. One ornate alabaster lamp had a close-fitting inner bowl which had a painted scene on its outer surface. Only when the wick floating in oil was lighted did the scene show through the outer wall. A miniature gold statue of Amenhotep III on a chain and a lock of Tiy's hair, contained in a nest of small coffins, have suggested to some Egyptologists that Tutankhamon was the youngest child of this royal couple.[39]

Much of the material crowded into the four small chambers was specifically funerary. The wooden life-sized standing statues, the flesh black and the garments gold, which stood before the blocked entry to the sarcophagus chamber were created for this purpose. Of a number of other statuettes two were in pairs, one with the king standing on the back of a black panther and the other with him standing on a reed float and spearing a hippopotamus in the water beneath (Plate 27); both pairs are funerary objects. The three beds, with their differing decoration of animal heads, symbolized the regeneration of the king, the cow his mounting to heaven, the hippopotamus, Taweris, the new birth (Plate 17), and the lion the new life. Anubis resting on his shrine (Plate 16) was the patron deity of all necropolises.

In the sarcophagus chamber the mummy of the king lay wrapped in linen, many amulets within the bandages, and the golden mask on his head (Plate 28). He was encased in a coffin of solid gold and in turn in two gold-plated wooden coffins with brightly coloured inlaid decorations. All these were placed within a red quartzite sarcophagus which was enclosed in four shrines of wood with gold overlay and with funerary texts inside and out. Each of the side panels had first been laid against the appropriate walls, and then assembled. Seeing the chamber with the shrines removed (Plate 40), one marvels at the small space in which the carpenters worked. This, in part, may account for their carelessness; hammer marks on the shrine show that they had scant respect for the fine craftsmanship of the panels they were assembling.

In a small room off the sarcophagus chamber was the elaborate canopic chest within a gold covered wooden shrine. It was guarded on each side by one of the four goddesses whose figures, with out-stretched wings, had stood at the corners of the sarcophagi of many of the kings of this dynasty. In the process of mummification it was the custom to remove the viscera and to enclose the liver, spleen, lungs and intestines each in a " canopic " jar. The lids of the jars usually represented the protecting spirits, one human, the others a baboon, a jackal and a hawk. In this tomb four cylindrical compartments were made in a block of alabaster, each capped by an alabaster head of the king. Within were four minature gold coffins which contained the royal viscera.

All this funerary furniture was carried and dragged up the valley from the edge of the cultivation, a road $2\frac{1}{3}$ miles long. Yet the valley so turned and twisted that the centre of the burial area, where Tutankhamon's tomb was quarried, was only 600 yards from the upper terrace of Hatshepsut's temple at Deir el-Bahri.

The mortuary temples of the Eighteenth Dynasty, with the exception of that of Hatshepsut, are known only from traces. Amenhotep I and Thutmosis II built rather small temples, while of that of Thutmosis I no trace has been discovered. Thutmosis III and Hatshepsut began their temples at about the same time. Thutmosis placed his at the edge of cultivation somewhat south of the causeway of Montuhotep II. The pylons and many of the walls were of mud brick, though both limestone and sandstone were used for certain walls and ceilings and granite for the doorways. Adjoining at the south was a chapel for Hathor. Today there is little but the mud brick walls to be seen. The modern road runs between the two pylons and most visitors go along it unaware that they are passing through the forecourt of the mortuary temple of Thutmosis III.

While Thutmosis built a conventional temple, Hatshepsut followed a different plan. Influenced by the imposing pyramid temple of Montuhotep II, her first plan was to imitate it, but this design soon was abandoned. Even at this earliest period Hatshepsut had removed a temple of Amenhotep I which may have been dedicated to Hathor; the new plan for her temple required the removal of part of the mountain. Senmut, an official of great ability who made himself indispensable to Hatshepsut, was responsible for the building from the beginning.

The plan he finally followed combined well tested architectural elements in a new design. By levelling off the slope he created two courts, one at ground level and one on a terrace above, while on a second terrace he formed a platform for the temple proper. Each court had at its western end a double columned portico, divided into two parts in the centre by the ramp which gave access to the terrace above. When the first Europeans visited this temple area such was its disrepair that its nature was not recognized; its present appearance, set against the background of the towering cliffs (Plate 2), which makes it the most striking temple in Egypt, is in a great part the result of the reconstructions of M. Baraize.

On the wall of the south wing of the lower portico is the record of the transport of the first obelisks quarried for Hatshepsut. While she was still regent Senmut was commissioned to quarry them. The pair are shown butt to butt on the deck of a barge which was more than 300 feet long and 100 feet wide, and each obelisk was 92½ feet in length. The barge was towed by three rows of nine ships, each with a complement of 32 rowers. On arrival at Thebes the obelisks were decorated with inscriptions which named Hatshepsut as king, for her coronation had taken place after they had been commissioned. She erected them at the eastern gateway of the temple of Amon at Karnak.

To the north of the ramp dividing the first terrace, the walls of the portico are decorated with a series of scenes showing the somewhat mythical history of Hatshepsut from her birth to her coronation. The lower register tells of her divine birth, the legend which was taken over by Amenhotep III and which was discussed earlier (p. 131). The upper register tells of her youth and of her coronation by her father Thutmosis I. Of the scenes and inscriptions on the wall only the handsome figure of Ahmose, mother of Hatshepsut, was left untouched by two waves of despoilers, those who took vengeance on Hatshepsut and the agents of Akhenaten. Careful examination by Egyptologists of the remaining traces has recovered most of the content of these scenes.

Among the texts is one describing Hatshepsut in her maturity. " Her majesty became more important than anything else. What was within her was godlike; her manner was godlike; godlike was everything she did; her spirit was godlike. Her majesty became a beautiful maiden, blossoming out. The goddess Uto, at this moment, applauded her divine shapeliness. She is a woman of distinguished appearance." Such was Hatshepsut's own estimate of herself.

To the north of this wing of the portico is the chapel of Anubis. Here the destruction by the detractors of Hatshepsut was not as complete as on the portico, and much colour is left on the remaining reliefs. Above the depictions of the queen were the figures of the protective deities, the vulture, Nekhbet, of Upper Egypt (Plate 6) and the hawk, He of Behdet (Horus), of the delta. The piles of offerings which Hatshepsut was shown presenting to the gods seated before her were untouched in the erasures and give some idea of the colourfulness of the decoration (Plate 7).

The south wing of the portico contains the record of Hatshepsut's proudest achievement, the expedition to Punt, on the Somali coast, in about the eighth year of her reign. This land was the home of the myrrh tree whose exudations were a necessary ingredient of the incense used daily in all Egyptian temples. Carved on the southern wall of the colonnade is a picture of the coastal village which the Egyptian expedition visited. Some of the sketches on which the reliefs were based were made on the spot.

As is usual in Egyptian portrayal of landscape, space and time are shown by arranging the material register on register. On the shore of the sea full of strange fish (Plate 21) the Egyptian envoy and his troop were received by the chief of Punt, Parohu and his obese and swayback wife (Plate 12). The trade goods brought were little different from those offered to primitive peoples in recent centuries, beads, jewelry, axes and daggers. Behind the family of the chief stands a saddled donkey with the humorous notation, " the ass which carried his wife " (Plate 13).

In the village the huts of the people were domed, set on stilts and reached by ladders. Under the trees of the forest were long-horn and short-horn cattle, baboons, leopards and, perhaps because the artist had mixed in some sketches of upper Nile fauna, a giraffe and a hippopotamus. The trees were ebony, dompalm, and those with resinous gum. This gum was collected, young trees dug up, their roots carefully wrapped, and put on ship for transportation to Egypt. The fleet returned northward along the coast, these goods supplemented by a representative selection of animals. Some inhabitants of Punt, a race related to the Egyptians, accompanied the fleet.

South of the wing with these reliefs was the chapel of Hathor. In the forehall a number of columns had capitals with the head of Hathor, with bovine ears, on two sides (Plate 25). On the slate-coloured walls of the rear chamber Hatshepsut was shown nursing at the udder of the Hathor cow. At the base of the side walls are a number of niches once closed by doors; on the walls of these Senmut engraved pictures of himself so placed that the opening doors would conceal them. Most of these escaped detection by those who sought to obliterate the memory of this able official.[40]

The colonnade of the temple proper on the upper terrace had a row of square columns against which stood great statues of Hatshepsut in the garb of Osiris. Access to the hypostyle hall was through a granite gateway, the inscriptions on it later usurped by Thutmosis III, who placed his own foundation deposit of model tools beneath it. Directly opposite was the sanctuary cut into the rock of the mountain. The doorway, only five feet wide, would not have been easy to enter by the priests, two abreast, carrying the bark of Amon on their shoulders. This means that the bark was much smaller than the scenes on temple walls would indicate. Egyptian art used size as an indication of importance and not as a scale relative to reality. The rear shrine for the deified Imhotep and Amenhotep, son of Hapu, gods of healing, was added in the Ptolemaic period.

To the south of the central hypostyle hall was the mortuary suite for Hatshepsut with a room dedicated to the cult of Thutmosis I, her father. Here, as elsewhere, her figure was often erased; where it was retained the cartouches of one of the first three rulers named Thutmosis have been substituted for hers. At the north end of the hall was a chapel to Re, open to the sky, an altar in the centre. These contiguous temples, as they have been called, continued to be a feature of Theban mortuary temples throughout the rest of the New Kingdom.

Whereas Montuhotep had planted his court with trees and lined the central avenue with statues of himself, in the guise of Osiris, the avenue of Hatshepsut's court was lined with sphinxes with heads of herself; just before the lower ramp there were two T-shaped papyrus pools. The only trees found were at the entrance of the lower court; they never grew large, as witnessed by the stumps still to be seen.

Hatshepsut, like Montuhotep, had a causeway going from the forecourt to a basin and canal at the edge of cultivation, where she had a small temple. Between the two causeways, slightly nearer to that of Montuhotep, excavators have found parts of a causeway of Thutmosis III. Some of the pavement with pits for trees which lined the avenue and the limestone wall of the northern side can be seen east of the modern road along the desert edge.

This approach, long known, has been a puzzle. The only known structure at the western end was a cave cut into the rock behind the north eastern corner of the platform of Montuhotep II; this contained a small painted chapel dedicated to Hathor (Plate 10). Within it stood a statue of the Hathor cow nursing Amenhotep II (Plate 11). An ostracon from the site tells of work on a structure in the forty-fifth year of Thutmosis III.

This ostracon, difficult to read, mentions features which do not fit the small chapel. Nor is there any explanation for the lower end of a ramp positioned between the two temples of Deir el-Bahri. All was made clear when, in 1961, the Polish architect Leszek Dabrowski, sent by his government to assist the Department of Antiquities in further reconstruction of Hatshepsut's temple, found evidence that the chapel for Hathor was only an adjunct to a larger temple. While the work is still proceeding, it is clear that Thutmosis III had built this above the upper terrace of Hatshepsut, north of the temple proper and in part behind her chapel for Hathor. The platform on which it stood extended almost to the rear part of the temple of Montuhotep II and was considerably above it. Much of it was on fill which has collapsed, leaving only the northern part of the temple which was built on solid rock. The now vestigial ramp had extended to it. The amount of evidence destroyed by early excavators, whose methods were not adequate to the situation, cannot be calculated.

The tomb of Hatshepsut as king in the Valley of the Tombs of the Kings lay almost directly behind Deir el-Bahri. While still queen of Thutmosis II another tomb had been made for her. It was at the end of a small valley at the south side of the peak, about two-thirds of the way up an almost sheer 300 foot cliff. Here by great effort a fine yellow sandstone coffin had been brought. Because of the change in her fortune it was never needed. This tomb was found in 1916-17 by the energetic searches of Howard Carter; in 1914 he had discovered, up a valley at the north end of Dra Abu-el-Naga, the tomb of Ahmose Nefertari, the queen of Ahmose and mother of Amenhotep I. Another queen of Ahmose's, Inhapi, had a cliff tomb south of Deir el-Bahri in which some of the royal mummies were later concealed. Behind the walls of the north colonnade on the lower terrace of Hatshepsut's temple was the tomb of Merit-Amon, daughter of Thutmosis III and wife of Amenhotep II. She died without issue soon after her brother-husband became king; her coffins were stripped of their gold covering by thieves. She was reburied by the priests of Amon about 1050 B.C. and was not again disturbed until her tomb was found by Winlock in 1929. There are many other of these cliff tombs made for the families of the rulers of the Eighteenth Dynasty, but because of their lack of decoration they cannot be associated with particular persons.

In the Nineteenth Dynasty the place of burial of members of the royal families was changed to a small valley south of Deir el Medineh and behind Medinet Habu. Here about eighty tombs of the queens and royal children of that and the following dynasty have been noted, but the original occupants of but few are known. The most spectacular of the tombs in which the wall decorations are preserved is that of Nefertari, the chief queen of Ramesses II. Because of the progressive deterioration of the painted plaster on some walls it is not open for general viewing.

The roughly quarried surfaces of the walls were covered with a layer of gypsum plaster and on a harder coating the figures were moulded in low relief and brilliantly painted. The queen is wearing a gossamer outer linen garment and a close-fitting inner one, this gathered about the waist with a tasseled sash. Over her shoulders was a broad golden collar and on her head a golden crown. This had a shell patterned like a vulture covering her dark wig and was surmounted by a solar disc and plumes simulated in gold. Her eyebrows and lids were blackened with kohl. The rouging on her cheeks is unique (Plate 68). Over the doorway to an inner

73. Fisherman with nets.

74. Men washing linen.

Both wall-paintings in the tomb chapel of the Sculptor Ipuy. Reign of Ramesses II. *Theban Tomb No. 217*

73
74

chamber is the vuture goddess Nekhbet (Plate 71) and at one side the figures of Harakhti (Horus of the Horizon) and Hathor, Chieftainess of Thebes (Plate 72). In a frieze of funerary gods one vignette shows Aker, two lions back to back, the rising sun between them, symbolizing yesterday and tomorrow. Only part is preserved, a young lion with his shoulder tuft and stylized mane (Plate 85).

The mortuary temples of Amenhotep II and Thutmosis IV, of which a few traces were recovered by careful archaeological exploration, lay to the north and the south, respectively, of the site Ramesses II later chose for his temple. Farther to the south Amenhotep III erected his great mortuary temple. The pylons and probably some of the walls were of mud brick; all walls have now disappeared. Several granite statue groups and smaller monuments were taken by Ramesses III for use in his temple, and it was at Medinet Habu that Daressy found the fragments of the colossal seated figures of Amenhotep III and Tiy, with their daughters standing in front of the throne. The reassembled statue is the largest by far in the Cairo Museum. Another pillager was Merenptah who quarried the temple of Amenhotep for much of the stone for his mortuary temple a little to the north-west. His famous " Israel Stele " was engraved on the back of a stele of the earlier king on which were recorded his building enterprises.

Here Amenhotep III described his mortuary temple. " Now his majesty was pleased to build a very great monument, without equal since the beginning of time. He built it to be a monument for his father Amon, Lord of the Thrones of the Two Lands, erecting for him an august temple on the starboard of Thebes, an everlasting fortress of sandstone, embellished with gold throughout, its floor shining with silver and all its doorways with electrum. It is wide and very long, adorned for eternity, and made festive with this exceptionally large stele. It is extended with royal statues of granite, of quartzite and of precious stones, fashioned to last forever. They are higher than the rising of the heavens; their rays are in men's faces like the rising sun... Its workshops are filled with male and female slaves, the children of chieftains of all the countries which his majesty conquered. Its magazines have stored up uncountable riches. It is surrounded by villages of Syrians, peopled with children of chieftains; its cattle are like the sands of the shore, totalling millions."

The site of this great temple never has been properly explored.[41] The modern road runs over its southern wall. In a slight mound at the rear are stumps of columns and remains of various statues. A little to the east another of the great steles has been set up in its original position.

There still stand the battered seated figures of Amenhotep III which measure about 65 feet from the base of their pedestals to the top of their heads; when they wore crowns which no longer survive, they were higher still. Since Roman times they have been known as the Colossi of Memnon. Tradition tells that the upper part of the northern statue, toppled to the ground by the earthquare of A.D. 27, used to emit a sound as it was struck by the rays of the rising sun. Greek travellers identified it with the Ethiopian hero whom Achilles slew in the Trojan War, Memnon, son of Eos, the dawn. It was she whom he greeted each morning. After Septimus Severus restored the upper part the song was heard no longer. On its great legs are Greek graffiti, including poems, telling of its fame. When the two statues were erected, it was the southern one which had the greater fame, for this was the " Ruler of Rulers ", served by its own priesthood. The Colossi, much as they were in Roman times, still stand as lonely sentinels on the way to the Theban necropolis (Plate 80).

To the south along the desert edge Amenhotep III built a sprawling town, with the palace complex a mile from the temple. The palace of the king had extensive harem quarters adjacent, while nearby were other palaces for Queen Tiy, for their daughter Sit-Amon, who became an associate queen in the latter years of the reign,

75. The court of Amenhotep III, Luxor Temple, with the apse of the chapel of the Roman legion beyond.

76. Decorated fatted ox, for offering in the Feast of Opet. West wall of the court of Ramesses II, Luxor temple.

and for the heir to the throne who became Amenhotep IV and then Akhenaten. Near the palaces were villas for the chief officials and smaller houses for the administrators of lesser importance. In the vicinity were homes of artisans and servants. To the north of the palaces was an audience hall for the king and farther north the temple area.

The buildings were of mud brick, but many of the walls and floors of the palaces were plastered and gaily decorated with painted designs, birds in the papyrus swamps, foreign captives, a calf romping through a meadow. On the ceilings were more formal patterns, one with spirals and heads of cows with solar discs between the horns, a motif said to come from Aegean originals, but actually long established in Egypt.

From the rubbish heaps near the administrative offices came more than a thousand mud seals which had been used on rolls of papyrus, dispatches and accounts which had come into the palace archives. Strewn about were pieces of buff pottery with blue painted decorations, some with animal heads on the necks. The finest had a free standing ibex head, attached to the vase only at the neck and tip of the horns, with the body painted on the shoulder of the vase.

On the fragments of many utilitarian jars were hieratic dockets indicating the nature and place of origin of the contents, and often the name of the official in charge of the bottling. Many were dated, most to the years 30, 34 and 37, the years of the three jubilees of Amenhotep III. In the temple area was a small chapel to Amon and special halls for the celebration of these festivals.

To the west of the town a graded road can still be traced; to the north it turns toward the mortuary temple and to the south bends again, running through the desert to disappear into the cultivation just north of the little Roman temple of Deir Shelwit. Nearby are the ruins of a small sun temple, perhaps contemporary with the palaces, which has never been explored.

On the edge of the cultivation before the town are mounds which were piled up when a great basin was excavated. The area outlined by the mounds is over a mile and a quarter long and almost half a mile wide. In actual size the basin may have been smaller, as allowance must be made for banks along the sides. From the middle a channel led off to the east; this may indicate the usual T-shaped lake, but it is more likely to have been a canal communicating with the river. This basin has been identified with a pleasure lake built for Tiy, but a recent study has made this unlikely; it may have been a harbour where ships discharged merchandise for the royal court.

When the court returned to Thebes after the Amarna revolution the old palaces were used again, but their importance and that of the town about them rapidly declined. The mortuary temples of Thutmosis II and Amenhotep, son of Hapu, were in the desert south of that of Amenhotep III, enveloped by the town. To the south of these the buildings were cleared away for a new mortuary temple which by the end of the Twentieth Dynasty had been dismantled. The remains indicate that it had been begun by Ay, then taken over and enlarged by Haremhab. Both usurped in turn a pair of statues made for Tutankhamon who may well have begun the temple on this site. One of the statues is now in the Cairo Museum; its face, though damaged, is one of the most expressive portraits of this king (Plate 52).

The earliest mortuary temple of the Nineteenth Dynasty also had three kings concerned with it. Here there was no usurpation; Seti I built one section to honour his father Ramesses I, but did not complete the temple before his death. Ramesses II continued work on it, making the same change from raised to incised relief as in the Hypostyle Hall at Karnak, but other enterprises took his attention, and he never completed the decoration. The pylons and walls of the courts, probably of mud brick, have disappeared. In this temple is the first known introduction of shrines where the barks of Mut and Khonsu might rest during the Feast of the Valley.

The part of Seti's temple which lay behind the courts, the temple proper, completely roofed except for the Re chapel, was about 175 feet broad and slightly less in depth. The mortuary temple which Ramesses II built for himself, known as the Ramesseum, was far more ambitious. The rear part, comparable with the preserved section of the temple of Seti I, was 200 feet wide and 330 feet deep; the two courts added another 200 feet in front of this. While much of the Ramesseum was quarried by the Ptolemies for their additions to the small temple at Medinet Habu, the west face of the First Pylon, the same face of the north tower of the Second Pylon and the pillars before it, and parts of the portico and the first two hypostyle halls still are standing.

On the faces of the pylons are depictions of the battle of Kadesh. On the Second Pylon are some details of the fray. A great many of the opposing warriors and their chariots are floundering in the river Orontes; several chieftains, mentioned by name, are being pulled out by their soldiers and the Hittite troops are hanging by the heels " the wretched prince of Aleppo ", slapping his chest to expel the water.

The prenomen of Ramesses II, used in the name of the temple, was Usermare-setepenre; the Greeks vocalized the first part as Ozymandyas. Diodorus, reporting in about 60 B. C. and using a source some 250 years earlier, gives a colourful description of the building, accurate in some parts and fanciful in others. At the time of the original account the temple still was in good condition. Beside the ramp leading to the gateway of the Second Pylon was a granite seated statue of the king, reported to be the largest in the land and without sign of deterioration. At the time when accounts of Belzoni's discoveries were exciting the British people, Shelley, taken by the description, wrote his well-known sonnet telling of its present shattered state. The trunk has tumbled from the throne and lies on its back, hardly recognizable (Plate 79).

The first hypostyle hall, less than one-third the size of the great Hypostyle Hall at Karnak, is better proportioned and does not seem so crowded. This may be because a few of the columns and the side walls are no longer standing. In the second hypostyle hall the central ceiling blocks are still in position. On them is a so-called astronomical representation, giving the seasons and the months, and in the centre the circumpolar constellations. The scene of the recording of Ramesses II's name on the sacred persea tree, in which Norden had seen Eve's temptation of Adam, is on the west wall of this hall.

At the sides and rear of the temple were storehouses built of mud-brick, mostly long corridors with vaulted roofs. The vaults were built without forms or centering. The heavy side walls were built to the desired height and the end wall rose some six feet higher. Against this, on top of the side walls, the vault bricks were laid, the first course at a slight angle and only one or two bricks high, conforming to the curve of the vault. The next course was leaned against the first, following the curve, and the work continued until the vault was complete. The bricks for vaulting were prepared by drawing the fingers across the wet surface before the mould was removed, so providing a key for the mortar.

The last of the mortuary temples of which more than traces remain is that of Ramesses III. He selected a site just south of the temple finished by Haremhab, and had to bend his temenos wall to accommodate it. It was built according to Ramesses on ground " holy since the beginning of time ", but he was not referring to the earlier town site of Amenhotep III, the scattered buildings of which he had to remove. The holy ground actually lay some fifty yards to the southeast.

Here was a temple built on what became known in the Twenty-first Dynasty as " The Holy Mound of Djeme ". In this site Hatshepsut began and Thutmosis III completed a small chapel to " Amon of the Place of Holiness ". A previous shrine of the Middle Kingdom was replaced; it had the same ground plan as the larger mountain chapel of Montuhotep III. Some of the consecrated limestone blocks from it were re-used in the walls of the Eighteenth Dynasty sanctuary.

At the front of this chapel was a peripteros with an open-ended sanctuary at the centre. The rear part had six rooms; one on the right hand side, with its own entrance, was for the statue of the king. The others, one suite with two rooms at the front and three at the back, were entered by a doorway immediately behind the sanctuary. The first of these rooms, and the largest, contained a double statue of Thutmosis III and Amon seated side by side on a throne.

At the beginning of the Twenty-first Dynasty there is a record of the visit of Amon of Opet to Medinet Habu every ten days, though in the temple itself it is mentioned only in inscriptions on later additions. The plan of the temple is the same as that of the first way station on the processional route of Amon of Southern Opet. This suggests that at the time of Hatshepsut there were already periodic visits to this chapel by the ithyphallic statue of Amon of Opet whose home was in Luxor Temple.

There is no inscriptional record of the fortunes of the Eighteenth Dynasty temple from 1050 to 750 when the Ethiopian rulers, followed by the kings from Sais, the Twenty-fifth and Twenty-Sixth Dynasties, made alterations and built a small pylon and portico before it. Burials of important persons about it, including Harsiese, proclaimed pharaoh at Thebes at the beginning of the Twenty-Third Dynasty, show that it continued to be a very sacred shrine. The Ptolemies made further extensive alterations and additions, including a great pylon. Antoninus Pius (A. D. 138-61) started, but never finished, a portico and forecourt before this.

Hakor, on columns he used to prop up the sagging roof, says that this temple was a " burial crypt for all his fathers, the gods of the necropolis, while Montu, Lord of Thebes, the Bull which is in Medamut, revives their members every day ". In the Ptolemaic period oaths were sworn by this Montu who had a shrine nearby. Even before the Ptolemaic period there were growing up fantasies about the shrine which told of it as the burial place of the eight primeval gods of Hermopolis and the home of the great snake Kneph, a beneficent genius, the Agathos Daimon of the Greeks. Later the north wing, added by the Ptolemies, became a Christian church dedicated to St Menas; traces of wall paintings concerning his life still can be seen.

As the site of his mortuary temple and its outbuildings Ramesses III selected an area 1020 by 670 feet. This area he enclosed with a mud brick temenos wall originally at least 60 feet high and 35 feet thick at the base. The Eighteenth Dynasty temple thereafter had no independent entrance through the temenos wall until one was cut in the Ethiopian period. The great wall was a fortification and the precinct could be entered only through high gateways on the east and the west. That such a protection was necessary was proved by the destruction of the western gate toward the end of the dynasty during an attack by marauders. These temenos walls were built after the completion of the mortuary temple in 1175.[42]

Before the temenos, on the central axis, was a quay at the end of a basin to which a canal led from the river; the present road to the temple ends over the position of this basin. Some yards in front of the temenos wall was a low crenellated sandstone wall decorated by Ramesses VI with scenes dedicated to the gods of the chief cult centres of Nubia and Upper Egypt. At the gateway in this wall were two porter's lodges decorated by Ramesses IV and VI.[43]

From the passage between these lodges the vista stretches through a succession of gateways into the midst of the temple, where the loss of the roof over the central part makes light what once was in gloom. Down this avenue once a year, during the Feast of the Valley, were paraded the barks of the Theban gods, led by that

77. The striding colossus
of Ramesses II,
south-east corner of the court
of this king, Luxor temple.

of Amon, followed by those of Mut and Khonsu and, for the first time on record, by that of Montu. Ramesses, when he was able to come to Thebes for the occasion, was purified and robed in the small palace on the south side of the first court, and then came into the court through a communicating doorway to greet his father Amon and officiate in the festival.

The majesty of Ramesses III was well set forth on the outer walls of the high gateway. The relief is higher than on any other pharaonic monument and the figures of the king are in heroic proportions. On the east faces of the towers he is smiting the enemy and dedicating them to Amon. In a register below each scene is a row of bound captives, alternating Nubians and Libyans on the south and sea peoples and those of the eastern Mediterranean littoral on the north. In the passageway the king drags his captives to present them to Amon. In a niche on the south Ramesses worships " Ptah... who is in the Mansion of Millions of years, ' United with Eternity ', who hears prayer ". " United with Eternity " was the ancient name of the mortuary temple of Ramesses III. Once the hair and beard of Ptah were inlaid with glazed blue tile and the posts of the shrine overlaid with gold; this was an ikon to which the ordinary people might come and pray.

This high gateway was patterned after Syrian migdol fortresses and, when the gates were closed, might give some extra measure of protection against attack. There was, however, no primary provision for the manning of the walls by the defenders. In the decoration of the rooms in the towers Ramesses, who appears as conqueror and priest on the outer walls, is shown in the intimacy of the harem. Though his royalty is signalized by his crown, Ramesses plays draughts with the girls, chucks some under the chin, has his arm round another and is fed sweetmeats by others. The maidens are clothed in elaborate headdresses and little else. The destroyed western gateway had similar scenes in its rooms. The mud-brick wall adjoining the gateway had in a thicker section other rooms and the approaches to the rooms in the central sandstone structure.

At one time there was a garden in the south-eastern corner of the temenos. It had disappeared when the burial chapel of the God's Wife of Amon, Shepenwepet I, was built about 730 B. C. The mud-brick structure, the eastern chapel in the row, has now also vanished and only the subterranean burial chamber gives evidence of its position. This is notable because it has the oldest known true vaulting of stone. To the west Amenardis I built her burial chapel of sandstone, with a central shrine within a roofed ambulatory and a small court in front. It was named picturesquely " The Vineyard of Anubis " of whom it contained a cult statue. Adjoining at the north was the tomb chapel of her successor, Shepenwepet II, with only the central shrine finished. Flanking it were the chapel of the next God's Wife, Nitocris, and of her mother Mehetenweskhet, the queen of Psametik I.

The First Pylon of the great temple, the finest of those of the pharaonic period still preserved, was once veiled by mud-brick walls which stood before it; evidence of these was recovered by careful excavation. On the fronts of the towers of this pylon, at either end, are traditional scenes of the king smiting his enemies before Amon and lists of towns and areas captured, all based on the conquests of Thutmosis III (plate 82). Toward the inner ends of the towers are two niches for the flagpoles. These were fastened at the top by bars extending through window-like openings, which had no other function. At the northern end of the pylon begins the stairway which mounts to the porch over the gateway and from which other stairs go to the tops of the towers.

A careful study of the reliefs on the temple walls reveals that many of the religious scenes were copied directly from those in the Ramesseum. The scribes responsible for the design went to the older temple and made copies of what they found, then put the scenes on the walls of the temple of Ramesses III, often in exactly the

78. Glazed ceramic bowl found in the tomb of the Fan-bearer Maiherpri, Valley of the Tombs of the Kings. About the middle of the Eighteenth Dynasty. Cairo Museum

same position. However, the Medinet Habu temple was somewhat smaller, 165 feet wide behind the pylon and 500 feet long. The difference in size and the varying plan of the temple proper required some adjustment in the placement of the reliefs. Moreover, there were religious scenes in the Second Court where Ramesses II had battle scenes in the corresponding positions. The ruined condition of the Ramesseum makes it impossible to tell just how far the copying went, but it was clearly extensive. Often mistakes in the inscriptions at Medinet Habu arose from misunderstanding those of the Ramesseum or from careless copying.

Although the religious scenes may have been derivative, the scenes of Ramesses III's battles were original. On the outer wall at the west and on the west end of the north wall are episodes of a Nubian campaign and of the Libyan war of Year 5. Eastwards from these, continuing to the Second Pylon, are a series of events associated with the repulsion of an attempted invasion by the Sea Peoples in Year 8. The most notable scene is the first sea battle known in history. The two navies met in a harbour in the north-eastern delta and the invaders were driven off.

Three registers show the sequence of action of an Egyptian and an enemy ship. In the upper register the invading ship, with a duck head on the high prow, has had its sail caught by a grapnel thrown from the Egyptian ship and is being drawn to it. In the crow's nest of the defending vessel an expert with the sling picks off the enemy. In the scene below, the mast of the enemy ship is tilting and the ship listing. In the lower register the ships have drifted so that they point in opposite directions to their original positions; the enemy ship has capsized; the mast is broken; and there is a great rent in the sail made by the grapnel. On the surface of the bay float the bodies of the slain invaders.

The sea peoples had two distinctive headdresses, one a helmet with horns and sometimes a ball on top, the other a bandeau into which many feathers were inserted. The latter was worn by the Philistines and the Danians. This attempt to invade Egypt was part of a great migration; while some of this great wave of warriors struck by sea, others escorted ox-carts with women, children and baggage along the coastal road coming from Gaza. These, too, were met and defeated by the Egyptian troops.

Only a small part of the migratory people were engaged in this attack. Their kindred had already settled along the coast to the north and others had landed on the African shore west of Egypt, displacing the tribes there. One Libyan tribe sought to migrate into Egypt in the eleventh year of Ramesses III. After they had penetrated eastward fifty miles beyond the border fortress which was built on a crag named " Start of the Country " to the second fortress " Sand Castle ", they were met by the Egyptian army and decimated. The warriors killed numbered 2175.

When an Egyptian soldier felled an opponent in battle, he cut off his hand, and, if the man was uncircumcised, his sex organs. After the victory each soldier was rewarded from the booty according to the number of these grim trophies he had collected. The counting of all the dead, the prisoners and the booty was done in the presence of the king who gave out the rewards for valour. The scenes show such an accounting.

In their defeat 2052 Libyans, men, women and children, were taken captive, together with horses, asses, goats and sheep to a total of more than 42,000, about two-thirds of which were dedicated to the estates of Amon. The labour and the wealth so taken was used in the construction of the temples and the maintenance of the widespread estates from which produce came into the temple storehouse. In Papyrus Harris I Ramesses III counts 62,226 persons whom he gave into the service of his mortuary temple; many of these were captives from his wars. It may have been their descendants, and the descendants of those enslaved captives of earlier

79. Fallen colossus, the Ozymandyas of Diodorus, a red granite statue of Ramesses II, named " Re of the Rulers ", Ramesseum.

generations, who made up the bands of foreigners which terrorized the countryside in the latter part of the dynasty.

By the time the temple was finished the wars were over and Ramesses was free to come to his temple in western Thebes for celebrations and ceremonies. Many of these took place in the First Court, the south side of which formed the façade of the adjacent palace. In the middle of the wall was the window for the royal appearance. When first constructed there was under it a row of heads of prisoners, sculptured in the round, suggesting that they lay prostrate beneath the feet of the king. When a wooden balcony was added in front of the window so that Ramesses could have a view of the court unobstructed by the columns, the central heads were removed. A panel beneath the window shows Egyptians and foreigners in contests of fencing and wrestling. One of the wrestlers is warned by the referee not to commit a foul, as he is in the presence of Pharaoh.

The central block in the panel is the one from the Ramesseum which the Medinet Habu artists had copied. When Daressy made repairs to the temple he found a gap, and taking the block which the Ptolemies had quarried from the Ramesseum and brought to Medinet Habu, he trimmed it to fit the available space and set it in position; it fits with only a slight difference in scale.

On the northern side of the court the square pillars had against them squat figures of the king, not intended to be a portrait, but to symbolize kingship itself. Their identity is made clear by working the hieroglyphs of the prenomen of Ramesses into the decoration of the crown. The small figures of a prince and princess on either side of each statue again show that in Egyptian art size depended on the importance of the object and the needs of composition.

In the mortuary temple of Ramesses III each court and hall is higher than the one before, mounting up to the sanctuary for the bark of Amon. On the upper walls of three sides of the Second Court before the portico are scenes of great religious festivals. To the south is the Feast of Sokar, the god of the Old Kingdom necropolis at Sakkara, and on the north the Feast of Min. The latter combined a harvest festival with fertility aspects and the commemoration of the earlier kings.

In the feast Ramesses III is carried from his palace, seated on his portable throne, by officials and princes, accompanied by officiating priests, courtiers, musicians, dancers and a military guard. At the shrine of the god the king presents the morning offerings, then the ithyphallic statue of Min-Amon-Kamutef is carried on a float. Before the god go the king and queen and preceding them the white bull, the god's living symbol. Divine emblems and the statue of the deceased kings are carried in the parade. At one point four doves are released and instructed to go to the four corners of the earth to inform the gods that Ramesses III has become king. After songs and the recital of ritual the king is handed a ceremonial sickle with which he cuts a sheaf of wheat, the ears being fed to the bull. Then the god is returned to his shrine where the king performs the final rites of the festival.

In the register below the festival scenes on the north wall, the barks of the Theban gods come from their shrines to meet the bark of the king. The extensive texts give little information; Amon promises a multitude of blessings on Ramesses III and the king recounts his benefactions to the god. An inscription at the right compares the stability of the temple with the eternal order of the universe. " As long as the sky arches over the land and the sea and the bright sun shines, (as long as) the sun bark makes its daily journey and the ground waters encircle the Two Lands, so long shall the Mansion of Usermare-meriamon (the prenomen of Ramesses III), ' United with Eternity ', in the estate of Amon, continue to be the palace of the Lord of Gods (Amon)."

On the walls of the terrace, the portico of the temple proper, the main scenes are memorials of the coronation. Below is a procession of princes, left unnamed

80. The " Colossi of Memnon ", statues of Amenhotep III before his now vanished mortuary temple. The far colossus was the " vocal " Memnon; the near one bears the name " Ruler of Rulers ".

by Ramesses III. Later Ramesses IV put his name before the first figure and afterwards Ramesses VI identified the next two figures with himself, adding the names of his sons before the figures of some of the following princes. His eldest son and heir added his name in a cartouche during the few months of his rule.

Beyond the portico the temple proper had three hypostyle halls before the sanctuary of Amon. Over these was a high roof with a clerestory in the first hall. On the sides were many chapels and rooms and two contiguous temples.

On the south of the first hypostyle hall was the treasury, a suite of five rooms. The entrance was concealed by a panel across which the wall reliefs were continued. It was held in position by ties through holes in the edge of the stone doorway. Within the rooms are pictured temple furniture, a harp, chests, sphinxes and figures of the king holding offerings, all gold or gold-covered. Bags of raw gold, marked with their weight and source, are shown stacked up, as well as rings of gold and silver in orderly rows. Ingots of copper, shaped like animal skins, are laid out in order. If only a small part of the treasure shown on these walls was actually stored in these rooms, the riches were great indeed. All has long since disappeared; perhaps the jasper hand found in the vicinity was part of a statue with gold decorations, treasure which the thieves removed (Plate 89).

The admiration of Ramesses III for his predecessor Ramesses II led him to make a chapel for the bark of the earlier king next to the treasury. No earlier king not related to the reigning monarch was ever so honoured. At the time when the temples were being stripped of their treasure, it was reported that the bronze fittings of the double doors of the treasury had been stolen. No such doors exist in the treasury proper and it must have been the double doors of the sanctuary for the bark of Ramesses II which were despoiled. At the same time the fittings were stripped from the doors of the " slaughter house " on the opposite side of the hall. Here, in a room partly open to the sky for better ventilation, the meat offerings were kept until needed for the meals of the gods. Next to this room was a chapel for the bark of Sokar; the statue of the god Ptah still standing there had originally been made for the temple of Amenhotep III. At the east end of this row of chapels was one for offerings to the living king with his sons and daughters, all anonymous, bringing gifts to Ramesses III and his queen, in whose cartouche her name was never inscribed.[44]

Off the rear of this hall were two sanctuaries for barks, at the south for Montu and at the north for Amon of " United with Eternity ", the god of the mortuary temple. This Amon was Ramesses III himself and statues of this god existed before Ramesses' death. This dual role of the king is strange to the modern mind, but the ancient Egyptian saw no incongruity in the ruler making offerings to himself as a god.

The second hypostyle hall had an astronomical ceiling similar to that in the same position in the Ramesseum. In the south wall was the entry to the royal mortuary suite, one of the contiguous temples. Coronation ceremonies for Ramesses III in the underworld are among the scenes on the walls, with others showing copies of sections of the Book of the Dead. One room has another copy of the astronomical ceiling at the Ramesseum, copied with various errors.

On the opposite side of the second hypostyle hall was the doorway to the Re chapel, the second contiguous temple. This, like many chapels to the sun god, was known as a " Sunshade ". The main room was open to the sky and once had an altar at its centre. At the north end of the vestibule there was a stairway going up to the terrace above the rooms at the sides and rear of the temple proper.

Beyond the third hypostyle hall were the sanctuaries for the barks of the Theban Triad, Mut at the south, Khonsu at the north and Amon in the centre. A pedestal on which the bark rested is at one side of the centre room; it was found underneath

81. Glazed tiles from the main doorway of the palace of the mortuary temple of Ramesses III at Medinet Habu, showing bound prisoners, a Syrian and a Negro. *Cairo Museum*

the floor. It may have been made for the sanctuary of Amon of " United with Eternity ", for a dedication to this Amon is on one end, while on the other is an inscription to Amon of " Blessed through Monuments ", the Festival Hall of Thutmosis III at Karnak. This Amon almost certainly was identical with Thutmosis III himself.

To the north of the sanctuaries is a room with nine niches for the statues of the Ennead of this temple. Rooms at the rear were for the storage of various pieces of temple furniture and emblems used in services and festivals. In the Ptolemaic period some of the rooms still roofed were used as offices for officials and notations they wrote on the walls are still visible.

The palace south of the First Court had its counterpart at the Ramesseum, except that the latter had no bed chamber. The palace of Ramesses III had at its centre a reception hall, with the king's private apartments behind. Even here he kept the appearence of majesty; his living room had a dais, still preserved, on which stood his throne. To the east of this was the bedroom, a bed niche at one end. On the west was a bath. To the west of the king's apartment was a smaller one for the queen. Behind them both were three suites of two rooms, wardrobe and bath for other women in the entourage. The original palace was found to be too small and was enlarged after a few years. Only the ground plan of the palace was found by the excavators; they built up low walls on the foundations of the second palace, and these give a good idea of the architectural layout (Plate 86). Though the walls were of mud-brick, the decorations of the palace were rich and the main doorway, of stone, had many inlays, among them glazed tiles depicting bound prisoners (Plate 81).

The south wall of the temple had a calendar of offerings for the set feasts. On the west wall of the south wing of the First Pylon were two scenes of Ramesses III enjoying the sport of hunting (Plate 83). In the upper scene he is driving across the desert in his chariot, picking off wild game with his arrows. Below he is in the marshlands, standing on the tongue of his chariot, driving his spear into a wild bull. One bull has already been killed and another is dying. The realism of these hunting scenes places them among the best examples of Egyptian art.

The cult of Ramesses III continued down to the end of the dynasty. By this time the most valuable fittings had been stripped away, either stolen or sold in exchange for food supplies to support the offerings to the gods and pay the wages of the temple personnel. In letters and dispatches of this period the mortuary temple of Ramesses III had become known by the abbreviated designation of " The Mansion ". Within its precincts was the centre of the necropolis administration. Near the ruins of the western gate stood the office and residence of Butehamon whose name is known from many records. The pillars of his central hall have been set up in their original place.

The mortuary temples built by the successors of Ramesses III in the Twentieth Dynasty were less substantial and only a few remains of them have been found. After the end of this dynasty the rulers of Egypt were no longer buried at Thebes, except for a few whose suzerainty was recognized only locally. Just to the south of Medinet Habu a small temple, which had no relation to the deceased kings, was erected in the Ptolemaic period. Dedicated to Thoth, it is now known as Kasr el-Agouz. The outline draughtsman who laid out the design on the walls had a sure eye and steady hand, but the sculptor who followed him did some of the poorest work of the Ptolemaic period.

After the eleventh century B. C. no more names were added to the lists of the Lords of the West. The great millenium of Thebes had come to a sorry end and, with the collapse of the administration of the temples and tombs, those who had led The Southern City to world power were no longer honoured and protected.

82. Ramesses III ceremonially smiting prisoners, First Pylon of the mortuary temple at Medinet Habu, south tower, east face.

The Houses of Eternity

THE GODS LOVED EGYPT. The sun-god Re shone every day, seldom hiding himself behind clouds. In summer heat the north wind brought the cool breath of life. In the middle of summer Hapi, the inundation, swelled up from the river, watering the fertile land so that plants would start their growth as the days became cool. Not far below the surface the primeval ground water could be tapped, filling lakes and wells and providing water when the irrigation basins had been used up. Food plants grew rapidly and densely, barley, emmer and wheat for bread and beer, grapes for wine, fodder for cattle. In the pools grew the lotus and in the fields other flowers, many heavy with perfume, ready for making bouquets which the people loved. Bees provided honey and other sweetening was obtained from the carob pod. From flax came fibres for the weaving of linen cloth which was made from gossamer fineness to service weight. The fish of the river and the game of the desert provided food and sport. The mines in the desert gave gold, silver and copper. The Lebanon had timber to supply Egypt's greatest lack and a land as rich as Egypt was easily able to afford this and other imports.

The green band along the banks of the river, the marshes of the delta, the yellow sands of the desert hills, the ever blue skies by day and the brilliant stars by night— no Egyptian could imagine a more perfect paradise than the Two Lands. And surely paradise itself would be like this, another Nile valley.

The view of the after-life held by the earliest Egyptians can only be surmised from their burials. In their graves were placed jars of food and slate palettes on which they ground their eye paint. Like most primitive peoples they had a belief in some sort of a continued existence where these would be needed. As the country became unified, the kings built larger tombs, culminating in the pyramids. These had chapels for the presentation of offerings needed for the sustaining of life in the next world.

About the pyramids the members of the royal family and the officials of the government were given their own burial sites and tomb chapels. This clustering of the tombs of the members of the court has given rise to the interpretation that at this period the kings alone were immortal and that the rest obtained immortality only through them. Certainly the oldest texts treat the king as a god who came into the next world to be with his fellow gods. The earliest of these texts describe him ascending to the sky to dwell with the gods in the stars, but other texts speak of existence in the underworld. At all times in the history of Egyptian ideas of the after-life, there existed simultaneously differing conceptions of the other world which

168

to modern minds appear to be contradictory. This happened in part because, as new concepts arose, the old were never entirely discarded.

No written records have survived to make known to us the thoughts of ordinary people about the future life. However, the evidence of the tombs of private persons of the first three dynasties near Helwan and Turah, independent of any royal tomb, shows that these people expected immortality in their own right. Other tombs were grouped about the pyramids, not because their occupants had to depend upon the ruler for immortality, but because the court was expected to continue its function in the other world. Even more important, their position also gave those buried near the monarch the privilege of receiving in their chapels offerings first presented to the king.

It is true that the funerary texts used by the kings in their pyramids from the end of the Fifth to the end of the Sixth Dynasties had derived from versions in the tombs of non-royal persons, but the texts for royal use had already developed considerably by the time the first known copies were made. They may have stemmed from a common inheritance, the texts in the pyramids having been adapted from those for non-royal use. With the decentralization of government, persons of position and means built their tombs near their provincial homes, providing for their own funerary offerings rather than receiving them from offerings first presented to the king.

The earliest known tombs in Thebes come from the end of the Sixth Dynasty. The reliefs which have survived follow patterns established in the Memphite necropolis but show the work of provincial craftsmen. Some fragments suggest that artisans trained in the north worked in Thebes. Throughout the early part of the Eleventh Dynasty the steles of both private persons and royalty were work of provincial artists, as their strange forms show.

The unification of Egypt under Montuhotep II again made available to the Thebans artisans trained in Memphis. The king employed these in his mortuary temple, but such craftsmen were not always available to nobles whose tombs were quarried in the nearby hills. The remaining fragments of decoration of the tomb chapel of the Vizier Dagi (T. T. No. 103) [45] and of the tombs of the Chancellor Kheti (T. T. No. 311) and of the Princess Neferu (T. T. No. 319) show painted bas-reliefs and wall paintings of excellent quality. On the other hand, the wall paintings in the tomb chapel of the Custodian of the Royal Harem, Djar (T. T. No. 366), were done by a less skilled artist. In the middle range of skill in execution are the wall paintings on the pillars of the tomb chapel of General Intef (T. T. No. 386) now being excavated by the German Archaeological Institute.

All of these tombs, and others of the period, were in the sides of the nearby hills or in the floor of the valley not far from the causeway leading to the temple of Montuhotep II, so situated that offerings from the temple might easily be brought to them.

The unfinished tomb of Montuhotep III was at the base of the cliff somewhat to the south of Deir el-Bahri; north of the tomb, on a spur of the hill, not far from the tomb of Queen Inhapi, an official of this king, Meket-re, built a tomb chapel. Whatever decoration may have been on the walls has disappeared, but in a side room was found a group of models. The careful work of Herbert Winlock ensured that they were removed and restored with proper attention. These magnificent wooden figures can be seen in the Cairo Museum and in the Metropolitan Museum in New York in almost their original condition.

The largest model shows Meket-re seated on a porch with his scribes and overseers inspecting his cattle as they are driven past. Another shows a stable where cattle are being fattened by forced feeding. Two model houses have porticos with gaily decorated columns and ceilings, the courtyards in front of them planted with trees.

Several groups represent buildings about Meket-re's estate. There is a granary and a bakery, the latter showing the preparation of bread and beer. In a spinning and weaving establishment the process of turning flax into cloth can be followed through the different stages. Another building has a carpenter's shop. In all of these models there is detailed attention to the tools and work in progress.

For business journeys Meket-re was provided with two pairs of ships, one in each pair with sails set for going southward against the current and the other with sails furled, mast lowered and oars manned, for faring downstream. An escort of kitchen boats provided food for the travellers. Four yachts were provided for more casual trips and one small boat was used for fowling and fishing in the marshes. The commercial fishermen had two canoes made of bound reeds between which they dragged a net to catch fish more rapidly than could a sportsman with a spear (Plate 4). Several offering bearers were among the models of which the best were two well-made figures of women, 28 inches high, bearing crates on their heads, one containing food and the other drink.

These well carved and painted models are a far cry from the paddle-dolls with clay lumps for heads and hair of twisted string ending in clay balls found in many Eleventh Dynasty tombs (Plate 84). They were hardly playthings for children; more likely they represented Nubian dancing girls or concubines. Their bodies show tattooing and there were beaded girdles about their waists. Such tattooed bodies have been found in Nubia, though of a much later date, and the styling of the hair still is to be found among Nubian women.

All of these models were placed in the tombs so that the deceased might enjoy familiar surroundings in the next world. By magic they would turn into the things they represented, servants going about their usual tasks and animals to be slaughtered for food. Tomb walls showed similar scenes in paintings and reliefs which later almost entirely replaced the models.

One class of models continued, small servant figures known as shawabtis or ushebtis, a name which underwent a metathesis and a change in meaning among the Egyptians. The first name came, perhaps, from the wood of which they were made; the second means "answerer". These appear first in the Ninth Dynasty and served as substitute mummies in case the body of the deceased were destroyed. Later, still keeping the mummiform shape, they became servant figures of a particular sort. In Egypt most citizens were liable to a kind of *corvèe*, enforced labour on government projects. These figures, usually one for each day of the year, were to answer if the deceased should be drafted for labour in the next world. Not only were they placed in the tombs of ordinary people; they were placed in royal tombs as well. Royal figurines, especially in the Eighteenth Dynasty, were often works of art. Those of private persons were usually made of faience with a blue glaze. Later the forms deteriorated and even those made for royalty were crude, such as the ones from the burial of Queen Henuttawy of the Twenty-first Dynasty (Plate 43).

When the court moved to Lisht at the beginning of the Twelfth Dynasty, a royal cemetery was established nearby and most of the officials were buried in the vicinity of the rulers they had served. From this period only one decorated tomb has been identified in the Theban necropolis. Yet there were other burials, for somewhere in the necropolis was found the blue glazed figure of a hippopotamus, with the plants of its pool painted on its side (Plate 44).

In the Twelfth Dynasty a tomb chapel was made for Senet, the wife of Intefoker, Vizier of Amenemhat I (T. T. No. 60), who had a tomb in the necropolis at Lisht. Senet, who survived him and died in the next reign, was buried about half way up the hill of Sheikh Abd-el-Gurna. A long corridor extends into the hillside and in a room at the end a shaft leading to the burial chamber was let into the floor.

The walls of the corridor and the end room were painted, rather crudely, though

83. Ramesses III hunting desert game (above) and wild bulls in the marshes (below), First Pylon of the mortuary temple at Medinet Habu, south tower, west face.

84

quite an improvement on those of Djar. None of the pigments is very bright and the scenes seem dull compared with those of later tombs in the vicinity. Though the scenes of daily life derive from those of the Old Kingdom tombs, there are many new details of the funerary ceremonies which are common to the tomb chapels in the Eighteenth Dynasty.

The scenes at the entrance show planting and ploughing, irrigation by men carrying buckets suspended from a yoke, the grain harvest and the vintage. Most of the north walls show the pleasures and occupations of daily life. Where Intefoker once appeared in scenes of fowling and fishing from reed canoes in the marsh his figures have been removed.

This erasure of his figure and sometimes of his name from the tomb walls is a phenomenon not easy to explain. It seems almost certain that the tomb originally was his, though it is possible that it was only through convention that his figure was shown. Senet was also named in his tomb chapel at Lisht, but too few fragments remain to tell whether or not his figure was erased there. Such a mutilation of the figure of the owner is common in Theban tomb chapels. In one of the finest of these, that of Rekhmire, vizier in the latter years of Thutmosis III and the early years of Amenhotep II, the name and figure of the deceased were erased throughout and at ground level were additionally defaced by a covering of red paint. Kenamun, Head Royal Steward and, because his mother was a nurse of Amenhotep II, foster-brother of the king, suffered the same fate and in his tomb most of the figures of his wife were obliterated as well. Another influential official, the Steward of Queen Tiy, Kheruef, never finished his tomb nor was he buried in it; in most instances his name and figure were removed.

Such examples could be multiplied. On the whole, there has been no attempt made to connect the erasures with known historical events. A change in political fortunes may have brought disgrace on an official, as certainly happened to Kheruef during the Amarna revolution. Since the tombs were under royal patronage, the destruction must have been done with the approval of the administration or even by its order. This vengeful action in so many cases suggests a political instability only occasionally shown in other records.

To return to the tomb of Senet. Though it is only speculation and not history, it is possible that Senusert I believed Intefoker to be involved in the assassination of his father, either actively, or by failure to protect the king, or merely by favouring the other claimant to the throne.

The marshes where Intefoker indulged in his sport also produced food for general consumption. Here men are catching fish in a draw net, while others are working a trap net for birds. This was placed on the ground and baited. One man kept watch and when a good number of fowl were feeding he gave a signal to three men hidden in the rushes to pull the net closed.

Following a scene of Intefoker hunting game in a desert preserve, the walls present the domestic offices of the bakery and the slaughter house. The bakery made both bread and beer and it is not always possible to discern which product is being produced. But here the process of brewing is particularly well illustrated. The grain, usually first malted, is ground on a slanting stone, a deep channel at the bottom collecting the flour. This is sieved. Dough is mixed and long narrow pottery cones are filled with it. These operations are all performed by women. Then the men take over and the cones are stacked horizontally on a grill under which a brush fire is lit to give the loaves a partial baking. The man tending the fire is saying, " I'm doing what you wished, but look! here's the trouble. The fire-wood is green. Look! I'm going to curse."

The partially baked loaves are then pounded in a mortar together with an equal quantity of dates. A workman complains about the dates he has to use. " This

84. Wooden " doll ", perhaps representing a nubian dancing girl. Eleventh Dynasty. *Cairo Museum*

85. Forepart of a lion, one of the pair symbolic of the god Aker. Wall-painting in the tomb of Queen Nefertari, Valley of the Tombs of the Queens.

lot of dates in the bin is stale. If only I could see it swell up and become fresh." The pounded bread and dates are mixed with water to constitute a mash which, when it has stood for the proper time, is strained and the wort collected in a jar. The remaining draff was used for food, sometimes eaten while still moist, sometimes pressed into cakes and dried. A boy with a bowl begs the brewer, " Give me some draff; I'm starved." The brewer curses him, " Damn you and damn the one who bore you through the hippopotamus charm. You eat more than a king's ploughman. You're already stuffed." After the beer had been fermented properly it was bottled in pottery jugs which were then stoppered.

In the Moscow Mathematical Papyrus, found by a member of the Abd-el-Rassul family near Deir el-Bahri, eight of the twenty problems are concerned with beer-making and the relative prices of grain and dates used in the process. One of these, translated into modern terms, goes as follows, " A man exchanges for emmer a jug of beer made of equal amounts of barley malt and dates. The beer has the strength of two jugs to the gallon of ingredients. The dates are worth three times as much, and the emmer two and two-thirds times as much, as the barley malt. How much emmer did he receive? " The answer is three-eighths of a gallon of emmer.

In the slaughter house a fowl is roasted on a hand spit over a charcoal fire and meat is grilled on a brazier. Strips of flesh are cut from a slaughtered ox and hung on a line to dehydrate, an ancient ancestor of jerked beef. The skin of the animal is scraped and pounded in preparation for tanning. All these familiar household affairs are similar to those shown in Meket-re's models of only a century earlier.

Norman Davies noted that the rear part of the tomb chapel of Senet and Intefoker showed traces of a hot but almost smokeless fire. He believed that this conflagration had taken place in ancient times, but it may have been a relatively recent occurrence, explained by a story related by James Bruce, who had been attacked by the people of Gurna.

" A number of robbers, who much resemble our gypsies, live in the holes in the mountains above Thebes. They are outlaws, punished by death if found elsewhere. Osman Bey, an ancient governor of Girgé, unable to suffer any longer the disorders committed by these people, ordered a quantity of dried faggots to be brought together, and, with his soldiers, took possession of the face of the mountain where the greatest number of these wretches were. He then ordered all their caves to be filled with this dry brush-wood, to which he set fire, so that most of them were destroyed; but they have since recruited their numbers, without changing their manners."

The tomb chapel of Senet stood alone on the hill, as far as evidence shows, for about four centuries.[46] Then, beginning with the Eighteenth Dynasty, this area on the hill and a quarry to the north-east of it, as well as the hillsides of Dra Abu-el-Naga, Khokha and Gurnet Murai and the low-lying desert before them, were used for tomb after tomb until they were literally honeycombed with chapels and passages to burial chambers. Often the quarrymen broke from one tomb into another and the tunnels of grave robbers, ancient and modern, added other passages. Court-yards of a larger tomb were used by later generations to quarry smaller chapels. Thus the large sunken court of the tomb chapel of Kheruef had the entrances of eight intrusive tombs off it and four others containing enough decoration to be given numbers were broken through into the tomb of Kheruef or into the later intrusive tombs. In addition to these, a number of small rooms were quarried into parts to receive later burials.

All tomb chapels which have some decoration or from which has come some notable discovery have been given numbers and more than 400 of these have been listed. Some from the Eighteenth Dynasty have excellent bas-reliefs which, if finished, were originally painted. With few notable exceptions these are little known.

86. Palace of Ramesses III, Medinet Habu, with original stone work re-erected in place and mud-brick walls built up on the original foundations.

174

87

88

Despoilers cut out many details for sale to collectors. Under the situation which existed in the earlier days of exploration, this was unavoidable, but it is disturbing to discover that one of the finest reliefs showing Queen Tiy, found and photographed in 1903 by Howard Carter, was ruined by rapacious thieves who cut the head and bust from the wall and sold it to a leading European museum a few years later.

Until after the middle of the last century most of the known tomb chapels were inhabited by the local people and today many a dwelling in Gurna is in a tomb or in an extension from it. This explains some of the damage the tombs have suffered.

If the stone surface was good, the decoration was painted directly on the smoothed walls or on a gypsum wash applied to them. Often no attempt was made to smooth off the stone. It was left rough and a heavy coat of plaster was applied to get an even surface for painting. A cheaper method was to coat the rough walls with mud plaster and apply gypsum to that. Several hundred unnumbered tombs in the necropolis now with rough walls were once finished this way.

Many of the New Kingdom chapels have, after the entry, a transverse hall extending equal distances from the doorway, and opposite the door a passage extending to the rear, often with a small room at the end. At the end of the passage or opposite it in the additional room there usually was a niche to hold a statue of the deceased and his wife, or a statue group cut out of the living rock.

These tomb chapels were prepared as everlasting places of rest for the deceased and his family. These monuments have led some who have studied them to conclude that the ancient Egyptians were possessed by a morbid preoccupation with death. Just the opposite was true; they were so in love with life along the Nile river that they sought to assure its continuance forever.

Yet even in this hope there was some scepticism. A number of tomb chapels have the text of songs sung to the accompaniment of a harp which reflect this spirit. One of these " Songs of the Harper ", from the tomb chapel of Thothemhab (T. T. No. 194), goes thus:

I have entertained you since you came on earth,
While your natural power continued.
Never stop doing what you desire,
Until the day you peg out.
As for those who have passed on since creation,
None has ever come back again.
When their names are searched out by enquiry,
Not even a brick of their houses is found.
Their faces know no holiday to fulfil their dreams;
Their goods have been left to others.
They are departed; they have passed away.

The Vizier of Thutmosis III, Rekhmire (T. T. No. 100), who continued in office into the next reign, showed on the walls of his tomb chapel the responsibilities of his office and its rewards. Uniquely, the ceiling of the back passage of his tomb slopes up to the rear, paralleling the slope of the hill. This added much wall surface to an already large tomb.

In the front hall are scenes of his induction into office and an accompanying text tells of this and the duties of his position. There were two viziers, one living in Thebes and one in the Northern Residence.[47] In general, except for the administration of the particular frontiers, their duties were the same. With the royal treasurer the vizier administered the entire section of the country. Since there are

87. Seti I worshipping the sun-god Re, drawing on a pillar in the tomb of the king, Valley of the Tombs of the Kings.

88. The northern constellations, the bull and the driver representing Ursa Major, painting on ceiling, burial chamber of tomb of Seti I, Valley of the Tombs of the Kings.

no corresponding texts on the duty of a treasurer, we do not know the exact division of duties, but apparently the collection of taxes was the duty of the vizier, while the treasurer kept the storehouses and vaults.

The vizier regulated trade with foreign countries, equipping ships and bargaining for trade goods. He arranged for the comfort and protection of the king when travelling. All legal matters were under his jurisdiction and many cases came to him for judgment. His servants had to be as incorruptible as he, showing no partiality, receiving no favour and standing aloof from all with whom they had official business. Regulation of farm lands and supervision of irrigation came under his jurisdiction. Full records were kept of all matters and these had to be filed in the proper archives, to be given only on receipt. Confidential papers could be seen by the vizier alone and could not be removed from the archive.

With all this in his charge Rekhmire must have been a busy man and only with good organization could his work have been accomplished. The following excerpt from his biography may sound somewhat smug but it does show his high sense of social responsibility and personal integrity.

" I judged (impartially) between the pauper and the wealthy. I rescued the weakling from the bully. I warded off the rage of the bad-tempered and I repressed the acts of the covetous. I cooled down the temper of the infuriated. I wiped away tears by satisfying need. I appointed the son and heir to the position of his father. I gave bread to the hungry, water to the thirsty, meat, beer and clothing to him who had none. I succoured the old man by giving him my staff and caused old women to say, ' What a gracious act! '

" I hated evil acts and never committed one. I caused liars to be strung up by the heels. I was guiltless in the sight of God. No informed person said about me, ' What has he done? ' When I adjudicated weighty claims, I caused both parties to settle peacefully. I deprived no one of justice for reward. I was never in any way deaf to the empty-handed and I swear I never took a bribe from anyone."

Other scenes in the hall showed the collection of taxes and gave the kinds and amounts coming from the district administrative centres, but all are too badly preserved to give much economic information. The usual hunting scenes and agricultural occupations are shown and Rekhmire pictures the sacred furniture he sent to the temples.

The finest of the paintings in this hall is a group of panels showing foreign peoples bringing their merchandise and tribute. These peoples, with their varying costumes and products, appear in one of the best scenes of this nature, of which there are several examples in the tomb chapels of the Eighteenth Dynasty.

From such scenes it appears that foreign delegations had to be led by one of their chiefs, if not composed of them; certainly the dignity of the Egyptians demanded that they receive no one whose standing was less than that of an aristocrat. In the top panel the chiefs of Punt bring in the same products which were brought back not many years earlier by Hatshepsut's expedition. There are myrrh trees and myrrh, ebony, pelts and exotic animals, ostrich plumes and eggs, ivory and apes (but no peacocks). The people of the Aegean isles and coastlands carry golden vases of exotic design and decoration so much admired in Egypt. Nubian products are similar to those from Punt except that there is no myrrh; instead there are giraffes, cattle and hunting dogs. From Syria come other vessels of gold, horses and chariots, and animals rarely seen in Egypt, the Syrian bear and elephant. In the lower panel are captives and hostages taken in military campaigns to the south and north.

On the beginning of the south side of the passage are the workmen and warehouses attached to the temple of Amon. Into the temple are brought jugs of wine and lengths of linen. Further on there are workshops, those devoted to rope mak-

89. Red jasper hand, originally attached to a statue, found at Medinet Habu. Eighteenth to Twentieth Dynasties. *Cairo Museum*

90. Glass bottle, from the tomb of the Fan-bearer Maiherpri, Valley of the Tombs of the Kings. About the middle of the Eighteenth Dynasty. *Cairo Museum*

91. Green schist statue of the hippopotamus goddess Taweris. Twenty-fifth Dynasty. *Cairo Museum*

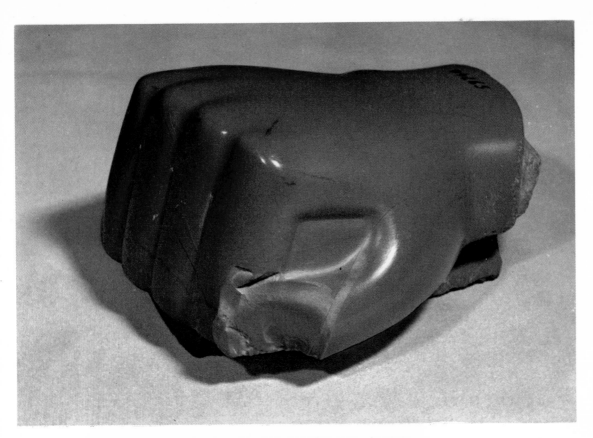

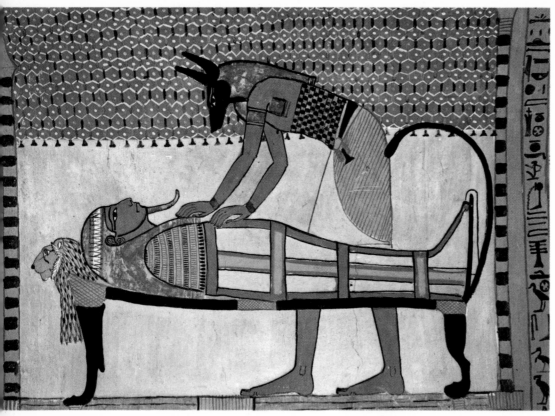

ing, leather work and the skilled craft of the cabinet-maker. The process of fine gold-work is shown from melting the metal and pouring it into moulds to the burnishing of vases. The bellows for the fires under the crucibles are operated by foot, but since there is no return-spring to expand them, the workmen have to pull them into the inflated position by attached ropes. Brick-making and building have been discussed in an earlier chapter. The scenes showing the sculptors' studios have been partly destroyed, but in what remains we can see the finishing touches being put on royal colossi and a sphinx.

These examples give only a faint idea of the wealth and variety of ancient industries preserved on the walls of the various tomb chapels. The similarity of the same type of scenes from tomb to tomb suggests that the artists had rolls of papyrus which had on them scenes customarily used in the decoration of tomb chapels and that these were drawn on as the occasion demanded. In some cases there may have been copying from one chapel to another, but the basic sources were available elsewhere. The skill of the artists varied from tomb to tomb and from period to period and the costumes worn by affluent officials and their families represented the style of the day. Only in the elaboration and addition of minor details was there any scope for the imagination and originality of the individual artist; otherwise the representations show the executive skill of the artisan only in reproducing a set and conventional theme.

Much of the remaining walls of the passage is given over to funerary rites. A large section is devoted to the memorial meal for the dead, attended by family and friends. In this the men and women are separated and served by musicians and youths of their own sex. How far the scene represents actual events and how far it should be interpreted symbolically is difficult to decide. Rekhmire's mother, for instance, who had died some years previously, is shown seated on a chair being served with wine. The guests, however, are seated on mats laid on the ground.

The musicians accompanying the singers, and often singing themselves, play on the harp, the lute and the tambourine. The guests wear cones of perfumed fat perched on their heads; the heat of the body melts the fat so that it runs down over their hair and shoulders. The young servants pass them floral collars and bouquets and serve them with food and wine. The wine seems the more popular and there is evidence that on these occasions many of the guests found pleasure in getting drunk.

In such scenes, here and in other tombs, artists paid more attention to the women and girls than to the men and boys and the former show more grace and more variation in attitude than the latter. In the tomb of Nakht, Astronomer of Amon in the reign of Thutmosis IV (T. T. No. 52), one of the three guests sitting on a mat is turning to offer a taste of her fruit to one of her companions who is hiding her own fruit (Plate 51). In the same reign the deceased Accountant of the Granary of Amon, Djeserkareseneb (T. T. No. 38), is being offered a floral necklace and a bowl of wine by his daughters while a young woman harpist entertains (Plate 49). One of the guests at this memorial meal is being presented with a floral necklace (Plate 50).

Variations in styles of dress are shown in these scenes. The women feasting in memory of Nakht wear dresses which cover them well, while the guests and performers at Djeserkareseneb's funeral have considerable décolletage. The serving-girls are nude except for a necklace and a narrow girdle worn low on the hips. Indeed, in this and in the style of their coiffure they show similarities with the Eleventh Dynasty paddle-dolls, though the serving-girls are not tattooed.

The end of the south wall of the passage in the tomb chapel of Rekhmire has the fullest representation of a funerary procession shown in an Eighteenth Dynasty tomb. Some of the elements of this ceremony go back at least to the Fifth Dynasty, while

92. Red granite statue, found near the sanctuary of the bark of Amon built by Alexander the Great, at the Luxor Temple, and often identified with this king but actually almost a century later.

93. The funerary god Anubis resuscitating the mummy of the deceased, the Servant of the Place of Truth, Sennodjem, wall-painting in the burial chamber. Reign of Ramesses II. Theban Tomb No. 1

94. "Opening of the Mouth" ceremony performed in front of the mummy of the deceased, wall-painting in the Tomb chapel of the Royal Sculptors Nebamon and Ipuky. Reign of Amenhotep III. Theban Tomb No. 181

others appear for the first time in the tomb of Senet or even later. The full significance of these episodes is not always clear, but apparently they began only after the embalming process and wrapping of the mummy was completed.

Careful examination of a large number of mummies in the light of the limited documentary evidence which has come down to us makes it possible to determine the method used to preserve bodies. As soon as possible after death the corpse was delivered to the embalmers. In a few cases there seems to have been some delay, perhaps because death took place in one of the few places where embalmers were not near at hand, and decomposition had set in. Through an incision made in the left side of the abdomen, the organs other than the heart were removed. They were separated, dried and packed in the four canopic jars. The brain was removed through the nostrils with a long-handled narrow spoon. Then the body was packed inside and out with dry natron, a mixture of sodium carbonates which occurs naturally but is often contaminated with varying quantities of sodium chloride and sodium sulphate.

The desiccation took forty days, at the end of which period the salts were removed and the body washed. From the end of the Eighteenth Dynasty onward an attempt was made to restore the body to a more natural appearance, the extent depending in part on the station and prosperity of the deceased. Padding was introduced into the muscles of the limbs, and the cheeks filled with pads. Onions or stones were placed under the eyelids. The wrapping with bandages was elaborate, and at various times not only royal mummies but those of private persons had many amulets bound between the layers of bandage.

The full preparation of the mummy and the funerary ceremonies took seventy days. When ready for burial the mummy was placed in the coffin which was put into a catafalque mounted on a sledge; this was pulled by oxen to the tomb. The wall paintings show a great number of rites on the journey. These were designed to prepare the deceased for the proper introduction into the next world. There were visits to shrines of funerary gods, offerings made to and for the deceased, all these accompanied by the appropriate spells. Dancers performed, one group wearing crowns of a reed frame, similar in shape to the white crown of the king.

A number of times there appears a wrapped object, often pear shaped, sometimes with a human head protruding, often placed on a sledge following the catafalque. This has been interpreted as a representation of an unmummified corpse with legs drawn up in the foetal position, as in burials of the prehistoric period.[48] But it is difficult to understand such a survival, as it implies the existence of two bodies. This wrapped object, called the " teknu ", may have represented the placenta of the deceased, since the placenta was considered to have an identity with the child at birth.

On one of the walls of the passage of Rekhmire's tomb the almost endless episodes of the " Opening of the Mouth " ceremony are depicted, by which the mummy was magically revivified; the same ceremony was used to bring statues and reliefs to life. When the rites were completed, the person lived again in his house of eternity and in the next world. The relation between these two is not clear to us and probably was not to the Egyptians. The spirit of the deceased could come into the tomb chapel and partake of the offerings and have communion with those gathered for the memorial meal.

Most of the burial chambers of the private tombs in Western Thebes, except those of the workmen who lived in Deir el-Medineh, were crudely constructed and finished and could be reached only by tortuous passages. Very few had funerary texts and only one with decoration similar to that in a tomb chapel is known. This is the burial chamber of the mayor of Thebes, Sennefer (T. T. No. 96), who held office under Amenhotep II. Access to the chamber is by a stairway descending from one side of the court of the now inaccessible chapel.

95. Container for eye-paint, small wooden figure of a man carrying jar. Eighteenth Dynasty.

The ceiling of the main chamber was left rough by the quarrymen and the covering plaster followed the undulations in the rock. Part was decorated with a grape-vine and the uneven surface gave added charm to the pattern. A very fine granite statue group of Sennefer seated beside his first wife Senetnay, who was royal nurse, is in the Cairo Museum. Standing between them against the chair is their daughter Mutneferet (Plate 48). Sennefer appears here as a somewhat obese moon-faced man in the prime of life. All three figures wear wigs appropriate to their age and sex. Offering inscriptions which run down the skirts of Sennefer and his wife show signs of wear from the offerings laid on their laps through the years.

It is interesting to compare the statue with a picture of Sennefer on one of the columns of his tomb chamber, where he is seated under a persea tree with his second wife Meryt sitting on a mat by his side (Plate 54). Before him is a table with jars of beer and wine. In the statue he appears bare from the waist up; in the painting he wears a tunic. In both, gold bands are about his upper arms and gold bracelets adorn his wrists. About his neck is a "choker" of several rows of gold rings or shells, probably a present from Amenhotep II. Between his breasts he wore, strung on a cord, two heart shaped medallions, unique ornaments which were his proudest possession. The painting shows that one was gold and one was silver.

The tomb chamber was admired by Greek tourists and in another picture one of them has painted on one of the medallions, in good hieroglyphs, the name Alexander. Among the funerary scenes shown was the voyage to Abydos. More often in picture than in reality the mummy of the deceased was taken down river from Thebes to this city which was believed to be the burial place of Osiris. On the voyage north the barge with the deceased and his wife, shown as living persons, was pulled by a boat manned by oarsmen, who took advantage of the current; on the trip upstream the towing ship has the sail set to catch the north wind (plate 8).

The tomb of Sennefer, on the hill of Sheikh Abd-el-Gurna, is one row or level above the tomb of Rekhmire; on the level above the latter is the tomb chapel of Kenamon, Head Steward of Amenhotep II (т. т. No. 93). This chapel has suffered considerably from the persecution of the deceased and from the smoke and destruction caused by its use as a dwelling. Were it not for this damage in composition, in use of colour and in imaginative adaption of the old designs it would be one of the finest in the necropolis.

On the lap of Kenamon's mother sits the infant Amenhotep II, his figure that of a miniature adult. The stool beneath his feet consists of a group of kneeling, bound captives. Over his head the protective bird is neither the falcon nor the vulture, but the goose of Amon.

Another scene shows gifts to the king, the finest examples of the products of the royal workshops for the year, presented to Amenhotep on the first New Year's Day of his reign. They consist of statues of the king in various woods and stone, one of his mother and one of his great-grandfather, Thutmosis I, as well as sphinxes with the head of the king, stone vases and gold jewelry and vessels. Of these there was a single example of each kind, but of other objects, shields, quivers, bows, chariots and other battle equipment there were large numbers.

In the passage are remnants of a hunting scene which, in its original state, was the most striking presentation of the subject ever executed in the Theban necropolis. In most examples, the game is shown in a fenced area, a kind of corral into which beaters have driven the desert animals. Usually they are neatly arranged in registers with horizontal ground lines, as in the tomb of Senet. In the hunting scene in the chapel of Rekhmire the ground lines are no longer straight, but meander like paths; the animals are still rather stiff and arranged in groups, the head of the animal in the rear projecting a bit forward of the one immediately in front.

On the wall in Kenamon's chapel no corral is shown nor the usual arrows show-

96. The Servant of the Place of Truth, Nebenmaat, his daughter Hol beside him, playing draughts with his wife Meretseger, wall-painting in his burial chamber. Nineteenth-Twentieth Dynasty. Theban Tomb No. 219

97. The funerary god Anubis attending the mummy of a fish, wall-painting in the burial chamber of the tomb of the Servant of the Place of Truth, Khabekhnet. Reign of Ramesses II.

187

ered by the hunter, and the ground lines appear as desert tracks. These divide the composition into segments of varied size and shape fitting the animals shown. Along the tracks plants and shrubs grow in all directions. A pair of ostriches and their young feed on the ground and nearby jackals run in and out of their burrows. The calf of a wild cow lies curled up and a hare hides under a bush. A pregnant wild she-ass has been chased by jackals and has begun her labour; as she drops her foal a jackal stands by ready to seize it. The largest and best preserved of the vignettes shows a dog holding an ibex at bay. The gradation of the colour in the grey coat of the ibex and the dappling of the paint gives an excellent representation of the thick hair of this animal.

In the tomb chapel of Kenamon, as in many others, there are scenes of the presentation of offerings for the deceased and the gods. In the tomb chapel of Minnakht, the Overseer of Egyptian Granaries (T. T. No. 87), still farther up the hill, the only wall with painting at all well preserved shows servants bringing meat and bread offerings for the sustenance of the owner of the tomb (Plate 60). Jars of wine and beer are standing in vine covered shelters to keep them cool and before each is a small stand stacked with bread, a servant purifying it by pouring a libation and burning incense in a brazier. Two porters bearing a chest mounted on poles are preceded by a man who is purifying the way and another who is holding two formal bouquets. Often the figures of the offering-bearers become almost pure decoration, arranged on each side of the funerary stele in the end wall of the hall, as in the tomb of Nakht (Plate 58).

Offerings heaped on tables are often more elaborate than those shown on the wall of the tomb of Minnakht. One such pile of offerings, with cuts of meat, flowers and vegetables, placed before Osiris, is shown in the Nineteenth Dynasty tomb chapel of Userhet (T. T. No. 51), the High Priest of the mortuary temple of Thutmosis I (Plate 64). The simpler conceptions of the Eighteenth Dynasty have been abandoned and the desire for showiness has taken over.

One part of the funerary scene in the tomb chapel of Minnakht shows the villa of this official, before it steps descending to an excavated pool on which floats a boat carrying the coffin. Such pools, stocked with fish, with lotuses growing and birds swimming, appear regularly in tomb chapels. Similar ponds are sometimes shown in front of the tomb itself. Those which have been found in front of chapels of the Ramesside period are diminutive and pathetic affairs: the basins made of pieces of stone were less than a yard long and half as wide and not more than four inches deep. Beside each was the stump of a palm, the trunk never more than three inches through.

In the lower left corner of the funerary scene in the chapel of Minnakht is a group of mourning women wailing, beating their breasts and throwing dust on their hair (Plate 47). Again this depiction can be paralleled many times in the chapels in the Theban necropolis. Often the wife of the deceased is shown weeping before the mummy of her husband, as in the chapel of the two sculptors, Nebamon and Ipuky (Plate 94), who lived at the time of Amenhotep III (T. T. No. 181). These two men plied the same craft, held much the same offices, and successively married the same woman, Henutneferet. The two coffins do not represent the two men, however, but only two episodes in the " Opening of the Mouth " ceremony. The mummy has a formal bouquet before it and on its head the same cone of scented fat that was placed on the heads of the guests at the funerary banquet.

Several groups of mourning women appear on a wall of the chapel of the vizier Ramose (T. T. No. 55), a contemporary of the two sculptors, who lived, as did they, into the reign of Amenhotep IV. One group of five mourning women is seated, tears running down their cheeks, while they throw dust on their heads (Plate 46). There is more charm in this painting than in that of the women in the tomb of Minnakht.

Only one wall of Ramose's chapel was painted; the other two decorated walls were intended to be done in bas-relief, but were left unfinished and the other wall surfaces were never begun. The work of the sculptors shows care in modelling and sharpness of line. However, the subjects depicted, in a large part Ramose and his relatives, are static, since they are shown only that they may partake of the benefits accruing to Ramose. The fine figure of Ipuia, the mother of Ramose, is well executed, but has no particular individuality, presenting her as a comely young woman (Plate 33). There is no real difference between her features and those of Werel, shown with her husband, the Overseer of Royal Horses, Maiy (Plate 35). The work of the sculptor in this tomb is technically of the best in Egypt, but the subjects gave no real opportunity for the artist to express his creative abilities.[49]

The chapel of Ramose received its last decoration in the Amarna period. On the rear wall of the hall Amenhotep IV was shown, on the left of the doorway, in the conventional manner, but on the right the Amarna style was used, though the new name of the king had not yet been adopted. In the latter the faces of the king and Nefertiti have been hammered out, but their outline is clearly visible and the usual anatomical peculiarities appear. The rays of Aten, shining above the royal couple, extend life to their nostrils. The monarch stands in a window of appearance bestowing honours on Ramose, while behind the vizier, sketched in by the outline draughtsmen and never carved, appear the courtiers and foreign visitors. It was only on the figures of the king and queen that the sculptor had begun his work. Though a change in artistic style had accompanied the political change, the artists had lost none of their skill and had been freed from some of the ancient conventions, though the new ones brought restrictions of their own.

Another official contemporary with Ramose was given a tomb chapel even larger than that of the vizier. This was Kheruef (T. T. No. 192), whose position as Steward of Queen Tiy gave him great influence. The rear part of his chapel was planned to be the same in size and design as that of Ramose, while before it there was to be a great open court surrounded by a portico, with an entrance on the side opposite the door of the hall. The court was quarried, the hall completed, the passage roughed out and the portico of the court begun, but the quarrymen were plagued by the poor and brittle quality of the stone. The wall of the rear portico, the entrance to the hall beyond and the front entrance to the court were the only parts decorated and these reliefs have suffered greatly from deliberate destruction in ancient times, from the action of salts in the stone in certain parts and from modern robbers. The technical quality of the relief is as good as that in the chapel of Ramose and may have been done by the same artists; the content, however, is of much greater interest.

The left of the wall of the portico pictures the celebration of the first jubilee of Amenhotep III, the right half the celebration of the third. In the first festivity there is a troupe of dancing girls with successive movements of the dance set out. Here is a liveliness so lacking in the chapel of Ramose, as in the bending and swaying of the dancers (Plate 38), who were accompanied by singers and musicians. The seated directors of the performance clap one hand on the knee to indicate the time and raise the other up and down to signal the note. In the celebration of the third jubilee there are, accompanying the religious performance, the sports of boxing with bare fists and an ancient stick game in which each opponent seeks to fend off the other's blows by skilful use of the staff. This game, still played today, is one of graceful action rather than of attack.

In the front entry way Amenhotep IV appears making an offering to his father and mother. It is still being argued whether the older king was shown alive or dead; the sadly damaged state of the wall does not aid the solution. One portion which is well preserved shows the hand of Tiy about the wrist of Amenhotep III (Plate 39).[50]

Another of the better preserved Theban tomb chapels is that of Menna, Scribe of the Royal Fields about the time of Thutmosis IV (T. T. No. 69). In this office he had charge of all records of the king's agricultural domains. His tomb, at the lower north-eastern end of the hill of Sheikh Abd-el-Gurna, is one of those most frequented by present-day visitors. In the back passage is one of the best executed and best preserved scenes of spearing fish and hunting wild fowl in the marsh lands. As usual, these sports are shown as two episodes, the figures of Menna standing on reed canoes facing each other, a clump of papyrus between them in which the birds have hidden their nests, though they were not always safe here from predatory cats and ichneumons. Menna throws curved hunting sticks or boomerangs in an attempt to bring down the ducks and geese (Plate 56), a feat requiring no mean skill. He was so fond of his family that he had them shown with him in his canoes; in one of them his small daughter, kneeling between his legs, leans over the side to pluck a lotus bud. This is one of the most charming figures the ancient artist has painted.

As might be expected in a chapel of an official of Menna's responsibility, there is, in the hall, a fine series of scenes of the harvest. There follow in succession the reaping, the carrying of grain to the threshing-floor in rope baskets, the piling up there of the ripe heads (Plate 55), threshing with oxen, winnowing and the reckonning of the measures of grain harvested. In the last scene it is apparent that ancient bureaucracy had the same problems as face its counterpart today; four men measure the grain while eight are needed to keep the tally. Small intimate details of agricultural life add charm and interest to the scene: a labourer who has fallen asleep under a tree, a woman picking fruit with her babe swathed against her breast, two girl gleaners pulling each other's hair because one has trespassed on the territory of the other and a girl extracting a thorn from a companion's foot.

In the Twenty-sixth Dynasty there was a revival of ancient art and the classical language. Montuemhat, the most influential man in Thebes in his lifetime, built for himself a great tomb in Asasif, before Deir el-Bahri (T. T. No. 34). He, or his artists, admired the harvest scenes in the tomb of Menna and copied them in relief. This is known, however, only because a number of small incidental pictures, such as the woman picking fruit and the quarrelling gleaners which had survived an attempt by thieves to remove the whole wall, came on the market in the past two decades; many reached museums in the United States.

The full extent of the tomb of Montuemhat, its forehall and sunken court, its subterranean halls and corridors, became known only in recent years. It is vaster than any royal tomb. However, it combined both chapel and tomb chamber; to make a strict comparison one would have to include the king's mortuary temple and his tomb. By such standards most of the royal establishments would be somewhat larger. Two other vast underground tombs with courts were quarried for contemporary officials, Harwa (T. T. No. 37) and Petamenope (T. T. No. 33), both of which had been open at the time of Pococke's visit. These also have extensive and winding corridors. Montuemhat and Petamenope had the walls of these passageways covered with a great variety of funerary texts. Both took enormous precautions to conceal their burial chambers. The way to these was camouflaged by two false chambers, the real one having its entrance through the ceiling of the second, blocked by stones built into one end of that room. Nevertheless, tomb robbers managed to get through into the real burial chamber.

After the Twenty-sixth Dynasty the use of decorated tomb chapels was abandoned; only one of later date, belonging to the Ptolemaic period, is known in the Theban necropolis. Its decoration is slight and is confined to the entrance-way.

98. The housewife, Songstress of Amon, Djetmaat-iouesankh, making an offering to Osiris, and

99. Pouring a libation to the gods of the underworld, vignettes on her funerary papyrus. Twenty-sixth Dynasty. *Cairo Museum*

However, soon after the beginning of the first millenium B. C. the mummy was frequently enclosed in a moulded mummiform case. This was made by wrapping linen strips about a mud form and stiffening the linen with glue. The case was then slit almost the full length of the back and the lower end was left open. It then was covered with gesso and the features of the face and the head painted in (Plate 100). On the body were painted funerary scenes and texts and the name of the deceased. After the wrapped mummy had been introduced into the case, it was laced up the back and a board fitted to the opening at the foot.

It was usually enclosed in a wooden mummiform coffin, sometimes in two. These, too, have the head painted and the name and titles of the deceased inscribed down the front. When excavating the tomb chapel of Kheruef five of these coffins were found in a small chamber cut into the floor. One mummy, that of a youth, was not enclosed in the sort of case described. The only mummy to be unwrapped for study proved to be that of a woman who had died in childbirth; the foetus had been placed between her thighs. The colours on the cases, except where the applied varnish had yellowed, were as bright as the day the mummies had been laid away more than 2500 years ago.

From the Eighteenth Dynasty onward various funerary texts were written on papyrus rolls and placed in the coffin with the deceased. These have been given the name "Book of the Dead", though no two copies contain the same "chapters", as the different compositions have been designated. Nor do the same chapters always have similar texts; there are many versions of each composition and most of them are corrupt. All were concerned with the well being of the deceased in the after world. The 125th chapter contains the "negative confession" in which the deceased denies that he has committed personal or social sins or transgressed against the gods. The whole tenour of these protestations, which have precedents going back to the earliest Egyptian records of standards of personal conduct, show respect for personal property, chastity, honesty, fair dealing, and a responsibility for one's fellows and the rights of the gods.

Many of the references are obscure and many others require an understanding, as far as this is possible, of the enormous complexities of Egyptian mythology. Here is an extract from the short version of Chapter 110 as it appears in the Mortuary Temple of Medinet Habu, with some of the mythological references omitted. The section is entitled "Entering in peace and receiving the good path in the Field of Offering."

"I exist there like the god who is there, inundated with its water. I eat of its bread. I traverse its lake; I ferry across in the boat of the god. I know the cities and the nomes thereof. I cultivate emmer and barley there that I may have sustenance there...Lo, I have ferried across and rest...I row in its lakes to its cities. I ward off the mourners so that they may fight. My speech is potent and my spell is pointed that they may not prevail against me. I know the lakes and the Fields of Offerings where I am. I am strong there; I am glorified there. I reap there; I copulate there. I row in its lakes; I draw nigh its city; I live in its field...I remember and I do not forget; I am alive!"

Even in this short passage there is much repetition. The deceased, here Ramesses III, proclaims his knowledge of this land and insists vigorously that he is not dead.

Many of the funerary papyri are richly illustrated with pictures which supplement various chapters, reminding one of the illuminations in medieval manuscripts (Plates 98 and 99). Many of the papyri were made to order for a specific person, but others were commercial products with blanks left for the name of the deceased. When such a roll was purchased the names were supposed to be filled in, but often some blanks were overlooked, and there are instances where a woman's name has been put in the blanks while all the pronouns in the pre-written document are masculine.

100. Head of mummy covering of the woman Tebra, painted on gesso surface over shell of linen stiffened with glue. Twenty-Sixth Dynasty. *Cairo Museum*

In mentioning a few of the numerous tomb chapels in the Theban Necropolis no reference has been made to one district, now known as Deir el-Medineh, anciently called " The Place of Truth ", in the floor of the valley behind the hill of Gurnet Murai. This small community, founded early in the Eighteenth Dynasty, was inhabited by artisans called " Servants in the Place of Truth ", the quarrymen, the draughtsmen, the sculptors and the painters who were responsible for the preparation of the tomb of the reigning pharaoh.

These workmen were divided into two gangs, designated the " right " and the " left ", like the two divisions in a crew on a ship. Each was under the charge of a foreman who had an assistant and the records of each gang were kept by a scribe. These men were paid in kind by the government in the form of a regular ration of emmer and barley. They also received supplies of water, fuel, fish, vegetables, oil and clothing as well as their tools. Their dwellings were crowded together within a walled area and were reached by narrow streets. They must have been dark, but the people spent most of their daylight hours outside the walls. The house of Sennedjem, in the south-eastern corner of the enclosed area, measured about 28 by 61 feet so it was not as cramped as it appears.

The gangs alternated their work periods of ten days. When they were engaged in work on a royal tomb, the men of the gang did not return to their homes at dusk, but spent the night in huts above the Valley of the Tombs of the Kings where their food was brought to them by members of their families. The reason for this isolation is hard to determine, as a walk of no more than twenty minutes along the mountain path would have brought them to their village.

On the rough mountain-side above the valley these men built crude shrines from stones lying about, approximately a foot square and slightly deeper, within which they placed small steles, each bearing the name and figure of the man who had dedicated it and sometimes the name and figure of a god. As the men prayed before these shrines they faced the peak; this was deified and was one of the popular gods of the people of the village.

In the royal tombs the decoration on the walls was carried out as soon as the quarrymen had smoothed off the surfaces. In the tomb begun and then abandoned by Setnakht, the texts were carved and painted as far as the corridor had been quarried. The high degree of skill of the funerary artisans indicates the existence of a school in which they were trained.

Indeed, there was a school for scribes in the village. The schoolboys, instead of using expensive papyrus, did their exercises on flakes of limestone and the teacher used these for his instruction. When the flakes were finished with they were discarded and great numbers of them consisting of written exercises, drawings, trial pieces of sculpture and so on have been recovered. Many personal accounts, letters and other records were written on such flakes. Great numbers of these *ostraca*, as they are called, have been recovered. When they have been fully studied, we shall have more knowledge about the people of this village and their life than about any other ancient community. Scholars who specialize in this field can recognize the handwriting of each scribe and pupil, know about their families and their personal affairs, and can identify the houses in which they lived.

Because the scribes kept some of the papyri they wrote, and more importantly, because many of the documents once housed in the depository at Medinet Habu were removed to tombs for safe-keeping, a large number of the important documents found in Thebes come from this village and from nearby tombs. Unfortunately, most of them were discovered by modern villagers and all too frequently were torn and broken in the marketing.

The workmen themselves decorated their tombs, located up the mountainside just west of the village. In many the chapels were constructed above ground. They were small, built of mud-brick or stone rubble and capped with a pyramid. Most were found in ruins, but the burial chambers, which were usually decorated, have often been preserved in good condition. The mummies were interred with their choice possessions, a practice going back to prehistoric times. Where primitive men placed in their graves slate palettes for the grinding of eye paint, the men and women of Thebes were buried with their cosmetic jars, often exquisitely formed. Sometimes they are in the form of fish or animals; some show a young girl stretched out as the handle of a container. One unusual wood carving of the Eighteenth Dynasty shows a kneeling man just about to rise with a burden on his shoulders; this is a jar which was used for eye-paint (Plate 95).

Most of the tombs have been violated and their contents stolen; such objects as have been left are often broken. Fortunately one tomb in Deir el-Medineh was found intact, that of the worker Sennedjem (T. T. No. 1), who lived in the reign of Ramesses II. His tomb was only a few yards from his house. At the west end of the court, levelled off in the slope, there were three chapels, the central one his, the side ones for his sons. The entrance to the burial chamber and adjoining rooms was in the floor of the court. Within these rooms were discovered the coffins of Sennedjem, of his wife, and of one son, two of them still on the sledges on which they had been dragged to the tomb. The wooden door into the burial chamber was painted on both sides, and the colours of this, and on the coffins and other funerary furniture, remain bright today. Sennedjem's bed, his chair, some tools, including cubit measures, and six walking sticks were buried with him; most of the objects are in the Cairo Museum.

The vaulted burial chamber has on the walls various painted funerary scenes and the pictures of Sennedjem and his family. On one end of the chamber is a vignette which belongs to Chapter 110 of the Book of the Dead. Here Sennedjem and his wife are sowing, ploughing and harvesting in the underworld, while about the fields flows water in canals and on the banks grow the trees these people knew in life. Another scene shows the god Anubis, or a priest wearing a jackal mask, bending over the mummy on a bed administering the necessary services to bring the dead to life (Plate 93).

Not all the burial chambers in other tombs are as brilliantly coloured as this; some are quite subdued. In a nearby tomb belonging to Sennedjem's son, Kha-bekhnet (T. T. No. 2), the mummy on the bed being given the usual ministrations is that of a fish, not a man (Plate 97). In much the same style is the scene from the contemporary tomb of Nebenmaat (T. T. No. 219), where the owner is playing draughts with his wife (Plate 96).

The execution of the paintings in these tombs is less expert than in most of the tombs of the higher officials of the same period. One tomb in the Deir el-Medineh group in which chapels were quarried into the hill is that of the sculptor Ipuy (T. T. No. 217), who also lived in the reign of Ramesses II. Here the drawings, especially of living creatures, are not very expert, but the subject matter is lively and often amusing. One of the owner's duties was to make furniture for a chapel of Amenhotep I. The artist shows the workmen climbing over an elaborate wooden shrine or canopy which they are finishing. On the top one man is smoothing off the surface while nearby one of his fellows has fallen asleep on the job. A third man is trying to rouse him before the master notices. A fourth workman on top of the shrine has just dropped a maul on to the toes of one of the workmen on the ground; he is jumping around on one foot while the foreman beside him yells to the careless one above to watch out. Working beside the man with the injured toes is another who pauses long enough to have an attendant apply eye paint, used both as a protection and as an ornament. Such incidents do not appear in the chapels of the more dignified officials.

Other homely scenes appear in this tomb, the owner with a kitten in his lap, while under the chair of his wife the mother cat is shown full face, an unsuccessful attempt at such a depiction. In one corner the laundry men are doing the wash (Plate 74); elsewhere on the walls are goatherds with their flocks, each man carrying his belongings in a cloth sack tied on the end of a stick which he bears over his shoulder, fishermen dragging a net from their boats (Plate 73), men irrigating a garden with shadoofs, others picking grapes and treading out the juice for wine. Many of these themes were illustrated in the more formal paintings and reliefs in the tomb chapels of the Theban officials, but those in the tomb of Ipuy have their own peculiar charm.

The villagers had their own temples, one dedicated to Amenhotep I. These have disappeared. In the Ptolemaic period a new temple was built on the site of an earlier one. The reliefs are carefully executed and almost perfectly preserved. They do not show excessive roundness which characterized so much of Ptolemaic relief.

Mummification did not end with the abandonment of the tomb chapels. Indeed, there are many records from the third and second centuries B. C. of families of priests whose chief source of income was the performance of services for the dead. Many demotic papyri are concerned with these matters, and there is one list, written in both demotic and Greek, which gives the names of over 130 heads of families, all of whose mummies were under the care of a single priest and his son. Such bodies were piled up in tombs and chapels whose original owners had long since been dispossessed. Most of the mummies so cared for were those of ordinary people. In the Roman period a portrait of the deceased painted on wood was placed over the head and bound in the wrappings. While most of these portraits come from the vicinity of the Fayyum, the earliest known, of the first century A. D., were found in Thebes.

By this time Thebes had become a provincial village. The priests still sought to carry on the ancient rites in the vast halls at Karnak and Luxor, but with the appearance of Christianity the old religion officially died. Churches were built in the temples; tombs became hermits' cells and even monasteries. Amon was no longer worshipped, though his name was not quite forgotten.

When the ruins of the Christian buildings were cleared from Hatshepsut's mortuary temple, it was discovered that the "Northern Monastery", the meaning of the Arabic name Deir el-Bahri, had been dedicated to a Christian martyr whose name was Phoebamon, a combination of the Greek *Phoibos* and the Egyptian Amon. Thus at the place where the bark of Amon so long had rested in his annual Feast of the Valley, where the god of Thebes had so long been honoured, the name of the man whose faith the early Christians remembered was the same. Phoebamon is a partial translation of the name borne by the deity whose power built Thebes, the one to whom the kings of the Egyptian empire dedicated much of the nation's wealth, the Foremost of Ipet-esut, the King of the Gods, Amon-re.

Conclusion

As THE VISITOR TO THEBES walks westward from the alabaster base of the naos of
Senusert ɪ in the temple of Amon at Karnak, passing along the aisle on the central
axis, he makes his exit through the gateway of the First Pylon, before which stand
the remains of a building whose statue bases bear the names of early Roman em-
perors.   In his walk he has passed through two thousand years of history, by monuments of rulers who bore the famous names of Hatshepsut, Thutmosis, Amenhotep, Seti, Ramesses and Ptolemy.   Gone are the precious stones and gold which
once adorned the buildings and the massive ruins are only shadows of their pristine
glory.

Once this temple was the home of the most powerful god of the most powerful
nation of the second millenium B. C.   When Waset, Thebes, was a small provincial
village and Amon a god of slight importance, Ipet-esut, the temple of Amon at
Karnak, was a primitive shrine.   As the power of the Theban nomarchs expanded
and eventually extended over the whole of the Two Lands, the power of Amon
grew as well.   In the Twelfth Dynasty he became firmly entrenched as the prime
national god.   As the kings of the Eighteenth Dynasty continued their conquests
following the expulsion of the Hyksos, holding the allegiance of princes and peoples
from the Fourth Cataract of the Nile to the banks of the Euphrates in Syria, Egypt
became the first empire and Amon the first universal god.

The fortunes of Amon became the fortunes of Thebes and the god's temple Ipet-
esut and the surrounding city Waset became synonymous.   Artistic styles were set
in the temple ateliers.   National policies were decided in the palaces and chan-
celleries of the city and in·its archives were preserved the records and the wisdom
of ages.   Thebes was the administrative capital of Upper Egypt and, at times, of
the entire land; in its heyday it was always the chief religious centre.   It was no
idle boast that Thebes was the Mistress of Every City and Amon the King of Gods.

It was evident to the rulers of Theban origin and to their successors in the Nineteenth and Twentieth Dynasties that their successes in battle were owed to Amon,
and that he brought prosperity to Egypt.   It was only a just repayment that much
of the wealth and a great part of the captives taken in the conquests be dedicated
to Amon.   Through these gifts his temple was continually enlarged and the increasing number of his landed estates, from which came the produce which filled the
temple warehouses, were manned.   Thus the temple of Amon in Thebes became
the largest ever built and most probably the richest.

So that Amon might bestow his favours on the deceased kings, those of the Eleventh Dynasty and of the Seventeenth, Eighteenth, Nineteenth and Twentieth Dynasties were buried in the Theban necropolis and many of them erected great mortuary temples there. Not far distant from these great numbers of the officials of the country received the benefits of the offerings first made to Amon and to the rulers.

Various estimates have been made of the population of ancient Egypt, none having a claim to accuracy. One based on the probable productivity of the land places it at six million. The population of the city of Waset never perhaps exceeded twenty thousand and was probably no more than half that for most of its history.

The rulers of the Nineteenth Dynasty established their residence in the northeastern delta so as to be able to protect their Asiatic frontier more effectively. Thebes began to decline then, though the temples of Amon and other gods received large additions under this dynasty and the next. The reasons for the ultimate decline of Thebes, and of Egypt, are not clear, but the chief causes seem to have been the rise of new and powerful states in hither Asia and a period of low Niles. With the productivity of the fields reduced, resort was had to the robbery of the riches of temples and tombs. Many descendants of captives broke their bonds and, joined by disaffected peasants, roamed the land.

By the end of the second millenium Amon was losing his authority, though Tjekerbaal of Byblos still stood in awe of him, and he was worshipped in the Sudanese kingdom near the Fourth Cataract. His worship in Thebes, and the upkeep of some of his estates, continued into the latter part of the first millenium. Under Nekhtnebef and the Ptolemies who succeeded to the throne shortly after him there was a renewal of activity in building and refurbishing the holy places of Amon, but by then he was again only a local god. No other Egyptian god replaced him in pre-eminence.

The records on the extant buildings, and those from the finds of papyri, steles, statues and other antiquities coming from Thebes constitute the greatest source of information which scholars possess for the reconstruction of ancient Egyptian culture and of the history of the Middle and New Kingdoms. The collections of Egyptian antiquities in the museums of the world have been assembled largely from Theban sources. This preponderance of material from Thebes gives a one-sided picture of the importance of Thebes in relation to that of other centres, but the Egyptologist is obliged to work with the materials available.

Increasing numbers of visitors are coming to Luxor to see the extant monuments, the greatest number and mass of such remains of historical antiquity in any such area in the world. As the singer in the " Song of the Harper " lamented, there are few mud brick dwellings of the people and the kings remaining. However, the temples, the tomb chapels and the tombs were built to last for eternity. Only in Egypt, and particularly in Thebes, has any people come so near to realizing this end.

Notes

1 The view that Amon was located in Thebes from early in history is contrary to that generally held by Egyptologists. The great scholar, Kurt Sethe, in *Amun und die acht Urgötter von Hermopolis*, 1929, advanced the theory that Amon came originally from Hermopolis and was brought to Thebes by an Intef after he had conquered the town, a political move to strengthen his power. However, the first evidence of the actual inclusion of Amon and Amonet in this group of eight primordial divinities comes from the end of the Twenty-sixth Dynasty, about 550. Sethe did not then know that the conquest of Hermopolis had taken place later than he judged, under Montuhotep II, nor did he know or make use of the earlier appearances of Amon in Theban inscriptions. Moreover, he gave little weight to another late tradition, in the demotic Papyrus Berlin 12603, that Amon and Amonet were added to the eight Hermopolitan deities, making ten. This tradition is as valid as the other. G. A. Wainwright, in a review of Sethe's book in the *Journal of Egyptian Archaeology*, XVII (1931), pp. 151 ff., took a sceptical view of Sethe's position and his objections seem even more valid in the light of modern knowledge. The statement of Paul Barguet, *Le Temple d'Amon-re à Karnak*, 1961, p. 2, that " déjà à la IIIe dynastie sans doute, Karnak était un lieu consacré à Amon ", though undocumented, is closely in accord with my own views.

2 The war against the Hyksos may have lasted longer than is usually reckoned. How long Kamose lived after the foray in his third year is not known. The fall of Avaris is usually put early in the reign of Ahmose. Yet the neglected colophon on the Rhind Mathematical Papyrus tells of fighting in the eleventh year of an unnamed king. Since the main text on the papyrus is dated to the thirty-third year of the Apophis whom Kamose opposed, this can only be of a successor. At the beginning of the civil year eleven occurred the unseasonable phenomena of thunder and rain on successive days. On the twentieth of the first month " the Southerner " (probably a better reading than " General ") invested the frontier fortress of Tjel, near

modern El-Kantarah, and entered it a few days later. Some three months later Heliopolis was entered; was this the last pocket of Hyksos resistance? The sailor Ahmose of El-Kab relates that after the first attack on Avaris there was further fighting south of this city, which fits in well with this picture. Assuming that Kamose and Apophis died about the same time, this brings the final conquest of the delta toward the middle of the reign of Ahmose, whether year eleven be his or that of his Hyksos opponent. If " the Southerner " refers to the Theban king, the latter seems more likely. That Ahmose did not fully succeed in quelling Nubia in his latter years seems indicated by the Nubian campaign of Amenhotep I soon after his accession.

3 A description of this manuscript was published by Giuseppe Caraci, " Un Italiano nell'alto Egitto ed in Nubia sul finire del secolo XVI ", *Archivo Storico Italiano*, Serie VII, Vol. XI (1929), pp. 29-76, 231-67. The visit to Luxor is described on pp. 61-72. I owe my knowledge of this article to Dr. and Mrs. Erich Winter, of the University of Vienna.

4 Protais, quoted in Lord Lindsay, *Letters on Egypt*, I, 1838, p. 390, spelled the second Cama, which Vansleb, *Nouvelle relation... du voyage fait en Egypt*, 1692, p. 411, renders Sciama. James Bruce, *Travels to Discover the Nile*, I, 1790, p. 122, gives them as Shammy and Tammy. Lindsay, *loc. cit.*, gives Shama and Tama as his vocalization. Richard Lepsius, *Briefe aus Aegypten*, 1852, p. 284 (English edition, *Letters from Egypt*, p. 258), writes Schama and Tama. Neither of these names seems to have any meaning in Arabic, and they are unknown to the present inhabitants of Gurna. They now call the colossi *El-Salamat*, " Salutations "; Lepsius, *op. cit.*, p. 415, n. 38, in his letter of January 25, 1845, insists that this is a corruption of *El-Sanamat*, " Idols ". Yet on the title page of his Guest Book (Ger., *Fremdenbuch*, see *op. cit.*, p. 272) illuminated by him, and dated Christmas, 1844, he gives a drawing of the two colossi, with the superscription " El-Salamat ", though perhaps only because this suited his purpose. This Guest Book, with an

"Advice to Travellers" in both German and English, giving as well a short history of Egyptology, is in the possession of Zaki Mohareb in Luxor. The German text of the introductory "Advice" was published by Said Reute, *Ein Fremdenbuch aus Theben*, Berlin, 1909.

[5] Hieroglyphs include ideograms, picturing something or action, and phonograms, giving consonantal sounds. The former are often used to determine a word; the round disk of the sun follows many words for time. The latter represent not only the twenty-two monoconsonantal signs, the alphabet, but also combinations of two or three consonants together. Sir Alan Gardiner, *Egyptian Grammar*, shows about 700 hieroglyphs including some which are only varieties of the same sign. The total known is more than double the number in this list.

[6] This account is given by Howard Carter in *Annales du Service des Antiquités de l'Egypte*, III (1902), pp. 115 ff, and summarized in his *Tomb of Tut-ankh-Amen*, I, pp. 72 ff. A different account, telling of the removal and return of the mummy and of the theft of the funerary boat is told by E. A. Wallis Budge, *By Nile and Tigris*, II, pp. 365 ff. Budge, Keeper of the Egyptian and Assyrian Antiquities of the British Museum, made many trips to the Near East to gather material for the Museum's collections. The frankness of his account is especially fascinating. Certainly he encouraged surreptitious excavation in various parts of Egypt. He defended himself by maintaining that Egypt was not prepared to pay for nor care for these antiquities, and that they were safer in the British Museum than in private hands.

[7] One of the great problems in working about the Theban necropolis is the mass of limestone chippings. When a tomb was quarried, these were dumped outside the entrance, and excavators have been able to do little more than move them short distances. Unless an excavation to bedrock or virgin soil has been made on the spot used for a dump, tons of this refuse may be piled on top of some undiscovered tomb or monument. A few recent excavators have tried to move this refuse to the desert edge, but this is a costly and not always possible operation.

[8] It is uncertain who invented the "curse". Many have suspected that it was Arthur Weigall, who was at the time one of the correspondents of the London newspapers who was not admitted into the tomb, a situation against which he rebelled. In his *Tutankhamen*, p. 136, he rightly denies that there was any curse written on the walls of the tomb, but had already weakened this denial by recalling, p. 89, that he had prophesied Lord Carnarvon's imminent death because of his disrespectful attitude toward the dead king. Weigall had followed Carter as Chief Inspector of Antiquities of Upper Egypt. To him great gratitude is due for his efforts to preserve the Theban monuments, particularly the private tombs, which he protected with doors and to which he gave the present numbering sequence. He had many valuable insights into the meaning of the antiquities, but his approach in his longer works is that of a journalist rather than that of a scholar. He was dismissed from

the Service of Antiquities shortly before the First World War because of alleged illegal dealing in antiquities. His friends maintain that he was the scapegoat for the real guilty persons, high officials of the governing power.

[9] Actually, there were only twenty-eight cantos. The Egyptians arrived at the number 1,000 by counting in units to ten, in tens to one hundred, and in hundreds to one thousand. The poem is a precious composition; in each canto the first and last words are puns on the canto number.

[10] Each nome but two has accompanying it a figure in *schoeni*. In all but two, which have figures in half a *schoenus*, the number is an integer. The only publication of these figures, Pierre Montet, *Géographie de l'Égypte ancienne*, 2e partie, Paris 1961 has taken them as square *schoeni*, which, with other figures, he believed to indicate the area of the arable land. The resulting areas are incompatible with such areas today, which are in excess of what there were four thousand years ago. The total of the *schoeni* is 81 or 82, depending on whether, in one nome, one uses the Senusert figure or that on fragments of a copy made by Amenhotep I. From a votive cubit found at Karnak, it is learned that the length of Egypt from Elephantine to Per-hapi, just south of Old Cairo, was 86 *schoeni*. But Upper Egypt ended at Ity-tawy, modern Lisht, a little more than twenty-five miles farther south. As the length of a *schoenus* was about 6.75/ miles, this figure works out exactly. The two nomes for which no length is given were overlapped completely by adjoining nomes. It is obvious that each figure must be given to the nearest integer except in the two cases noted, and that they were calculated so that together they would give the correct total distance. Other figures accompanying these lengths have not been explained.

[11] The rise of the ground waters follows the crest of the Nile by about a month and a half and is higher than the level to which the river has then fallen.

[12] High on the south wall of the passage is an inscription of Bonaparte's expedition giving the latitude and longitude of the chief temples of Upper Egypt and on the opposite wall a record of an Italian scientific party of 1841 giving the magnetic deviation of the compass. Access to the top of the north wing of the pylon is by a stairway beyond the north side of the First Court and can be found by going through the doorway in the north wall.

[13] See The Epigraphic Survey, *Reliefs and Inscriptions in Karnak*, I, II, Chicago, 1936. This is the only temple in the Karnak complex which has had adequate publication; otherwise, only desultory attention has been given to the ancient records and the publications often leave much to be desired. The same situation holds for the Luxor Temple and the mortuary temples of Seti I and Ramesses II.

[14] A "monument" is rather an elastic word in the ancient inscriptions. It could refer to a great temple, a stele, or a small piece of temple furniture, such as a vase.

¹⁵ The original nature of the flail is not certain. It has also been called a flagellum and a fly whisk. A similar instrument, made up of three fox skins tied together, is certainly a fly whisk; one is carried by Mereruka, shown in his tomb chapel at Sakkarah, dated to the beginning of the Sixth Dynasty. However, since as a royal insignia the flail is usually in company with the shepherd's crook, another view is that it represents a stick with leather thongs attached trailed behind the shepherd to collect gum exuded by certain shrubs. The crook as a hieroglyph is *heka*, meaning " ruler ", the pronunciation reflected in the Greek name for the Asiatic infiltrators into Egypt in the Second Intermediate Period, " Hyksos ", from the Egyptian words meaning " rulers of foreign countries ". It is not certain that it is an insignia of royalty for any reason other than its meaning as a hieroglyph. A similar situation occurs in the sign for " life ". This originally was a sandal strap, the name of which had the same consonantal structure as the word for life; it was therefore used to represent this abstract word. The popular designation of this sign as the " Key of life " is therefore quite fanciful. And the only identity between the shepherd's crook and its use as an insignia of rule may be that both the crook and the word " to rule " had a similar consonantal structure.

¹⁶ One scholar, who has since recanted, maintained that the list was only a corrupt copy of the lists of Thutmosis III, though even casual attention to the earlier publications would have shown this to be untrue. Part of the list is written boustrophedon, the lines to be read alternately right to left to right. Many familiar Biblical places, such as Megiddo (Armageddon), Gibeon and Gaza appear, as well as others which are obscure. A " Fort of Abram " in the Negeb may be named after the ancient patriarch.

¹⁷ When the foundations of the smaller columns of the Hypostyle Hall were rebuilt, it was discovered that these great shafts rested on uncertain foundations of other small blocks of Akhenaten. Similar stones were removed from the foundations of the east face of the north tower of the Second Pylon. So far more than 15,000 of these small blocks with Amarna decoration have been discovered, many retaining much of the original paint. Others were built into later buildings at Karnak and some have been found at the Luxor temple. Those from Karnak are now stacked in a building to the west of the temple of Khonsu, awaiting study, but scholars are discouraged by the knowledge that many thousands more still remain within the fabric of the Second Pylon.

¹⁸ Between a third and a half of the blocks of this sanctuary have been recovered, most from the Third Pylon, but at least one from the Ninth Pylon, and others show that they were re-used in an unknown building of Ramesses II. They now rest in rows, in their approximate relative position within each course, in the museum area of Karnak north of the First Court. A manuscript describing them, written by the late Pierre Lacau, with drawings by Henri Chevrier, awaits publication.

¹⁹ The Festival Hall had its own cult image, Amon of " Blessed through Monuments ", who was so deeply revered that he was memorialized on a pedestal for the bark which Ramesses III placed in his mortuary temple at Medinet Habu.

²⁰ " God's Land " was the name used both for Punt, part of present day Somali, and for Syria.

²¹ One wall was removed by Legrain and set up as the north wall of the room north of the sanctuary. To protect the colour in the figures of the gods and on the few hieroglyphs not destroyed by Thutmosis III, this room has been roofed and locked. It will always be opened on request to the attendant guard.

²² This is the Lateran obelisk in Rome, 105 feet tall, surpassing by eight feet the standing obelisk of Hatshepsut at Karnak.

²³ The inscription indicates that the monument should have been set up in the mortuary temple of Amenhotep III on the west side of the river. While it may have been brought over to Karnak from there, it seems more likely that it was made in the Karnak shops which produced the royal monuments and was never taken to its intended position. Such, too, must have been the fate of a stele marking the north-west boundary of Nekhen, the next nome south, from the reign of Senusert I, which was found in Karnak a few years ago.

²⁴ " Stretching the cord " was the first ceremony in the building of a new temple. Stakes were pounded in at the corners where the walls were to come and a cord was stretched round the outline of the intended building. In the Eighteenth Dynasty at Medinet Habu, Thutmosis III left a series of scenes of the progressive ceremonies at the start of a new building. The next step was the strewing of natron about the area where the temple was to be built, a ceremony of purification. Next came the act of hacking the earth with a hoe. This may be equivalent to turning the first spade of earth, but a similar scene on a wall built by Nekhtnebef in front of this temple suggests a different interpretation. Here the point of the hoe rests on a platform of four mud bricks, the earth of each wetted with a different liquid, wine, milk, beer and water, while shown above the hoe (i. e. resting on the ground at the side) is a rectangular object the same length as the brick platform. In my view this represents the king digging a hole for the foundation deposit. The four bricks are laid first, followed by the box with the commemorative objects. The last act in the Thutmosid scenes is striking the first brick, harking back to the time when temples had mud brick walls.

²⁵ The meticulous work of excavation and the detailed records kept by Clément Robichon in his exploration of the buildings within the temenos of Montu have earned him the admiration and gratitude of all Egyptologists. Many are unable to accept all of his interpretations, but they admire the care with which he examined and recorded the evidence, preserving many details which in the past would have been

overlooked or considered unimportant. His colleagues have written the texts of the excavation report of the volumes, *Karnak*, 1; *Karnak-Nord*, III, IV; all published by the Institut Français d'Archéologie Orientale, Cairo, which sponsored the excavations.

[26] The "Horus" name was the first of the five names of the Kings' titulary in the periods of Theban power. The first kings of the Eighteenth Dynasty, Ahmose and Amenhotep I, had as their Horus names "The Bull in Waset" and "The Bull who Subdues the Nations". Beginning with Thutmosis I, the kings began their Horus name with "Mighty Bull", followed by an epithet, and henceforth every male ruler used this prefix down to Takelot who omitted it in his Horus name. The full Horus name of Amenhotep III was "Mighty Bull, Appearing in Truth". One manifestation of Montu, the god of the Theban nome and later the Theban war god, was that of a bull. The fact that the bull was first used in the Horus name of the king at the beginning of the Eighteenth Dynasty and that Amenhotep III gave the second part of his Horus name to the temple he built for Montu suggests that there was at least a partial identification of the "Mighty Bull" with Montu. However, when Amenhotep IV changed his name to Akhenaten and proscribed all gods but Aten, he continued to use "Mighty Bull" in his Horus name, so evidently such an identification was not made by him.

[27] The results of the study were given to me verbally by Professor H. W. Fairman a few days after the examination was completed and he kindly gave me permission to summarize them before publication. He intends to have the study, with all the details, published as quickly possible, and it may appear at about the same as time as this book. Those who wish to follow more closely the arguments published up to the end of 1961 should consult the *Journal of Egyptian Archaeology* 47 (1961), with articles by H. W. Fairman, pp. 25-40, and C. Aldred, pp. 41-65. References in these articles note previously published material. Plans have been announced for the examination of the mummy of Tutankhamon to determine whether or not there is any resemblance in the skeletons indicating a family relationship.

[28] The original shrine had the same ground plan, with only a slight difference in measurements, as the Eighteenth Dynasty temple of Hatshepsut and Thutmosis at Medinet Habu.

[29] This translation is not very certain. Herbert Ricke, the excavator of the shrine, suggests that the reading "jubilation", if this is correct, was given because the statues of the ithyphallic Amon show him with his right arm upraised, similar to the hieroglyph of the man with upraised arms which determines words for jubilation. As an alternative translation he suggests the reading "family", as this shrine also housed the statues of preceding kings of Egypt which were paraded in the Feast of Min. More attention will be given to this feast in the next chapter.

[30] The presumption is that the canals would not have been excavated to the great depth nec-

essary to have them filled at the lower levels of the river. In 1488 B. C., the fifteenth year of Hatshepsut and Thutmosis III, the beginning of the Feast of Opet, the fifteenth day of the second month of the Season of Inundation, fell at the beginning of October (Gregorian calendar) when, according to the observations made before the building of the Assuan dam at the beginning of the present century, the river was still close to its high point. But by the end of the Twentieth Dynasty, in 1085, the beginning of the Feast of Opet was at the first of July (Gregorian calendar) when the river was close to its lowest point. At the time when Herihor built the river bark of Amon there would have been no water to float it in the canals when the Feast began, unless the bed of the canals were about three feet below the lowest level of the river.

In the time of Thutmosis III the Feast of Opet lasted fifteen days. By the time of Ramesses II it started on the nineteenth day of the second month of the Season of Inundation and lasted twenty-four days. Ramesses III added three days to its length.

[31] This interpretation of the Roman sanctuary, often thought to be a church, is drawn from U. Monneret de Villard, "The Temple of the Imperial Cult at Luxor", *Archaeologia* xcv (1953), pp. 85-105. The conclusions reached by the author belong to a field of scholarship beyond my competence, but on the observable evidence they seem convincing. Remains of the Roman forum and other buildings are on either side of the Luxor Temple.

[32] No detailed study of these erasures has ever been made. A worth while research project would be the careful examination of all the erasures in the Luxor Temple, supplementing the record with comparisons with other temples defaced during the Amarna period to see if the erasures were consistent. Certainly in some cases the erasures were made by semi-literate persons who hacked out words which had the same appearance as the name of Amon. In the Luxor temple there are later erasures due to superstition and these would have to be distinguished from those of the Amarna destruction.

[33] For the route taken by the inspectors I have followed a suggestion made to me in a letter by Elizabeth Thomas, whose book on the tombs of the Theban kings and queens appear will shortly. In plotting this route I have accepted the thesis of Weigall that Royal Tomb No. 39 (or one near by) was that of Amenhotep I. If the tomb found by Howard Carter up the valley off the north end of Dra Abu-el-Naga is the place where Amenhotep I was buried, it is difficult to fit the itinerary given in Papyrus Abbott to the geographical situation.

[34] The papyrus which contains this record has an interesting history. The lower part, now in the Pierpont Morgan Library, once belonged to Lord Amherst of Hackney. It was in his possession in 1870, when it was seen by the Egyptologist Samuel Birch of the British Museum, but there is no published account of how it was acquired. Early in 1936 Jean Capart, curator of the Egyptian section of the Musées Royaux

in Brussels, began his examination of some Egyptian antiquities presented by King Leopold III, objects which had been acquired by Leopold II just before his accession in 1865. Among them was a wooden funerary statue with a hole in the bottom. Exploring this, Capart discovered that it contained a papyrus. He carefully withdrew it, expecting it to be a copy of the Book of the Dead. Instead, it turned out to be the upper half of the Tomb Robbery Papyrus which had been in the Amherst collection.

[35] There is in private hands a fairly large group of these reliefs which has never been published. Responsible Egyptologists are making plans to publish them as soon as possible, and when this has been done a more coherent picture of the temple decoration should emerge.

[36] The local people named the tomb Bab el-Hosan, " Tomb of the Horse ", after the way in which it was found. The figure of the king in jubilee garb wore the red crown of Lower Egypt, and one might expect another with the white crown of Upper Egypt. Is it possible that there is an undiscovered " tomb "?

[37] This feast gave its name to the tenth month of the year, which came into Coptic as Pauni " The One of the Valley ". Other months of which the names were Theban in origin were the second, Paophi, " The One of Opet ", the seventh, Pamenoth, " The One of Amenhotep (I) " and the ninth, Pachon, " The One of Khonsu ". To this list perhaps may be added that of the third, Hathor, and the eleventh, Epiph, which derives from the goddess Ipet whose temple was beside that of Khonsu in Karnak. Thus, the names of four to six of the months of the civil year, as finally adopted, came from Thebes. This calendar, perpetuated by the Christian community, is still the agricultural calendar of Egypt.

[38] The most lucid translations of these texts are in Alexander Piankoff, *The Tomb of Ramses VI*, 2 Vols., (Bolingen Series XL, 1), *The Shrines of Tut-ankh-Amon* (Bolingen Series XL, 2), the latter also available in a paper-back edition and *The litany of Re* (Bolingen Seres XL, 4).

[39] This parentage would have been possible only if there had been a co-regency of twelve years for Amenhotep III and Amenhotep IV-Akhenaten. The chronology used in this volume does not allow for this overlapping, but the question is still under debate. Tutankhamon died in the ninth year of his reign, at the age of about nineteen. Akhenaten reigned seventeen years; thus Tutankhamon was born about the eighth year of Akhenaten's reign. Amenhotep died in the thirty-eighth or thirty-ninth year of his rule. Assuming a maximum co-regency of twelve years, the birth of Tutankhamon could not have been earlier than the thirty-fourth year of the reign of Amenhotep III. Tiy and Amenhotep were already married in the second year of the reign; Tiy would hardly have been younger than twelve at her marriage. Thus it seems certain that even under the shortest possible chronology Tiy could not have been younger than forty-five at the theoretical time when Tutankhamon was born. A much older age of Tiy at marriage, or a shorter co-regency, if any, would make it almost impossible for Tutankhamon to have been the son of Amenhotep and Tiy.

[40] While it is generally believed that Senmut died before the decease of Hatshepsut, and that his detractors immediately attacked his monuments, a statue found at the end of 1963 indicates that Senmut was honoured for some time after the memory of Hatshepsut was attacked. It should be noted that the Cairo statue of Senmut with the princess Neferure on his lap, shown in plate 19, has an inscription indicating that this statue was to receive a reversion of offerings from those presented to Thutmosis III. While Senmut was attached to Hatshepsut, he could have been loyal as well to Thutmosis III. The whole theory of the conflict between these two co-regents needs to be restudied.

[41] In early March 1964, Herbert Ricke and his assistant, Gerhard Häny, of the Schweizerisches Institut für Agyptische Bauforschung und Altertumskunde, began a survey of the site of the temple of Amenhotep III with the object of making clear the architectural plan of this structure.

[42] The mortuary temple of Ramesses III is the only temple in Egypt which has been published completely both epigraphically and architecturally. The work has been carried out by expeditions of the Oriental Institute of the University of Chicago. The reliefs are published by the Epigraphic Survey, *Medinet Habu*, 7 Vols., 1930-1964, and a volume on the High Gate is in preparation. A number of skilled Egyptologists, artists, and photographers have contributed to these volumes; the Field Directors have been Harold N. Nelson, Richard A. Parker, and George R. Hughes. The present writer became Field Director at the beginning of 1964. The architectural survey was under the direction of Uvo Hölscher, the publication *The Excavation of Medinet Habu*, 5 Vols., 1934-1964. The various scratched and painted inscriptions are found in William F. Edgerton, *Medinet Habu Graffiti*, 1937. The only translation of the texts yet published is William F. Edgerton and John A. Wilson, *The Texts in Medinet Habu Volumes I and II*, 1936.

[43] Throughout the buildings of Ramesses III at Medinet Habu Ramesses IV added marginal inscriptions, all copied from similar ones of Ramesses III except for the changed titulary. A considerable number of these were usurped by Ramesses VI, and the same practice was followed in other Theban temples. This has been taken as evidence of the persecution of the memory of Ramesses IV by Ramesses VI. I cannot accept this conclusion; there are many such inscriptions of Ramesses IV which were not altered, and it must be emphasized that in no place was a scene showing the figure and name of Ramesses IV ever touched by Ramesses VI.

[44] The fact that in Medinet Habu wherever the queen or princes and princesses appear, the places for the names are blank, has given rise to much speculation. This is often coupled with the harem conspiracy at the end of the reign in which Ramesses III either was seriously injured or poisoned, and from which attack he did not recover. This conspiracy involved the succession,

and in the trial afterwards a prince was found guilty in the affair, and allowed to commit suicide. However, there is no reason to believe that Ramesses had never decided on his successor, and thus could not name a queen who was the mother of his heir. Nor is there reason to suppose that the king had forbidden the names of any of his family to be inscribed on the temple walls. There is a much simpler explanation; orders were given to copy the Ramesseum reliefs, but no orders were issued to insert the names of the family of Ramesses III in place of those of the family of Ramesses II, and so the workmen left blanks, awaiting instructions which never arrived.

[45] This abbreviation stands for *Theban Tomb* and the number assigned. There are now 410 numbered tombs in the Theban necropolis exclusive of those in the Valley of the Tombs of the Kings, which has 58 numbered tombs, and the Valley of the Tombs of the Queens, which has 75 numbered tombs. However, in these last two groups the greater number have no decoration. There are hundreds of tombs of Theban officials where there is no decoration remaining, and of which there is no record.

[46] Davies believed that other tombs in the vicinity belonged to the Twelfth Dynasty and were re-used in the Eighteenth. This is possible, but there is no evidence to support Davies' theory.

[47] There certainly were two viziers at some, if not all, of the time in the New Kingdom; see Weil, *Das Viziere des Pharaonenreichs*, p. 65. There were two viziers, one of the south and one of the north, shown on a wall of one of the rooms built by Thutmosis III at Karnak, and two viziers appear in the bark in which Amenhotep III stands in the ceremony of the first jubilee shown on the wall of the tomb chapel of Kheruef; the latter evidence was unknown to Weil. There were also officials who were called the Viziers of Upper and Lower Egypt. In the twenty-ninth year of Ramesses III, during the strike of the necropolis workers, To, who had been vizier of Upper Egypt in the sixteenth year, was made Vizier of Upper and Lower Egypt. Since there is no evidence of three viziers, it seems probable that the vizier who was at the court of the ruler was senior to the other. There was another vizier, Hori, at the time that To held his superior office.

[48] This " foetal position " may have had no relation to the position of the child in the womb, but represented the position in which the Egyptians slept. The shortness of the Egyptian beds suggests this, and the head rests, so common among the surviving pieces of Egyptian furniture, show that they slept on their sides.

[49] Modern appreciation of the art of the ancient Egyptians varies among the beholders. The Theban tomb chapels most visited by tourists are those of Ramose, Nakht, and Menna; in the latter two wall-paintings are protected by glass. When Wim Swaan was taking photographs in the chapel of Ramose, a group of people stopped outside the entrance and sent one man inside to advise them about the worth of the place. He took one quick look around, went to the doorway and called out, " Nothing here worth seeing ". A few minutes later a young couple entered, and the wife remarked, " I like this so much better than the tombs with glass where they have made those terrible restorations in bright colour ". The wall paintings in the chapels of Nakht and Menna are, of course, original, and have not been touched up.

[50] The history of the discovery of this tomb is interesting. In 1886 Adolf Erman, who, at the age of thirty-one, was making his first trip to Egypt, was led by his donkey boy through a twisting robber's passage into a part of the portico which is now known to be only the right section. By the light of a candle he made a sketch drawing of what was above the debris, copying the inscriptions. He gave this material to his friend and teacher Brugsch to publish. Soon afterwards robbers broke up a large section of the wall in an attempt to cut out the heads of the king, queen, and princesses. Probably most of these were not successfully removed; a block with the heads of two princesses came into the possession of the Berlin Museum early in this century.

In 1923 Davies published, in the *Journal of Egyptian Archaeology*, IX, a photograph of a scene over the entrance doorway showing Amenhotep IV, his mother Tiy standing behind him, making an offering to Atum. This had been discovered more than ten years before, apparently by Winlock. Davies remarks that he and Gardiner had once visited the part that Erman had seen, but they did not know exactly where it was, and he thought it was a separate tomb. In 1941 Ahmed Fakhry, then Chief Inspector of Antiquities for Upper Egypt, and the late Zakariah Ghoneim, then Keeper of the Theban Necropolis, as a result of enquiries about the source of decorated parts from tomb chapel walls then appearing on the market, rediscovered the portico, and had it cleared and protected. Fakhry published an excellent preliminary report in *Annales du Service des Antiquités*, XLII (1943). The court and rear rooms, and the approach to the entry-way, were still filled with debris. In 1957-59 a joint effort of the Department of Antiquities and the Epigraphic Survey of the Oriental Institute of the University of Chicago made a complete clearance of the tomb and the later chapels opening on to the court. A full publication of the architecture and the scenes of the Tomb Chapel of Kheruef is in preparation by the Epigraphic Survey.

Bibliography

Except for the early travel books, all the works listed below are currently available. Works referred to in the notes have not been repeated here. Many of the books listed have full bibliographies. A brief notice of all scenes and inscriptions and of all known records of these, whether published or unpublished, will be found in the following:

PORTER, BERTHA, AND MOSS, ROSALIND L. B., *Topographical Bibliography of Ancient Egyptian Hieroglyphic Texts, Reliefs and Paintings*. I. *The Theban Necropolis*. Part 1, *Private Tombs*. Part 2, *Royal Tombs and Smaller Cemeteries*, Oxford, 1960, 1964. II. *Theban Temples*, Oxford, 1929. (Vol. II lists only material published to 1928. A second, expanded edition, with a notice of all the material on the temple walls, is in preparation).

EARLY TRAVEL BOOKS

BRUCE, JAMES, *Travels to Discover the Source of the Nile*, I, Edinburgh, 1790

DENON, VIVANT, *Voyages dans la basse et la haute Égypte*, London, 1807

LINDSAY, LORD, *Letters on Egypt, Edom, and the Holy Land*, I, London, 1838

LUCAS, PAUL, *Voyage du Sieur Paul Lucas au Levant, on y trouvera entr'autre une description de la haute Egypte*, I. The Hague, 1705 — *Voyage du Sieur Paul Lucas fait en MDCCXIV par ordre de Louis XIV*, II, Amsterdam, 1720

NORDEN, FREDERICK L., *Travels in Egypt and Nubia*, London, 1757

POCOCKE, RICHARD, *A Description of the East*, I, *Observations on Egypt*, London, 1743

PROKESCH, ANTON VON, *Erinnerungen aus Aegypten und Kleinasien*, Vienna, 1829

VANSLEB, P., *Nouvelle relation en forme de journal d'un voyage fait en Egypte*, Paris, 1677

WILKINSON, J. G., *Materia Hieroglyphica*, Malta, 1828

MODERN WORKS

ALFRED, CYRIL, *The Egyptians*, London, 1961 — *Middle Kingdom Art in Ancient Egypt*, London, 1950 — *New Kingdom Art in Ancient Egypt*, 2nd ed., London, 1961

BONNET, HANS, *Reallexikon der ägyptischen Religionsgeschichte*, Berlin, 1952

BREASTED, JAMES HENRY, *Ancient Records of Egypt*, 5 vols., Chicago, 1906, reprinted, 1961. — *The Development of Religion and Thought in Ancient Egypt*, Chicago, 1912, paperback reprint, 1961

BRITISH MUSEUM, *Introductory Guide to the Egyptian Collections*, London, 1964

CARTER, HOWARD, *The Tomb of Tut-Ankh-Amen*, 3 vols., London, 1923-1933, reprinted, 1963

ČERNÝ, JAROSLAV, *Ancient Egyptian Religion*, London, 1962

DESROCHES-NOBLECOURT, CHRISTIANE, *Tutankhamen*, London, 1963

DONADONI, SERGIO, *Arte Egizia*, Turin, 1955 — *La Religione dell'Egitto antico*, Milan, 1955

DRIOTON, ÉTIENNE, AND VANDIER, JACQUES, *L'Égypte* (" Clio ", Les peuples de l'Oriént méditerranéen, II), Paris, 4th ed., 1962

FORMAN, WERNER AND BEDRICH, *Egyptian Art*, London, 1962

FOX, PENELOPE, *Der Schatz des Tut-ench-amun* Wiesbaden, 1960 — *Tutankhamun's Treasure*, London, 1951

FRANKFORT, H., *Ancient Egyptian Religion*, New York, 1948.

WILSON, JOHN A., *Before Philosophy*, Harmondsworth, 1949

GARDINER, SIR ALAN, *Egypt of the Pharaohs*, Oxford, 1961

HAYES, WILLIAM C., *Cambridge Ancient History*, Revised Edition of Vols I & II, fasc. 3, *The Middle Kingdom in Egypt*, fasc. 10, Egypt, *Internal Affairs from Thutmosis I to the Death of Amenophis III*, 2 parts, Cambridge, 1961, 1962 — *The Scepter of Egypt*, 2 vols, New York, 1953, 1959

HELCK, W., AND E. OTTO, *Kleines Wörterbuch der Aegyptologie*, Wiesbaden, 1956

HOUSTON, MARY C., *Ancient Egyptian, Mesopotamian and Persian Costume*, London, 2nd ed., 1954

KEES, HERMANN, *Das Alte Ägypten*, Berlin, 1955 English translation available.

LEFEBVRE, GUSTAVE, *Romans et contes égyptiens*, Paris, 1949

LEWIS, BERNARD, *Land of Enchanters*, London, 1948 Ancient Egyptian stories translated by Battiscombe Gunn.

LHOTE, ANDRE, *La peinture égyptienne*, Paris, 1954

Lucas, A., *Ancient Egyptian Materials and Industries*, 4th ed. revised by J. R. Harris, London, 1962

Mayes, Stanley, *The Great Belzoni*, London, 1959

Mekhitarian, Arpag, *Egyptian Painting*, Geneva, 1954

Neugebauer, O., and Parker, Richard A., *Egyptian Astronomical Texts*. I, *The Early Decans;* II, *The Ramesside Star Clocks;* Providence, Rhode Island, 1960, 1964

Parker, Richard A., *A Saite Oracle Papyrus from Thebes*, Providence, Rhode Island, 1962

Posener, Georges, *Dictionnaire de la civilisation égyptienne*, Paris, 1959

Pritchard, James B. (ed.), *Ancient Near Eastern Texts*, Princeton, 2nd ed., 1959. Translations of Egyptian texts by John A. Wilson.

Riefstahl, Elizabeth, *Thebes in the Time of Amenhotep III*, Norman, Oklahoma, 1964

Säve-Söderbergh, Torgy, *Faraoner och Människor*, Stockholm, 1959

Schäfer, Heinrich, *Von ägyptischer Kunst*, 4th ed. revised by Emma Brunner-Traut, Wiesbaden, 1963

Sauneron, Serge, *Les Prêtres de l'ancienne Égypte*, Paris, 1957

Schott, Siegfried, *Altägyptische Liebeslieder*, Zürich, 1950

Smith, W. Stevenson, *The Art and Architecture of Ancient Egypt*, Harmondsworth, 1957 — *Ancient Egypt*, Boston, 3rd ed., 1952

Steindorff, George, and Seele, Keith C., *When Egypt Ruled the East*, Chicago, 2nd ed., 1957

Vandier, Jacques, *Manuel d'archéologie égyptienne*, 3 vols. in 6 parts, Paris, 1952-58 — *La religion égyptienne*, Paris, 2nd ed., 1949

Wilson, John A., *The Burden of Egypt*, Chicago, 1951. Paperback edition entitled, *The Culture of Egypt. — Signs and Wonders upon Pharaoh: A History of American Egyptology*, Chicago, 1964

Woldering, Irmgard, *Ägypten, Die Kunst der Pharaonen*, 1962

Wolf, Walther, *Kulturgeschichte des alten Agypten*, Stuttgart, 1962

Chronology

End of Predynastic Period, 3115

Protodynastic Period
Dynasties I and II, 3115-2686

Old Kingdom
Dynasties III to V, Memphis, 2786-2350
Dynasty VI, Memphis, 2350-2182

First Intermediate Period
Dynasties VII and VIII, Memphis, 2182-2160
Dynasty IX, Heracleopolis, 2160-2130
Dynasty X, Heracleopolis, 2130-2040

Middle Kingdom
Dynasty XI, Thebes, 2133-1991
Dynasty XII, Theban in origin, residence at Lisht, 1991-1786
Dynasty XIII, mostly Theban in origin, residence at Lisht until 1674, 1786-1633

Second Intermediate Period
Dynasty XIV, small independent kingdom in western delta, 1786-1600
Dynasties XV and XVI, two contemporary Hyksos kingdoms in the north, 1684-1567
Dynasty XVII, Thebes, 1650-1570

New Kingdom
Dynasty XVIII, Thebes, but administrative centre sometimes in the north, 1570-1320
    Ahmose, 1570-1546
    Amenhotep I, 1546-1526
    Thutmosis I, 1526-1512
    Thutmosis II, 1512-1504
    Thutmosis III, 1504-1450
    Hatshepsut, 1504-1482
    Amenhotep II, 1450-1425
    Thutmosis IV, 1425-1417
    Amenhotep III, 1417-1379
    Amenhotep IV-Akhenaten, 1379-1362
    Smenkhkare, 1364-1361
    Tutankhamon, 1361-1352
    Ay, 1352-1348
    Haremhab, 1348-1320
Dynasty XIX, administrative centre in northeast delta, 1320-1200
    Ramesses I, 1320-1318
    Seti I, 1318-1304
    Ramesses II, 1304-1237
Dynasty XX, administrative centre in northeast delta, 1200-1085
    Ramesses III, 1198-1166
    Ramesses IV, 1166-1160
    Ramesses V, 1160-1155
    Ramesses VI, 1155-1149
    Ramesses IX, 1141-1122
    Ramesses X, 1122-1112
    Ramesses XI, 1112-1085
    Herihor, about 1094-1088

Later Dynasties
Dynasty XXI, Tanis, 1085-945
Dynasty XXII, Tanis, 945-730
Dynasties XXIII-XXIV, 815-715
Dynasty XXV, " Ethiopian ", 751-656
Dynasty XXVI, " Saite ", 664-525
Dynasty XXVII, " Persian ", 525-404
Dynasties XXVIII and XXXIX, 404-380
Dynasty XXX, 380-343
Dynasty XXXI, 343-332

Macedonian and Ptolemaic rulers, 332-30
Alexander the Great, 332-323
Philip Arrhidaeus, 323-316
Alexander IV, 316-304
Ptolemy I Soter, 304-284
Ptolemy II Philadelphus, 284-246
Ptolemy III Euergetes I, 246-221
Ptolemy V Epiphanes, 221-180
Cleopatra VII, 51-30

Roman domination, 30 onward

Index